Praise for *When the Rer*

"In this intimate memoir, Dori Jones Yang takes a close-up look at the emergence of China in the 1980s, from backward country to world power. Beijing bureau chief for *BusinessWeek,* Dori was an eyewitness to the start of this historic transformation, and she tells the story with insight and verve."
—**STEPHEN B. SHEPARD**, former editor-in-chief, *BusinessWeek*

"Dori Jones Yang has given us two wonderful, East-West coming-of-age stories for the price of one: China's metamorphosis from poor Communist backwater to quasi-capitalist powerhouse, and her own journey from rookie reporter in the male-dominated world of business journalism to respected foreign correspondent. Both tales come with their share of great leaps forward and troubling setbacks."
—**SCOTT D. SELIGMAN**, author of *The Third Degree: The Triple Murder That Shook Washington and Changed American Criminal Justice*

"With refreshing candor, riveting detail and sharp insights, this beautifully told memoir breaks the mold of 'Western journalist-discovers-China.' Dori Jones Yang's wonderfully personal journey allows one to view this vastly different culture and increasingly powerful country as she did—with open eyes and heart, without prejudgment."
—**HELEN ZIA**, author of *Last Boat out of Shanghai: The Epic Story of the Chinese who Fled Mao's Revolution*

"This book is about two transitions—Dori Jones Yang's from student to Hong Kong bureau chief for *Business Week,* and China's from central planning to an open, market economy. Beautifully written, it portrays the victories and setbacks of both 'awakenings.'"
—**SHANTA DEVARAJAN**, professor of the Practice of International Development, Georgetown University

"Like all superb memoirs, Dori Jones Yang's is not only a candid reflection of her own character and experience, but an eyewitness account of an epic time in history. Her sensitive observations and skillful writing bring the yin-yang dualities of her life into a gratifying if sometimes hard-fought balance, to deliver a story that is sweeping yet intimate, ambitious yet humble, serious yet engaging."
—**CLAIRE CHAO**, author of *Remembering Shanghai: A Memoir of Socialites, Scholars and Scoundrels*

"As America's relations with China stumble today, looking back to the decade of Yang's encounter with China is more important than ever."
—**ROBERT A. KAPP**, former president, US-China Business Council

"Dori Jones Yang writes particularly eloquently about the 1989 Tiananmen Square crackdown; it marked the endpoint for China of a golden decade of economic reform and freedom while for her it was a betrayal by a country she had come to admire. This deeply personal book interweaves her desires for professional success, love, and motherhood and may inspire young women striving to balance these aspirations in their own lives."
—**JUDITH SHAPIRO**, co-author of *Son of the Revolution* and of *China Goes Green: Coercive Environmentalism for a Troubled Planet*

"Captivating! A pioneering female foreign correspondent, Dori Jones Yang captures the story of a young gal finding her way—as a journalist and as a woman. Her evolution intersects with dynamic world events, resulting in a mesmerizing tale of personal struggle, vibrant history, and real guts."
—**MARIANNE LILE**, author of *Stepmother: A Memoir*

"A riveting, insightful, personal account of a pivotal moment in history. Today, as China increasingly flexes its muscles on the world stage, this book provides a nuanced understanding of the challenges and promises presented by a complex global power that thinks and operates in ways so different from us."
—**LESLIE HELM**, author of *Yokohama Yankee, My Family's Five Generations as Outsiders in Japan*

When
The Red
Gates
Opened

A Memoir of China's
Reawakening

When
The Red
Gates
Opened

Dori Jones Yang

SHE WRITES PRESS

Published 2020
Printed in the United States of America
Print ISBN: 978-1-63152-751-7
E-ISBN: 978-1-63152-752-4
Library of Congress Control Number: 2020905896

For information, address:
She Writes Press
1569 Solano Ave #546
Berkeley, CA 94707

Interior design by Tabitha Lahr

She Writes Press is a division of SparkPoint Studio, LLC.

Dedicated to
my granddaughter, Maya,
and to American and Chinese children
who will, I hope, continue the approach
of mutual respect and understanding
between our two great nations

Contents

Foreword

⚭⚭⚭⚭⚭

Researching and writing this memoir felt like time travel—back to the most extraordinary period of my life. To enhance my memories, I reviewed my personal journals, appointment calendars, reporter's notebooks, and articles I published in the 1980s. This journey into the past brought back funny and fateful moments, painful and awkward episodes, and surprising insights into my own history and that of China.

To bring the story to life, I reconstructed conversations to the best of my memory and notes, trying to stay faithful to the tone and intention of both speakers. Before publication, I checked with many of the people mentioned in this book for accuracy and made changes as appropriate. Any errors are my own, as are my opinions.

Enjoy!

Prologue

⋐ᦱᦱᦱ⋑

U nder a warm white sky, Tiananmen Square bustles with the joy of anarchy. Nearly one million citizens of China, overcoming their fears, have gushed forth from their tiny flats into this open space at the center of Beijing. On this May day in 1989, an eager yet uneasy sense of amazement draws me to this familiar public space, now teeming with peaceful protestors. Televised images of this scene have been sparking imaginations all over the world this week; what will I find in person?

For a better view, I head for the huge portrait of Chairman Mao Zedong, the demigod who unified and stabilized China before disrupting it. His benign-looking face hangs on the imperial palace's monumental entrance called Tiananmen, optimistically named the Gate of Heavenly Peace, gazing south over the huge plaza.

History rises from every paving stone. This is the living heart of the most populous nation on Earth, the center of power of this country that calls itself *Zhongguo*, the Middle Kingdom, self-perceived source of all civilization and authority. I am approaching the exact spot where, for centuries, the messy lives of ordinary people met the closed corridors of their fearsome rulers. Here, Kublai Khan chose to build his fortress palace and reigned over the largest land empire ever. Here, Ming and Qing emperors ruled behind the red walls of the Forbidden City, whose front gate, Tiananmen, was almost always bolted shut. Here, Communist leader Mao Zedong declared a new people's republic and threw open the doors of the ancient palace, only to set himself up as a capricious dictator from a high-security compound next door. Its thick crimson walls separate the guarded courts of power from the ever-larger masses of people who now gather outside, in the huge square, demanding better governance.

When I reach China's main gate, at what feels like a turning point in history, I swivel to face the huge square filled with more protestors than have ever challenged any leader anywhere. Well, to my knowledge. The magnitude of the moment lifts my spirit far above my self-doubt. I have come as a journalist, empowered to gather all I see and hear into a first draft of history. For once, the everyday people of China are making the news, not its leaders.

Standing on a low-rise marble bridge under Mao's mien, I gaze in awe at the scene. Bright-colored tents dot the one-hundred-acre square. Starving students sprawl among the tents. Sympathetic protestors mill beneath red banners of their colleges. At the base of a stone obelisk called the Monument to the People's Heroes, self-appointed leaders with bullhorns squawk encouragement to the crowds, who seem mostly rather relaxed, even jolly, after five days of uninterrupted protest. Red flags flutter from every lamppost. An entrepreneurial street vendor dispenses fried-dough sticks from his cart to onlookers who have come to see the action.

To do these protestors justice, I will have to plunge into this sea of strangers, drawing on my language skills and whatever confidence I have built in my seven years as a reporter covering this country. Far outside my comfort zone, on the opposite side of the planet from my Ohio roots, I have come here alone, with no team of colleagues, just a clutch of editors back in New York, waiting for my reports to come flickering across the ocean.

An ambulance siren screams at the far end of the square, and I strain on tiptoe to see how a pathway opens for it to carry a hunger striker to the hospital.

"Aiya!" On the bridge beside me, a woman in a flowery shirt sounds like she's been gut-punched. I notice she has tears in her eyes. "These are our children! They are starving to death, and no one is doing anything about it."

"Is your son or daughter out there?" I nod to the sea of protestors.

"No, not mine. But every mother in Beijing feels the way I do. Don't you have a child?"

In my mind I see my two-year-old, standing in her crib, reaching her chubby arms out to me. I wince as I imagine that girl, grown up, starving herself in a public square. "I do," I answer.

This woman doesn't express surprise that I speak Chinese, but it registers on her face that I am a foreigner. She grabs my arm. "Thank you for reporting this news. You must tell the world." Her eyes blaze with urgency.

"I will." I pull the notebook from my waist. "I am a—"

"These are peaceful protests. No violence. Our children have stopped eating, for six days now. They are starving to death. The leaders have to do something!"

Her vehemence floods over me.

"Perhaps Zhao will help?" I say.

A second woman edges in. "Nobody knows where Zhao is! It was Li Peng who met with the students today. Did you hear?"

"What a joke," says an old man who can't resist joining the conversation. "He doesn't care about the students. Even old Deng doesn't care!"

Suddenly, I am surrounded by Chinese people eager to discuss politics—in public. They even dare to criticize the nation's most powerful leader, Deng Xiaoping.

"It's got to end soon," the first woman says. "They have to do something."

Still clutching my notebook, I don't scribble notes or ask names; I don't want to break the spell. Their leaders, normally suspicious of foreign journalists, have allowed hundreds of us into the country to cover what they thought would be a triumphal visit by the Soviet president, but Chinese college students surged into the spotlight instead.

The man shakes his head. "It's too late. Some leader is manipulating all of this."

"Not true! This is spontaneous!" says a young man in jeans, joining our group. "I was out there with my friends until yesterday. No one told us to protest."

"Nonsense," says the older man. "It's all about a power struggle. Otherwise, they would have ended it days ago."

For once, as a foreigner, I am not the center of attention. No one asks my opinion. They are being unbelievably open and trusting, talking politics with strangers on the street, and they want to hear each other. They have lived Chinese history and politics, so their understanding goes far deeper than that of any foreign analyst. Yet their government has, as usual, kept them in the dark about important decisions it has made.

"The army is coming, for sure," says another man. "I hear that they are about to declare martial law."

"Who has the guns? When people die, the world will know who killed them."

"No, no, no! The People's Liberation Army protects the people. They will not kill anyone."

I soak up their anxiety, their urgency, their candidness. The barriers that have kept me an outsider have fallen. These Chinese are reaching out and drawing me into their world—at its most fragile and sensitive moment.

I realize I have crossed the final border. This isn't just the biggest story of my journalistic career. It is my story, too, and I feel it from the inside out—like *baijiu* liquor that heats up your innards so much that your face flushes. Those are my children, too. In this very square, I once laughed when a stranger asked me to marry him. Now I have returned as the wife of a Chinese man, mother of a child whose blood runs back to the ancient origins of this country. As such, I am part of this family, related by marriage to both protestors and leaders.

These are my people, and their future is my future. The students of China—and their champions—are inspired by the ideals of my country, America. If they succeed, against long odds, at getting their government to listen to them, my heart will sing. If they fail, if their leaders quash them, I will be crushed, too.

Deng Xiaoping has shown them, by his daring example, how to defy the odds. During the ten years since he consolidated power, he has given his people a chance to thrive on a diet of reform and openness, flouting the teachings of Mao. Chinese students have studied abroad, scholars have exchanged ideas, private entrepreneurs have taken risks. Everything Deng has done seems to defy his six-decade commitment to Communism.

Now this generation, too young to remember Mao worship, has taken Deng's example of defiance in a direction he didn't expect. The citizens of Beijing are cheering them on. I am, too. None of us knows what their success might mean, but the cost of failure is unthinkable. On the irrational side of my brain, I still hope that some middle way might emerge.

Half a world away from the Ohio home where my parents quake about my safety, I am where I belong, in a nation in turmoil, on the brink of something unexpected. Only later will it hit me: what a fluke of fate it is to witness a shaft of the future shining through a hole in time. To feel the world tilt on its axis and throw you off balance, insisting that you rethink all your well-polished assumptions—that you chase history, stumbling and blind, into the unknown.

CHAPTER ONE:

The Red Gates Open

☙☙☙☙☙

野心, *yěxīn, ambition: In American English, a word that hints at get-up-and-go, goal setting, drive, determination, and potential self-made success. In Chinese, literally, "wild heart."*

This story began, this intricate dance of China and me and my awe of Deng Xiaoping, in Washington, DC, at the Kennedy Center for the Performing Arts on January 29, 1979, ten years before that memorable day in Tiananmen Square.

That wintry evening, I arrived for my first-ever gala performance bundled in a bulky pink coat and wearing a knit dress my mom had given me for Christmas. My only nod to the black-tie code were my low-rise black heels. Not that anyone would notice me. Of the two thousand–plus invited to the event, most were senators, members of Congress, administration officials, and other Washington luminaries; a few friends and I, worker bees at the National Council for United States–China Trade, were lucky to get free seats at the back.

Just five weeks earlier, following months of secret negotiations, President Jimmy Carter had agreed to end twenty-nine years of hostility and recognize Beijing's Communist government as the legitimate rulers of China. This evening, he was honoring China's leader, Deng Xiaoping, with a joyous celebration.

Back in college at Princeton, just three years earlier, I might not have cared. But after graduation, I had studied Mandarin Chinese intensively in Singapore, four hours a day, five days a week, for two years—even though it was nearly impossible for Americans to travel inside China. That experience, with Princeton-in-Asia, had changed the trajectory of my life. I was now in graduate school at Johns Hopkins, taking courses in advanced Chinese and international studies, as well as working part-time at the trade council, where I wrote articles for the *China Business Review*. With some earlier experience in journalism, I had placed all my chips on China, hoping it would one day open its doors to American reporters. To many, that seemed like long odds, betting I could find a job that combined journalism and China. But after Carter's decision, my hand was full of aces.

I followed the crowd into the opera hall and found my seat, near the back, under the overhang. Leaving my coat and program, I jostled up the aisle to ogle: an elegant Viennese chandelier shaped like a snowflake, acres of crimson carpeting, curving tiers of red-leather balconies. The guests were still streaming in when suddenly someone oohed and pointed to the balcony above my head. "There they are!"

Unable to see, I pressed my way forward, squeezing between tuxedos and ball gowns, diamond studs and French perfume, twisting my neck to look back and up. Finally, I reached a spot where I could see the presidential box on the balcony above. There stood Carter and his wife, but I only had eyes for the short man next to him: Deng Xiaoping.

I stared up, rooted to the spot, as people swarmed past me. First my face heated up, and then my breath went rapid and shallow.

To me, Deng was bigger than a rock star, higher than the chandelier, greater than the mild-mannered president who towered over his sturdy, five-foot-tall frame. With a receding hairline dyed black to hide his advanced age of seventy-five, Deng was wearing a simple Mao suit with a high collar, four pockets, and buttons down the front. On his shoulders rode the hopes of one billion people.

Deng's creased face hinted at years of suffering—two purges and a four-year exile to hard labor—but he was now smiling, clapping, and waving to us, an adoring crowd. Deng held no title higher than vice premier, but we all knew he was China's paramount leader, and he emanated a gravitas that commanded respect. A Communist since the age of nineteen and once one of Mao Zedong's close advisers, Deng had, since Mao's death, consolidated power, jettisoned most of Mao's crazy policies, and begun to open his country to new ways of thinking. If anyone could lift China out of poverty into prosperity, it would be Deng.

Although many of the gala guests had not yet found their seats, the orchestra struck up the US national anthem, and proud voices rose like bombs bursting in air. One man in the aisle sang the lyrics into my ear so lustily that I turned to see him. The crooner was Senator Ted Kennedy, with his distinctive craggy face. Normally, I would have been thrilled, but I pivoted my neck back to catch another glimpse of Deng, that rare Beijing duck. Charged by an aura of awe, I gazed until the leaders and their wives sat down, and then I returned to my seat.

John Denver, Shirley MacLaine, the Harlem Globetrotters—all the performances impressed me, but none moved me as much as the final act. Dozens of American kids from the National Children's Choir, dressed in their Sunday best, filed onstage and surprised us all by singing a well-loved Chinese song, "I Love Beijing Tiananmen," a pro-Communist, patriotic tune extolling the large central square in Beijing where military parades took place. I knew the lyrics, so I cocked my ears to hear if they would sing the final lines, "The great leader Chairman Mao leads all of us forward." Yep. These American kids were singing praise to Chairman Mao. US-China relations—the world, really—would never be the same. I shook my head in wonder.

When the show ended, President Carter and Deng walked out onstage and clasped hands high over their heads, a symbol of victory. We applauded like crazy.

It was a moment ripe with hope. After years of antagonism, the United States and China now had a chance for a fresh start. Along with a full-fledged US embassy in Beijing, Deng had allowed American correspondents to cover China. Every major US newspaper and magazine, I knew, would be looking for Chinese-speaking journalists with some knowledge of this massive, complex country that had been shut off from Americans for decades.

For me, that visit from Deng Xiaoping would always gleam with possibility. If China could emerge from isolation, I could overcome my natural reserve and transform myself, too, into someone my family had never imagined. If Deng could shake hands with the leaders of a country that had fought against all he stood for, I could defy expectations, too.

I was sneaking through a crack opened by a massive red gate, lured by some magnetic force. If my choices would upend my life in ways I could never have envisioned, I was ready to press my way in anyway. Unpredictable and perplexing, China was inviting me. I chose to go toward it, my eyes wide open, ready for anything, however the story might turn out.

෪෪෪෪

Three years later, Lew Young, überboss and editor-in-chief of *Business-Week*, poked his balding head around my office doorway. "Come talk to me." He aimed his finger at me, winked, and walked away.

I took a deep breath, lifted my fingers from the keyboard, and pushed back from my desk. All that week of January 1982, I had been hoping for this conversation. After two years of study for my master's degree, two visits to China, and a year toiling away as a low-level editor in New York, I wondered, *Has my moment come?* I jumped up and followed him.

More like a rangy Texan than the former Philadelphia engineer he was, Lew strode up the wide hallway—half a city block long. In his tie and vest, he generated a ripple of anxiety as he passed the open doors of his underlings, who looked up from their keyboards, startled. Trailing in his wake, I felt like a young cub scampering to keep up with the alpha male.

I hesitated before stepping into his large corner office on the thirty-ninth floor of the McGraw-Hill Building, overlooking Sixth

Avenue in midtown Manhattan. A whiff of newsprint rose from a tousled stack of papers on his large desk.

For a New York minute, my spirit pulled out, and I watched from the outside as a young woman with short wavy hair, dressed in a flowy black skirt and preppy plum sweater, took a seat facing her boss. The wall behind him proudly displayed a row of framed magazine covers. In his twelve years at the helm, Lewis H. Young had made *BusinessWeek* a "must read" for executives and the most profitable magazine in the country. Now he was expanding overseas.

"First," he said, "I just want to let you to know that we think you're great. I hear you're doing fantastic back there." His intense blue eyes blazed below reddish eyebrows.

Trying to collect myself, I edged back into the chair and nodded. "Thanks." I only half believed him. My transition into this editing job had been rough, and my inner critic had often forced me to retreat to the restroom to berate myself for being lazy and unproductive. Still, Lew's compliments were as rare as a taxi at rush hour.

"Now." He put two hands on his desk, fingers splayed. "I want to ask you, what kind of work do you want to do? You know, in the next couple of years?"

My breath caught in my throat. I knew exactly what I wanted: a transfer to the Hong Kong bureau, where I could cover China. Surely he knew that.

"I mean," he continued, "do you prefer reporting or editing? Do you want to stay here in New York or move to a bureau?"

"Well . . ." I stumbled. "What I really love is reporting. I'd rather do that than editing." I paused awkwardly. In fact, I disliked editing articles written by others. I had not become a journalist so I could have a desk job where I never got out and met people.

His hooded eyes regarded me without judgment.

Be articulate, I told myself. *Now is not the time for humility.* Though young and deferential, I already knew a lot, especially about China. "I'd like to move to an overseas bureau."

That was putting it mildly. Since long before that Kennedy Center moment, I had been dreaming of becoming a foreign correspondent and preparing with language study, travel, and on-the-job training in journalism. As a child in Ohio, I had started writing stories at seven, and my first job had been with my local newspaper. In high school, I had spent a summer with a family in France. During college, I had practically lived in the offices of *The Daily Princetonian*. When some expert told me to get "subject matter expertise," I had pounced on a fellowship opportunity to study Chinese in Singapore. That whetted my interest in China, which had led me to grad school and that part-time job writing for a US-China business magazine.

"Which bureau?" Lew was Mr. Clear and Concise, yet he was asking this open-ended question.

"Paris would be nice. I speak French," I started, noticing his eyebrows rise. "But my first choice is Hong Kong. Definitely." He was the boss, and I was messing with him. He grinned.

Unlike most major American news media, which had rushed to open bureaus in Beijing as soon as China opened up in 1979, *Business-Week* chose to cover China from the British colony. Two days earlier I had learned that our Hong Kong correspondent, Hal Ellithorpe, was trying to arrange a transfer back to the United States. This was my chance.

Yet at twenty-seven, I was young and untested. I had never worked in any *BusinessWeek* bureau, let alone produced stories on my own eight thousand miles away from my editors.

I sat tall, trying to look older than I felt in his presence. "China is the best story out there."

For me, the allure of China rose partly from the fact that it had been closed off for so long. During my childhood and youth, so-called "Red China" was hidden behind a Great Wall of isolation after the Communist victory in 1949. Americans were denied entry. Chinese people were barred from exit. News was skewed, filtered by state propaganda.

In the three years since Deng Xiaoping's celebrated visit, China had become America's new best friend. American businesses were scrambling to figure out how to profit from Deng's policy of welcoming foreign trade and investment. If I could get this posting to Hong Kong, I would have a front-row seat to this epochal shift in global relations.

Lew's shoulders relaxed, and he reached for his worn coffee cup.

"Let's hope that opportunity is at least half as good as everybody hopes. Every corporation in America is trying to get a piece of the action. One billion people. There's never been a bigger market. But China is so backward! They're all poor and brainwashed, right?"

I couldn't find the words for it, but I knew already that China was more complex than that. When I was growing up in the 1960s, I had been taught about totalitarian regimes, yet when I visited it, China did not seem monochrome and lockstep. It was neither an evil empire nor a socialist paradise, as some American scholars thought. But this wasn't the moment to contradict the big boss.

"You bet. China may not be the savior everyone is looking for," I countered. "Deng wants to give his people a chance to make their lives better, but Communists are notoriously bad at running the economy. Nobody knows when they might start another political campaign and blow it all."

"I thought all that bad stuff was over now that Mr. Deng has taken over." Lew leaned in. He was always most comfortable when discussing the news of the day.

"It's much better now. When I was in Beijing, most of the billboards were about the Four Modernizations, not Marxist slogans. But people are still skittish and not sure they can trust the government."

"You think Deng will really be able to keep it going, this Four Modernizations thing?" Lew clearly enjoyed the give-and-take.

"That's the big question, isn't it?" I answered, forgetting for a moment how much control Lew had over my life. "I just read a book by some Harvard professors. They claim China will become the next export powerhouse in Asia, just like Japan and Korea and Taiwan. But to me, that seems far-fetched."

"So you think all this excitement about China is overblown?"

"No, not at all! China could be a huge market for American business. But how could it ever manufacture stuff good enough to export? Chinese workers have jobs guaranteed for life. They've forgotten how to work hard."

"We'll see. It will be a great story to watch—and to cover." Lew regarded me as if he wished he were my age, heading off to report on this big story.

The big question hung silently in the air between us. Would he offer me the job?

Lew's face turned serious. "Here's my main concern. The Chinese are so secretive. They don't trust foreigners, especially foreign journalists. How would you get the real story?"

I paused. "It will be hard, no doubt about it. But I do speak the language."

He regarded me for a few moments, as if sizing me up. Quiet and soft-spoken, I did not fit the mold of an aggressive reporter. I had often been frozen by doubt, staring at the telephone and a list of people I needed to interview, unable to gather the courage to dial even one number. I kept that side of me secret—mostly.

"You can do interviews in Chinese?" he asked, his pale eyebrows rising quizzically.

"Yes, no problem. I did that in my last job." But behind my bravado, I wondered: How *would* I get Chinese people to tell me the real story? "Sometimes," I continued, more softly now, looking inside myself for answers, "sometimes you can gain people's trust by being . . ." I wondered how candid I should be. "By putting them at ease, by asking the right questions in language they can understand."

Had I blown it? Lew Young was one of the most hard-charging journalists I had ever met. The furrows in his forehead deepened, but his eyes softened.

"If we sent you over there," he said, "when would you be ready to go?"

The previous day, the heat in my New York apartment had gone on the fritz for the third time in a week—during the coldest freeze in January. A few months earlier, a thief had ransacked my apartment, stealing my violin and high school ring. Before that, a stranger had socked me in the face near Grand Central Station. I was ready to leave.

"Tomorrow?"

He laughed. "We'll see."

My hope took flight. I floated out of his office like a Chinese dragon kite.

❧❧❧

I barely slept that night, looking back and looking ahead. As the city lights streamed across my bed, I pondered: What was it about me, always wanting to fly off to distant places?

Nobody in my family had voluntarily sought out such adventures. The US Army had sent my dad to Burma and India during World War II, but he had hated it and longed for home. When my older brother graduated from college, he deliberately avoided going to Southeast Asia, which then meant fighting in Vietnam. In my family, Asia meant war and poverty.

Yet two weeks after graduating from college, I had confounded them all by flying to Singapore, half a world away, to teach English and study Chinese for two years. I felt no fear. Though my pay was puny, my teaching schedule allowed me to explore Asia on the cheap. I trekked the Himalayas in Nepal, explored ancient temples in Indonesia, marveled at Taiwan's marble gorge, and fed the sacred deer at temples in Japan. Breathing in the sights and sounds and smells of cultures I had never known, I developed a passion for going outside my comfort zone.

Still, I was stumped when a friend in Singapore asked me, "All of us Americans in Asia came here to escape something. What are you escaping?" Was I escaping something? Certainly not the things she suggested—my parents or childhood or identity.

Later, it occurred to me: I was escaping *ordinariness*. I had grown up the third of three look-alike Jones sisters in Ohio. I wanted to distinguish myself. I wanted to be *extraordinary*. I wanted to *be somebody*. Whatever that meant.

Flying off to the far side of the planet and exploring the jungles of Borneo by longboat wasn't a rejection of my placid childhood. It was reaching out toward what was, to me, the extreme unknown. I wanted to step out of the familiar and travel the larger world and write about it. I longed for a roller coaster ride of emotion, for euphoria and disaster, for love and despair.

If Lew gave me this chance, I would leave behind Little Me, the nagging voice that said, *I'm not important. Why should anyone want to talk to me?* I would cloak myself in this new mantle: *BusinessWeek*'s correspondent covering China. Maybe then I could really be somebody.

❀❀❀

The next day, Friday, January 16, 1982, the chief of correspondents, Keith Felcyn, called me into his office. He told me he had phoned our Hong Kong reporter and offered him a transfer back to the States. He showed me the memo he had sent to Lew Young, formally recommending that I be assigned to Hong Kong. I would be responsible for covering not only China, Hong Kong, and Taiwan, but also Southeast Asia, Australia, and India. That was about a third of the world's population! I could hire freelancers to help, but I would oversee them.

"Things still might fall through, but it looks pretty definite," Keith said.

Ecstasy zipped through me like a jag of lightning.

"Music to my ears," I said, trying to keep my cool. "When would I go?"

"We'd like you to overlap with Ellithorpe for a few weeks. Could you be ready by June?"

I smothered my doubts and grinned. "Whenever. I'll be ready."

That spring, I spent five months studying Cantonese, the dialect of Hong Kong, catching up on the latest news, and contacting China experts across the United States. I didn't have many belongings to pack.

Just before I left, I went home to Youngstown for a few days to visit my parents. My dad, who had encouraged me to pursue journalism starting in high school, was thrilled.

My mother's only words of advice: "Just don't marry a Chinaman."

I just chuckled. That sounded far-fetched.

CHAPTER TWO:

Disorientation

❦❦❦❦❦

鬼佬, *gweilo: a cheeky Cantonese term for "foreigner,"
usually translated as "foreign devil."*

Within a few days of my arrival in Hong Kong on June 19, 1982,
I felt like Alice in the looking glass. People spoke unintelligible
words, rules were wacky, expectations were upside-down, and I was
an alien.

I lived, temporarily, at the Mandarin Hotel, in the heart of the
Central business district, with its posh lobby where the rich and
powerful met for cocktails or high tea. My room was decorated with
fragrant flowers, a terry-cloth robe, and gleaming granite sinks. From
the window, I watched container ships and the Star Ferry crossing the
harbor. It was an oasis from the heat, humidity, and bus fumes in the
crowded streets of the city.

On hand to orient me was Harold Ellithorpe, a former freelance
reporter who had covered the Vietnam War. Still dressing in the

rumpled safari suit of a war correspondent, Hal was nearing retire-ment and had succeeded in getting *BusinessWeek* to hire him and arrange a transfer back to the United States.

When he came to the Mandarin Hotel to meet me for brunch the day after my arrival, he greeted me with a warm smile and a handshake. "Nice to meet you at last."

"Likewise," I said, feeling suddenly shy. I had worked with Hal remotely for more than a year, sitting in New York, editing stories he submitted from Hong Kong. I wasn't sure how he felt about a newbie like me.

A pleasant American with a round belly and a shuffling gait, Hal had the permanently sunburned look of a white man who had spent many years squinting into the tropical sun.

"The editors were happy with the China oil story," I added. We had just finished a long piece on how forty major corporations were preparing to submit bids to explore for oil off China's southern coast.

"Glad to hear that," Hal said, navigating me to the elevator bank and pressing a button for the top floor. He showed no frown of displea-sure about the amount of editing we had done. I had basically rewritten his whole story, adding in extra telephone reporting of my own.

At the restaurant, Hal introduced me to his wife and ordered a gin and tonic. I ordered a mimosa. It was a Sunday, not a work day. "Janie can help you get settled," Hal offered. "She has a friend in real estate who can find you a good apartment."

"Yes!" His wife smiled. "I can give you other names, too. Our doctor. My hairdresser. Even a manicurist. Well, if you want one." Glancing at my unretouched fingernails, she blushed.

I felt a rush of disorientation. Why would I want a manicurist? And did I look like I needed a better haircut? I probably did. My hair had frizzed out in Hong Kong's humidity.

By the time my omelet arrived, complete with British-style stewed tomato, my inner nerd was chomping at the bit. "So, what do you notice in China?" I asked Hal. "Are Deng's reforms really making a difference in people's lives?"

"Oh, China," he said, with a flick of his fork. "You never know what to believe."

"But what have you seen over the years? Do you notice a difference in the way people look in the streets and how they talk to you?" Hal had lived in Hong Kong since the fall of Saigon in 1975, and American journalists had been able to visit China for three years now.

"Well"—Hal savored a sip of his gin—"my sources tell me that what you need to watch is the big state-owned industries." He shoveled a chunk of fried egg into his mouth.

I cocked my head, only half surprised. "So, it's hard to get into China for reporting?"

He nodded. "Going there in person is a lot of trouble. Getting a visa and all that. Besides, all they tell you there is lies. You can find out much more here in Hong Kong. I'll introduce you to Father Ladany. He's been reading all that stuff out of China and knows what's what."

Stunned, I nodded respectfully, trying not to appear judgmental. Of course the Chinese government had a reputation for twisting the truth; it had proclaimed the Great Leap Forward a huge success even as millions were dying of starvation. But surely you could observe *something* by going to China. Now that it was more open, there had to be better sources than a Hungarian Jesuit writing a newsletter from Hong Kong.

At the end of the meal, Hal picked up the check. When I thanked him, he waved his hand. "Thank Father McGraw," he said, implying he would expense it to our company, McGraw-Hill.

Hal had agreed to stay on a full month to train me. My way of covering China, I vowed, would be different. I wanted to get to know it from the inside.

❦❦❦

The next morning, Hal took me to his office—my office—the *BusinessWeek* bureau in Hong Kong. He explained, with a mix of pride and shame, that he had set it up on a shoestring budget a year earlier.

In a summer squall, Hal and I waited at the hotel entrance in the taxi queue. Ahead of us were prim British bureaucrats, flamboyant Texan execs, and discreet Japanese salarymen. Silk ties, fitted suits, well-pressed shirts, subtle cologne, polished leather shoes—all made me feel out of place in my batik cotton skirt and sandals. *What do women foreign correspondents wear? Safari suits?* I wondered.

Our taxi drove us away from the sleek high-rise office buildings of Central east to Wanchai, a rabbit's warren of run-down buildings crammed together. Queen's Road East—hardly royal—was lined with open-fronted shops selling rosewood furniture, plastic pails, fine fashion, fresh fish, and financial services, as well as massage parlors, tailors, and barber shops. Old women laden with plastic bags and young men protecting their heads with briefcases dashed through mud-puddled alleys. The cab slipped down a side street lined with vegetable hawkers and turned onto another avenue, lined with dripping palm trees. A mob of signs jutted out from the buildings like fingers, with shop names in Chinese and English. Some had neon strips outlining the shapes of martini glasses and naked girls.

Red taxis, blue double-decker buses, and black Mercedes drove at top speed, screeching to a halt at every stoplight. I held on tight so I wouldn't catapult into the front seat, where Hal was conversing with the driver in pidgin English. I realized that I knew more of the local Chinese dialect, Cantonese, than he did, although I had studied it for only a few months in New York. Clumps of people waited at every light, more people per square inch than in midtown Manhattan. The streets had British names—Gloucester, Lockhart, Johnston—but the shop and building names were mostly Chinese. East had bumped up against West here for 140 years.

The cab swerved right under an overhead freeway and screeched to a stop in the shadow of the flyover, just off Hennessy Road. Hal pulled out some multicolored bills to pay the driver. I stepped out onto a sidewalk that was cracked and buckled.

The reek of urine seeped out of a low-slung building: the Canal Road public toilet. Exhaust fumes and cigarette smoke mixed with the stench. Honking horns and the roar of traffic from above banged on my eardrums.

"This is it, Chang Pao Ching Building," Hal said, pointing across the alley at a scrawny, gray, twenty-story structure. I looked up and managed to read a Chinese sign poking out of the building next door:

LITTLE SISTER LEUNG, SECOND FLOOR did not describe the services she offered.

This was where I would work, alone. It was a long way from the McGraw-Hill building in Rockefeller Center.

On the fifteenth floor, my wet sandals squeaked as Hal led me down a grimy hall to a small door with four signs by it, one of which read *BUSINESSWEEK*. Our Hong Kong bureau was a tiny room in an office shared with several random Chinese entrepreneurs. In it: a metal desk, a filing cabinet, an electric typewriter, and a telex machine. It stank of sweat and cigarette smoke. Through an unwashed window, I could see over the tops of grubby urban buildings to a sliver of the Hong Kong harbor and the misty mountains of Kowloon. Not the glamour I had imagined.

Hal gave me a quick demonstration of how to work the telex machine, which would be my lifeline to New York.

"First, I type out the article the usual way." He waved at the typewriter. "Then I take the copy over here to the telex machine and retype it." He sat down and poked a few keys. With a *clunk*, each key punched a pattern of holes on a long strip of yellow paper called a tele-tape. "I just got this machine. It's great." Hal grinned. "Before, I had to run over to the UPI office and ask them to send my copy. Now, I can just feed the tape into a reader on the machine, and ta-da! It goes off directly to New York!"

"Does it take a long time to type on that thing?" In our New York office, we had only recently begun using computers but still received stories by telex.

"Well, yes, but not as much as before. If I finish writing a story at, say, six p.m., it takes me until seven thirty to punch a tape and send it. Sometimes later. Janie complains when I get home late."

I must have looked dubious. Hal continued, "Way better than the old days in Saigon! For breaking news, we had to dictate our stories over the phone. Or send them by courier."

This telex machine was state-of-the-art international journalism in 1982. But I didn't relish the idea of late hours in the office—especially in this neighborhood.

✿☙☙✿

That evening, I had drinks with a journalist at Hong Kong's Foreign Correspondents' Club (FCC). Robert had formerly worked at the *China Business Review* in Washington, and we had friends in common, who had suggested I look him up. Now he had a great job as China economics reporter for the *Far Eastern Economic Review*, so we were both young Americans making our way in new jobs.

When we entered the main bar of the fabled club, then in Sutherland House, I stopped to soak it in. I had arrived. It had high ceilings, tile floors, and a well-stocked, wood-paneled bar, surrounded by swiveling leather stools on metal posts. Lively, chatting foreigners occupied almost all the seats. Smelling of wood polish, wet carpet, and Scotch whiskey, the bar felt very colonial—in this British crown colony of Hong Kong.

Along one wall were blown-up posters of cover stories written by FCC members. *Far Eastern Economic Review* and *Asiaweek* had quite a few; *TIME* and *Newsweek* were represented. So was *The Economist*. But not *BusinessWeek*. Not yet. It was an enchanting scene, a club for the privileged few, and I had earned the right to join, simply by becoming a foreign correspondent in Hong Kong. Would I one day feel at home here?

Robert found two stools at the bar and introduced me to a few of his friends, who welcomed me as one of their own and immediately exhorted me to join the club. They seemed like a motley crew, a mix of old-school British journalists, brash hard-drinking Australians, and stylish young Chinese and British women in advertising and public relations.

"Most of these guys are at the bar every time I come," Robert whispered confidentially, after ordering local San Miguel beers for both of us. "I don't know how they get any work done!"

With one conspiratorial grin, Robert put me at ease. But the people at the bar didn't look anything like my college buddies, grad school friends, or New York colleagues. I listened to their chatter, mostly gossip, wondering which might become my friends. It was hard to imagine.

Not only was I a long way from home, I was a long way from China.

༄ ✤ ༄

By Wednesday, my culture shock had intensified. That afternoon, Hal took me to meet two of his most trusted and admired colleagues. Typical of his crowd, he met them at a bar.

Hal and I took the subway to Kowloon—a modern underground system that made New York's screeching trains look dowdy. Instead of tokens, we used cards, purchased from a machine, and the cars were clean, air-conditioned, and graffiti-free.

The minute we emerged into daylight on Nathan Road, odors of flying grease from hot woks, bus fumes, and flowery perfume assaulted my nose. Kowloon was a sea of humanity, dodging, darting, ducking, and striding down Nathan Road, in clots, knots, and tangles. Stern, bearded Sikhs with turbans guarded banks. Windows sparkled with diamonds, gold necklaces, Rolex watches, stereos, cameras, and knockoffs of famous brands I had never heard of.

Hong Kong in 1982 was an odd mix of East and West, backward and modern, a paeon to capitalism on the edge of the world's largest Communist country. Though just twenty miles from the border, Kowloon had none of the socialist austerity of mainland China.

Once Hal and I entered the Sheraton hotel, the hubbub receded. Doormen and bellhops in uniforms smiled and bowed. Cool air rushed over my face, and the silence soothed my ears.

The bar, on the fourth floor, overlooked the harbor, but we turned our backs to the misty view. Taking a seat at the marble-topped bar, Hal introduced me to his two best friends: Bert, a former UPI reporter now working as a freelancer for McGraw-Hill's trade magazines, and Kevin, a columnist for the *South China Morning Post*.

"Bert was one of the last reporters evacuated from Saigon in April '75," Hal told me, as if that were last year. Bert smiled weakly and raised his scotch glass. He was so skinny that I thought he might fall off his barstool. I remembered watching those unnerving scenes of helicopters picking up frantic people in Saigon, seven years earlier. During my college days.

"And Kevin—he's a fixture in Hong Kong. He's been here for . . . what? Ten years?"

"Nah, going on fourteen years. Pleased to meet you, beautiful lady," Kevin said. "What can I get you to drink? Don't tell me you don't do hard liquor."

"Kevin was one of the first Western journos who went into China after Mao died in 1976," Hal told me. "He's really plugged in. He knows all about China."

"Nice to meet you," I said tentatively. "Um, gin and tonic?"

"A gin and tonic for the lady," Kevin said to the bartender. "They're sending girls over here now, are they, Hal? The times, they are a-changing."

You bet, I thought. *The male-dominated world of journalism is on its way out.* Just twelve years earlier, women at *Newsweek* had sued for the right to work as writers, formerly a job reserved for men, and now we were getting more opportunities.

Together, the four of us "drank lunch" for two hours. I didn't hear a single insight on China, just laugh-out-loud tales about encounters with wacky Chinese and deadlines missed because of drunken binges.

"So, why did they send you to Hong Kong and not Peking?" Kevin asked me.

I had wondered that myself. The *New York Times, Washington Post, Los Angeles Times*, UPI, and Associated Press had all opened bureaus in Beijing in 1979. "Because," I answered, as confidently as I could, "*BusinessWeek* covers business, not politics. Taiwan and Hong Kong are bigger trading partners than China right now."

"Ah, I see," he said. "Taiwan is an economics story. China is a political story."

I nodded sagely, as if I knew this already. But was it really that simple? It dawned on me that these two men were Hal's best news sources. That was why he had introduced me to them.

As I listened, the mist outside the windows grew so thick that Hong Kong Island disappeared completely. The gin took the edge off my screaming sense that I was a total outsider.

Hal was quiet as we walked back up Nathan Road. He was on his way out, as was his whole generation of Vietnam correspondents, most of them scarred by the war. I was an "occasional social tippler" in a world of "substantial imbibers"—in Hal's words.

After we returned to the Mandarin, my mind churned. Many of my friends back home in America were "China types"—people like me who had studied the language and the history of China and were fascinated with all the ins and outs of the news. To Hal and his journo friends, I represented a new, incomprehensible reality—a wave of idealistic young foreign correspondents, some women, some with master's degrees, many fluent in Mandarin. Ignorant about the details of the Vietnam War, we were arriving with the skills and eagerness to cover a new story: the emergence of China. Getting our news tips at the bar from other journalists wasn't going to work for us. At least, not for me.

But where—and how—would I find mentors, friends, colleagues, guides? My colleagues and mentors in New York were eight thousand miles away, and the closest *BusinessWeek* bureau, in Tokyo, was an expensive, four-hour flight away. In this city of five million people, I felt alone.

CHAPTER THREE:

Hong Kong Jitters

⤳⤳⤳

大班, *taipan, "big shot": a Cantonese term describing a powerful executive, used mainly for British overlords of Hong Kong trading firms.*

From the day I landed, I felt compelled to prove myself. Could I hit the ground running before Hal left in just four weeks?

During those first nights in Hong Kong, my shortcomings gnawed at me. I had never worked as a reporter in the field, with or without a bureau chief to guide me. I knew a lot about China, but my knowledge of other places in Asia was minimal. And my understanding of business was skimpy. I had only recently learned the meaning of "CEO." How could I cover banking and technology and the stock market?

I wanted badly to make it, to achieve and be productive. My all-girls high school, Hathaway Brown, had given me confidence. Princeton had trained me in how to compete in a man's world. But now I was in Asia, and I had been warned that Asian men did not respect women as Americans did, so I wasn't sure how I'd be received. I knew women had to work twice as hard as men to get the same recognition. The way to prove myself was to write memorable articles.

Much of what I knew about Hong Kong came from James Clavell's historical novels. *Tai-Pan* told the tale of a swashbuckling, opium-smuggling British trader and his American nemesis in the 1840s. Its sequel, *Noble House*, was set in Hong Kong in 1963 and featured descendants of those two rival trading families. *Taipan* means "big shot" in Cantonese, and the biggest of the bosses of British-owned trading companies was the head of Jardine Matheson.

As luck would have it, a taipan story broke just two days after I arrived in Hong Kong. Simon Keswick, the forty-year-old scion of the Keswick family, showed up in town, and Jardine Matheson announced that he would take on the number-two role at his ancestors' revered company. The Keswicks, related to the Scottish cofounder, William Jardine, had controlled the powerful trading company for generations. In recent years, an outside manager had run the company, which had prospered in real estate and merchant banking. Now, suddenly, the young master seemed poised to push him aside and take over as the next taipan.

This news set the colony's business community atwitter. It was a great story for Hal and me to work on together, although it broke only a few days before our Tuesday deadline.

The biggest issue in Hong Kong was fear for the future, and this news fed right into that. Britain had controlled the island since 1841 and signed a ninety-nine-year lease to occupy the bulk of the territory in 1898. The Chinese government considered the lease invalid, since it had been signed under duress when China was too weak to resist attacks by European powers.

Both the British and the Chinese residents of Hong Kong were obsessed by 1997, the date Britain's lease expired. Many commercial mortgages ran for fifteen years, and business decisions were being delayed because of uncertainty over land ownership after 1997. Many local Chinese had already fled once from the Communists, who had confiscated most factories and businesses in China. Business was the lifeblood of Hong Kong.

So if the colony's oldest and most famous British trading company, Jardine, was investing in Hong Kong—or taking its money out—that mattered. Pundits guessed that Simon Keswick's ultimate plan was to move Jardine's headquarters someplace safer. Most *BusinessWeek* readers could not name a single Chinese businessman, but they cared about the descendants of the British taipans.

"So, how do we get a quote from this guy?" I asked, lifting piles of newspapers off the one extra chair in our tiny office.

"No way," said Hal, swiveling from his desk. "He just landed yesterday. He won't be speaking to reporters today."

"Well, we could try. Shouldn't we call his office and see?"

Hal laughed. "Actually, I talked to Jardine's PR guy at the bar last night. He's an old friend of mine. He told me all about young Simon. Doesn't know much. Hates Asia."

"Could the PR guy get us an interview?"

"I doubt it. I'm sure Keswick has meetings all day," he began. Then, seeing my face, he added, "But I'll put in a call."

He did, and, as expected, the taipan-in-waiting didn't return our call. But Hal knew plenty of people in Hong Kong willing to comment. I watched him work the phones.

I sent a telex to Bruce Nussbaum, editor of the International Business section of the magazine in New York, pitching the story. Bruce told us to go ahead with a brief piece. I read all the local news accounts and took notes as I listened to Hal, and I drafted the piece myself. "I just came from New York, so I have a pretty good idea of what they're looking for," I explained.

Hal didn't seem to mind my pushiness. "Pretty good!" he said after reading it. He suggested a few changes and then guided me through the process of typing it up on the telex machine that afternoon. Bruce changed my lede, the journalistic term for the first few sentences of an article. Some editor in New York almost always did. But he kept most of the rest and ran it under the headline "Jockeying at Jardine to Be the Next Taipan." It didn't go beyond what others had written, but Bruce sent me a note praising it as "timely and lively."

During my year and a half in New York, Bruce Nussbaum had guided me and championed my dream of moving to Asia. Now in

Hong Kong, I could pitch stories to any section of the magazine, but International Business was the most obvious choice, so Bruce was the editor I wanted to please most. I knew he had my back.

I was off to a good start. At least I was in the magazine. Some reporters went weeks without getting in print. In a way, all of us foreign correspondents competed for space in the magazine. If the news was quiet in your part of the world, you had to bide your time.

⚜⚜⚜

That evening, I was sipping a cold beer in the paneled American Restaurant, watching a steaming plate of kung pao chicken land on the table. Across from me sat a young woman named Cindy, a redhead from North Carolah-na. She was two years younger, with easy laughter and relaxed banter. Despite the restaurant's name, it had some of the best Chinese food in Wanchai.

After all the male journalists I had met—and failed to relate to—I was hoping to meet some girlfriends to relax with. She seemed like a good possibility, but she made me nervous.

Having dinner with her was against the rules—at least, the rules as I had been taught. She worked for Seavex, a small company that found advertisers for *BusinessWeek* in Asia. My training as a journalist had warned against any fraternizing between the "editorial" and "business" sides. Socializing with a business-side person could expose me to charges that I was being influenced to write positive stories about companies that advertised in the magazine. But Lew Young himself had encouraged me to get together with Cindy, so here we were.

As we ate, I said nothing of the Jardine story I had just finished. It wouldn't be public till the end of the week. Likewise, Cindy did not mention the names of any advertisers; that reassured me. Instead, we talked guys and what it felt like to work in a field dominated by men.

"Have you ever dated a Chinese guy?" she asked.

"No, never." I thought for a minute. "In Singapore, there was a Chinese guy who seemed interested in me, but I was obsessed with someone else. He was kind of sweet, but some Asian men have a real attitude toward women. Back in New York—get this!—some Korean trade official invited me to a business lunch, ostensibly to talk about trade. He took me to his favorite restaurant . . ." I hesitated for dramatic effect. "The Playboy Club!"

"Oh, no!" Cindy gasped. "Do the waitresses really wear bunny ears and tails?"

"You bet," I reported. "Our waitress was about my age. Her cleavage showed as she delivered my iced tea. The Korean guy acted like there was nothing weird about it."

Cindy clamped her hand to her mouth to keep the chicken from flying out. "What about the guys on the thirty-ninth floor? How did they treat you? Not many women there, right?"

I laughed. "Oh, there are women editors, some really smart ones, all pretty low-level. Most of the men treated me with respect. But one time . . ." I hesitated, not sure if I should tell this story. Something in the sparkle of her eyes made me decide to go ahead. "One time, several of us editors were leaning over a table, looking at a layout. There's this one guy—an old man with wild white hair, well regarded for his economic analysis . . ."

"I think I know who you mean." Cindy grinned.

"I was focusing on the layout, and the next thing I knew, he wadded up a piece of paper and tossed it into my blouse, trying to hit my boobs."

She guffawed and almost knocked over her beer.

"And I never dress sexy!" I felt compelled to explain.

We laughed at the stupidity of clueless men who didn't know they were acting like jerks. Talking about it with Cindy took the edge off the offense I had felt at the time.

In 1982, women had just broken through many barriers in the workforce, and office-conduct rules were vague. A gender discrimination lawsuit at *Newsweek* had put pressure on all magazine editors to promote more women. Still, men held almost all the highest jobs at major newspapers and magazines—a legacy of decades when women were expected to stick to home and family. It didn't bother me that my bosses were men; that's just how it was. I knew I was breaking ground.

During college summers, I had worked under a female city editor at the Youngstown *Vindicator*, Annie Przelomski, but she was hard-edged and had to be, in that hardscrabble, industrial city news-room. In my field, she was the only role model I had. I admired her yet didn't want to end up like her: childless, chain-smoking, tough-talking, thick-skinned. But I didn't know what my other options were. I didn't want to be a sexy flirt. Or a country-club socialite. Or a high-heeled fashionista. Or a pearl-decked television newscaster. I knew what I didn't want to be, but I wasn't sure what I wanted to be. Substantive, knowledgeable, well read, competent, confident, respected by the men in my field. What did that look like in a woman under thirty?

Cindy and I relaxed as we traded war stories. Beneath her bubbly laughter, I could sense her depth and drive. Like me, she felt extremely lucky to have been given a substantive job in exciting Hong Kong. Finding Asian advertisers for an American magazine was also a new frontier. Lew Young had given us each a chance, and now we had to prove ourselves capable.

We were both adrift in a sea of unfamiliar faces, far from our roots and from the office environment of New York. I was glad I had breached the firewall and found her.

But here I was in Hong Kong! I needed to nudge myself beyond the familiar and get to know some Chinese people.

⚭⚭⚭

A few days later, just after noon, I stood in the lobby of the Mandarin Hotel yet again, this time looking for a woman called Mrs. Ng. An acquaintance in New York had insisted I ring up her mother, Julia Ng, once I got to Hong Kong. Although it seemed an unlikely con-nection, I had dialed the number, and Mrs. Ng had offered to take me out for lunch.

"Ng," I practiced to myself, as I looked around. It was a Cantonese name, and her daughter had taught me to say it correctly, with no vowels, just the phonetic sound *nnng*.

A small, sturdy, middle-aged woman, clutching her purse on her lap, stood up when I entered the lobby lounge. Clad in a belted floral silk dress, she had a quiet dignity that reminded me of my mother—although she couldn't have looked more different. Speaking in clipped British English, she suggested we "take lunch" at Luk Yu Tea House, the most famous dim sum place in Hong Kong, just a few blocks away. The Cantonese invented dim sum, but among themselves they called it *yum cha*—drinking tea.

When we entered, I inhaled a tantalizing aroma of steamed buns, vinegar, and ginger. On the ground floor, all guests were Chinese, and most tables were taken. The chatter was all in Cantonese. Wooden chairs scraped on the tile floor. Overhead air conditioners, mounted high on the wall, hummed. Clinking cups and plates competed with outdoor sounds of horns honking.

A waiter in a buttoned white jacket approached us, pointing to the staircase leading to the upper floor. Mrs. Ng spoke to him firmly in Cantonese, and he led us sullenly to a table in the back of the ground-floor section of the restaurant.

"Normally, you see, they insist that all foreigners sit upstairs," Mrs. Ng explained, as she straightened her skirt and sat down, placing her pocketbook on an empty chair. "I ordered *bolay* tea. Can you take it?"

"I'm not familiar with *bolay*," I admitted, as the teapot and two small cups appeared on our table. I reached for the pot.

"It needs to steep," she said, hovering her hand above it to keep mine away. Her tone was matter-of-fact, but I heard a rebuke in it. What kind of China expert was I?

A waiter, straight-faced and surly, pushed a wheeled cart next to our table. Mrs. Ng pointed to two small, round bamboo baskets, and the waiter put them on our table. Two sets of steaming buns. I was pretty sure I knew what was inside: barbecued pork in one set, yellow lotus paste in the other. "*Char-siu* and *lian-rong*?" I asked, mixing Cantonese and Mandarin.

Her penciled eyebrows went up as she poured me a cup of tea. She wore a large jade ring.

"I studied Cantonese in New York before leaving," I felt compelled to explain. "But mostly I speak Mandarin."

I wanted to get past her stiff exterior reserve, so I began to ask about herself and her life. She held her head high as she told me she was born in Hong Kong and graduated from Diocesan Girls' School and Hong Kong Baptist College. That made her a local elite in a city where many residents had fled from poverty in China. Her husband had run a small factory, but he hadn't made "real money" until he started investing in real estate in Hong Kong.

"That's why we could send our children to university in London and Boston."

More carts rolled by, with other dim sum specialties. Mrs. Ng pointed at her selections with a tilt of her chin and a brief Cantonese word. The food was steaming and delicious. Fat shrimp dumplings, spinach and crabmeat in a rice-paper bun, tofu rolls with pork in sauce, crisp flaky pastry with mashed dates, and a small bowl of honeydew-sago soup. I watched her to see which ones she dipped in vinegar and which she ate with more than one bite.

As we dined together, Mrs. Ng's stiffness melted. She began to give me advice.

"How much is your housing allowance?" she asked directly. "Oh, then you can't live on the Peak, or in Mid-Levels. You could try Happy Valley; that's close to your office. I'll give you the name of a rental agent who is more honest."

More honest? I thought. I assumed people were either honest or not.

"Most Hong Kong people can't be trusted. All they care about is money," she said, peeling the paper off the bottom of a fluffy bun. "They figure foreigners are dumb, so they add at least ten percent to the rent. Rents are so high now. Foreigners are partly to blame. They fly into Hong Kong with huge housing allowances. That unfairly jacks up the rents for local people."

Talking about money seemed to enliven her. But she gave me other advice, too.

"Don't bother trying to learn Cantonese. Foreigners can't pronounce it properly anyway. And it's only spoken in Hong Kong. Mandarin is more useful in China."

"You need to buy new clothes. Silk is the best for this climate. A lot of foreigners shop at Stanley Market. Good prices there."

By the end of lunch, which she insisted on paying for, the stiff, formal lady I had met at the Mandarin was gone. She was direct, directive, emphatic.

Not like my mother at all, I decided. But maybe the mother I needed, here in Hong Kong.

As we walked out of Luk Yu, she turned to me with one last piece of matter-of-fact advice. "Oh, and don't fall for a Chinese man. All they want is an American passport."

CHAPTER FOUR:

China's Back Door

⚛⚛⚛

*走后门, zǒu hòumén: go in through the back door. Find
an unconventional workaround if you can't get what you
want through official channels.*

I took Mrs. Ng's advice—well, about real estate, anyway. Since finding
a home in Hong Kong was a high priority, I contacted her "more
honest" real estate agent, who took me out to look at apartments for
rent in several neighborhoods. I fell in love with one of the first I saw.

Flat 9B at 5 Shiu Fai Terrace was a three-bedroom unit with a
wall of windows overlooking a green cemetery, the Happy Valley horse
racetrack, and a glimpse of the harbor and the mountains beyond. It
was on the ninth floor of a building, halfway up a slope in an area
called Mid-Levels. I had lived in twenty places in six cities but had
never had a home with such a spectacular view. Gazing out at a far
horizon made me breathe more deeply and spurred my imagination.

The agent assured me that it would take only fifteen minutes to
walk down the hill to my office, not mentioning how sweaty I would

feel after the uphill walk home. She said the rent was reasonable, since Chinese people considered the cemetery view to bring bad luck. The graveyard didn't spook me, but the rent did: about two-thirds of my salary! Fortunately, McGraw-Hill agreed to pay 70 percent of that, as a housing allowance.

What sold me on the place was how sunny and spacious it was. I quickly wrote a check to secure it.

I was hoping to share it with a roommate. Things were looking promising on that front. I had just met two other women, about my age, who quickly became my friends. Both were from Chicago, Midwesterners like me. One had come to Hong Kong to take a job as a paralegal, and the other worked as a copy editor at the *Asian Wall Street Journal* and had studied at the East West Center in Hawaii. Soon the three of us started hanging out together.

On bright, sunny days we would jostle our way onto a crowded ferry, wander along paved paths in hilly, green parts of the islands, and then come back for an evening of sunburned hilarity at Ned Kelly's Last Stand, a loud Australian bar with an amusing jazz band.

As I explored with my new friends, I could see that Hong Kong was the antithesis of mainland China. It was capitalistic, money-obsessed, pragmatic, efficient, international. Its richest rode in Mercedes with uniformed drivers and dined on fine food at fancy clubs. Everyday folks climbed up bamboo scaffolding for their construction jobs, shouted to be heard over ever-present jackhammers in the street, lined up for Jackie Chan kung-fu movies, and pawed over Cantopop cassette tapes at outdoor markets.

Hong Kong was the only city in the world that made Manhattan look slow-paced. Blurry bodies zipped along its wide sidewalks, weaving in and out so recklessly that out-of-towners like me could easily be elbowed, overrun, cut off, or shoved out into the traffic. At major intersections, a growing pool of people waited for the pedestrian cross signal, and the minute it switched to green, my body was swept along with the crowd at a breakneck pace. Everyone was in a hurry. Money-making was the common goal.

Taxis and trams, subways and buses made it easy to get around, but I also did a lot of walking. No need to go to a gym for exercise!

Construction everywhere, utility ditches, pipes, bulldozers. Always someone hosing down the pavement in the morning. Motorcycles parked on the sidewalks. Short skirts, long legs, high heels, long hair. Horns honking. Grime on streets, on clothes, on shoes, on my face, on my hands.

In the streets of Hong Kong, 1984

Hong Kong was and wasn't Chinese. Around 99 percent of its five million people were ethnic Chinese. But the British still ruled it as a crown colony, with a London-appointed governor and a supreme court filled with white-wigged expatriates. Signs were bilingual and reflected British usage: CARPARK, FLYOVER, ZEBRA CROSSING. Pirates still smuggled illegal immigrants from China in false-bottomed boats. Most Hong Kong Chinese considered themselves lucky to be living outside the borders of "mainland China."

As an American expatriate, I found it easy to get around. English was taught in the schools and spoken widely by local Chinese, with a distinctive, semi-British accent. English was enough to take a taxi, converse with a waiter, ask directions, and even shop in an outdoor food market. Across the border in China, by contrast, very few people spoke English, and expats who lived there had to learn Mandarin or else rely on interpreters. As a language geek, I enjoyed trying out simple Cantonese with taxi drivers.

I wanted to step out of the expat bubble, to find more Chinese friends like Mrs. Ng. I started at my office. Just outside my door, a young Hong Kong Chinese woman sat at a desk in the common area. She ran her own company, arranging exports for some small manu-facturers. Janita Tam chatted with me pleasantly, in excellent English. Later, I would hire her part-time to clip news articles I marked and file them for me. But when I asked her to join me for lunch, she declined. During eighty-plus years of colonialism, a barrier had grown up between locals and expats.

I wanted to get under the surface, to converse with Chinese people who would tell me the real story of their lives. I wanted to get "behind the Great Wall."

❧❧❧

Two weeks after my first article, an even bigger story broke. Britain's prime minister, Margaret Thatcher, announced that she was planning a trip to Beijing in September to begin discussions about the colony's future.

This news set off a tsunami of fear. The British promised they would never abandon Hong Kong to the grip of China's Communists, but the very prospect started an outflow of investors and capital. Penniless refugees had no hope of leaving the territory, but those with money scrambled to find a way out. Under the British, Hong Kong had been a stable haven, with clear rules, well-enforced laws, and wide-open opportunities for entrepreneurs to thrive. Now, it seemed, all that might end.

Hal and I got the go-ahead to cowrite a political analysis and interviewed experts to explain what these talks might mean. This time, I did a lot of my own reporting. When I called people on my contact list, I was pleased that most returned my calls promptly. The name *BusinessWeek* really did carry some weight in this town.

Since it was a "news analysis," we got a rare byline. Under Lew Young, *BusinessWeek* did not allow bylines for ordinary news articles, but he made an exception for news analysis, book reviews, and "letters from." It felt great to step out from anonymity. I knew my parents, back in Ohio, would see my name. Dad would be proud.

By the time Hal left, four weeks after my arrival, I felt on top of the world. The pace had been hectic, but that was life in Hong Kong. I had located an apartment I could afford, and I was eager to move in and enjoy its big, sunny windows and shiny wood floors. I had made some friends and loved my job. I was confident I could cope on my own.

But my ultimate goal was to report directly from China. That was proving to be frustrating. China's Communist leaders suspected all foreign journalists were working for their governments as spies, so they tried to keep close tabs on American journalists and prevent them from visiting off-the-beaten-track parts of the country.

The process of applying for a journalist's visa was onerous. You had to apply months in advance, explain exactly where you planned to go and whom you hoped to interview, and then accept a Chinese "minder" who would accompany you every step of the way—and would report to the Communist Party on what you did and said.

But when I went to apply, I found out there was a catch. I was told that China had a strict policy: foreign journalists must apply from their home country, not from Hong Kong. I could get a tourist visa in Hong Kong, but not a journalist's visa, which would allow official interviews.

It was a catch-22. Here I was, on China's doorstep, and I couldn't get a visa.

Frustrated, I slipped into China through the back door, just for a weekend. An American company, Beatrice Foods, was celebrating the opening of its factory in Guangzhou (formerly Canton), just three hours north of Hong Kong by train. Eager to see one of the first American investments in China, I skirted the rules. I got a tourist visa by identifying myself as "a housewife" and made it across the border just two months after I arrived. The whole time, I was looking over my shoulder. Was China's famous security apparatus tracking me? Apparently not. But I didn't want to take my chances again.

There had to be a workaround. I remembered the Chinese proverb "The higher-ups have their policies; the lower-downs have their workarounds."

Back in Hong Kong, I kept trying to reach the Chinese officials at Xinhua, the news agency that functioned as China's unofficial consulate. Finally, they agreed to let me join a government-sponsored tour with seven other Hong Kong–based foreign journalists. In September, we would visit northeast China, formerly Manchuria, home to much of the country's heavy industry. This part of China was known for gray skies and pollution, but for a business journalist, it seemed a good place to start.

I was relieved. At last, I would get an inside look at how China's economic reforms under Deng Xiaoping were affecting life on the ground. Yes, there would be minders and limits on access. But I had pounded persistently on the door to China, and they had finally let me in.

CHAPTER FIVE:

Behind The Bamboo Curtain

☙☙☙☙☙

老百姓, *lǎobǎixìng: literally "old hundred names," meaning the common people, or ordinary people, as opposed to government officials or military.*

I figured things were going well on my first official trip to China when, before breakfast on my first morning in Beijing, I got a proposal of marriage. The sky was high and clear that September day as I took an early stroll in Tiananmen Square. In front of the gate to the Forbidden City, a young Chinese guy, dressed in a typical blue Mao jacket, came up and asked me, in Mandarin, what country I was from.

My New York–honed instincts told me to pick up speed and walk away, but I had promised myself I would grab every opportunity to talk with the common people of China.

"*Meiguo*," I replied. America.

Delighted to hear me answer in Chinese, he told me he had come to Beijing from the nearby city of Tianjin to look for a wife.

"Look here." He pulled out a much-folded southern Chinese newspaper and pointed to what looked like a small classified ad, with a grainy photo. I could see a name, the age of thirty, and an address. "That's me! I placed this ad a month ago. Southern girls are richer than northern ones. But I've only heard from poor country girls! It's probably because my salary is low." The ad said his salary was equivalent to $20 a month. This guy did not look like someone sent by the Ministry of State Security. More like an enterprising—yet serious—goofball.

"How old are you?" he asked me, scrutinizing my hair and face.

"*Er-shi-ba*," I answered (twenty-eight), eager to talk to an ordinary man in the street.

He cocked his head, considering this. "Are you single?"

"I am." I flinched at where this conversation might be going.

"How much money do you make each month?"

"*Buhao shuo*," I answered. (Hard to say.) More than $20, for sure.

"Well, then, do you want to be my girlfriend?" His eyes gleamed as he leaned toward me.

I backed up and mumbled something about how I needed to get going.

"Where do you live?" he persisted.

"Hong Kong."

"Oh." He seemed only slightly deterred by the distance, more than a thousand miles. "It still might be possible. Write down your address." He whipped out a pen and a small notebook.

Hoping to get rid of him, I complied, confident that it was almost impossible for ordinary Chinese citizens to get to Hong Kong. I should have given him a fake address, but I didn't foresee that I would later receive letters addressed to "Beloved Comrade Dori."

What I loved best about China was the unexpected—the chance to connect with ordinary people across the borders of language, country, and culture. Unlike in Hong Kong, with its fast pace and global savvy, people inside China were more likely to stop and chat.

On this trip, as a reporter touring five industrial cities in

Manchuria, traveling with a group of international journalists, I knew my schedule would be filled with official activities. We would have sit-down interviews with leaders of a huge auto complex, a watch factory, a "furcraft" business, a film studio, a farm, and a "daily-use metals" factory that made razor blades in joint venture with Gillette. I planned to dutifully take notes. Interviews with government officials were important; they implemented policy. But my heart was with the folks in the streets, who were eager to converse with me—despite decades of propaganda about greedy American imperialists out to dominate the world. So I looked for every chance I could get.

A few days later in Harbin, China's northernmost city, I went out again for an early walk. Although it was September, the chill Siberian winds whipped through the city streets. Foolishly, I had brought only one pair of shoes, sandals. My toes turning into ice cubes, I was ready to turn back when a tall, pleasant man in his midthirties, clutching a book, approached me.

"Good morning," he said, in well-practiced English. "Do you speak English?" When I said yes, he continued, "Good. I study English by this book." *Advanced English.*

This time, communicating in simple English, I found a different sort of encounter. A worker in a railroad equipment factory, this guy was developing new skills.

"Why are you studying English?" I asked, as we started walking slowly along the street.

"I study Russian before. No good. Everybody study English now."

"You speak well. Can you use English in your job?"

"No no no." He shook his head emphatically. "Factory work not good. I want new job."

Now I was curious. Normally, Chinese assigned to a factory stayed for a lifetime. The system was rigid but provided security; it was called the "iron rice bowl." "What kind of job?"

"I don't know. Translator? Trade office?"

"Not at the factory?"

"No. Office-job pay is better."

His attitude showed how rapidly China was changing. For decades, individual Chinese had been forced to hew to the Party line—continuing revolution and class struggle—and to pretend they cared more about Party loyalty than about personal well-being.

During the Cold War, China was said to be "behind the Bamboo Curtain"—a take on the Iron Curtain in Europe. Now that the Bamboo Curtain was being parted, we in the West had a chance to see for ourselves what was going on behind it.

For the article I planned to write, I decided to look for examples of people whose lives were affected by Deng's reforms—evidence of how resilient and multilayered China was. I discovered them everywhere—even in this conservative, industrial part of the country. Nobody stopped me from approaching people in the street.

In the warmer port city of Dalian, I talked to a young peddler woman selling eyeglasses. Her tiny business was known as a *getihu*, individually owned. Just five years earlier, such entrepreneurship would have exposed her to charges of being a "capitalist roader," politically suspect. She told me she bought the glasses in southern China, where government-owned factories produced better-quality consumer goods, and then traveled more than a thousand miles by train to Dalian every spring to sell them on the street. Each fall, as the weather grew cool, she went back to her home in the south—"just like the swallows"—to visit her family and replenish her wares. She had a young son, whom she left with his grandparents.

"You must miss him," I said, sitting beside her on her plastic mat on the sidewalk so I wouldn't block potential customers. My dad was a retailer, so I thought of that.

"Oh, no, he's a naughty boy," she said. "Makes my mother so angry sometimes."

"You're lucky. In America, grandmothers don't usually take care of the children."

"Are you married?" she asked, squinting through a particularly ugly pair of glasses. Most of her products had clunky frames—black for men and orange or white for women.

"*Hai meiyou*," I answered. Not yet.

She smiled. "Good. That makes life easier." This surprised me. Many Chinese pitied me because I was still single and childless. Here was a strong woman daring to run her own business—and her own life.

In another city, Jilin, I chatted with a group of workers outside a watch factory. One asked me how much money I made. They earned fifty yuan a month, about $10, the price of one watch. When I demurred by telling them the cost of living was higher in America, one worker asked me to calculate how many watches I could buy with one month's paycheck. It was a good question—a better comparison than a dollar salary. After a quick mental calculation, I said twelve, although the actual number was much higher. They murmured in amazement. Such riches were beyond their imagining. It never crossed my mind—or theirs, I'm sure—that thirty years later, their sons might buy multimillion-dollar houses in American suburbs.

In every city we visited, streets were lined with outdoor stands and small repair shops owned by individuals. Although all factories were still government-owned, their managers talked openly about capitalist notions of profits, prices, and bonuses. Trade officials tried to persuade us their provinces were eager to attract foreign investment. Everywhere I went, I sensed a pent-up demand for change and an intense hunger for a chance to create a better life.

Many street corners had big billboards with political slogans in red characters, but the messages were not strident. Most referred to the "Four Modernizations" that Deng Xiaoping espoused. That policy of strengthening agriculture, industry, defense, and technology aimed to make China an economic power by the twenty-first century. Like most political slogans, that goal seemed far-fetched. China had an average per capita income of about $200 a year.

Maoist thinking was still widespread. The walls at a truck factory reception room were plastered with quotes from Chairman Mao. The manager talked about encouraging workers with bonuses, but he added, "The main key is ideology." The old ways of thinking were deeply ingrained in millions of people, especially in this region, which had benefited from Mao's policy of heavy industrial development.

Still, as I talked to more Chinese, many of my American stereotypes faded. They did not seem oppressed, looking over their shoulders, worried about censorship or government control. My professors had taught me that the Chinese were communal, putting the well-being of family and clan above self, and yet the ones I met in China eagerly embraced individual ambition.

I discovered something surprising about myself, too. When I interviewed people in Mandarin, I forgot that I was introverted. I have heard actors say they forget about stage fright the minute they begin to act. For me, speaking in a foreign language was like that. When I began to ask questions, my self-consciousness fell away and a confident reporter, much more fluent in Chinese, leaned forward with thoughtful, probing questions. Once I discovered I could count on that alter ego, I left my insecurities in my suitcase with my toothpaste.

Although I had been inside China twice before joining *Business-Week*, I realized that China was far more complex close up than it was from a distance. Reading the morning newspaper in America made it easy to analyze China and draw conclusions, as if it were a single entity. Actually observing the country on the ground made those generalizations seem superficial. Most important, although the state still controlled China's industrial strength, the entrepreneurial fervor of Chinese individuals—so obvious in Hong Kong, Taiwan, and Southeast Asia—had been unleashed. The genie was out of the bottle.

CHAPTER SIX:

Suspicions and Frustrations

ᴄᴓᴓᴄᴓ

麻烦, *máfan: bothersome, annoying, troublesome, frustrating.*

After the official tour of Manchuria ended, I spent an extra five days in Beijing. My goals were to make some contacts there, at the embassy and US businesses, and to figure out how I might report from Beijing in the future.

I stayed at the Jianguo Hotel, Beijing's first foreign-built joint-venture hotel, which had just opened its doors. A low-slung, motel-style building with an artificial brook between its wings, it was a replica of a Holiday Inn in Palo Alto, California. When I walked through its glass doors, I couldn't believe I was in China. Its doormen and bellhops wore sharp, modern uniforms and smiled when they greeted me in English. It had a French restaurant called Justine's and a bar called Charlie's.

After checking in, I strolled along China's main central avenue, which runs east–west through the city center. Commuters in identical white-collared shirts wove in masses through wide bicycle lanes. The central lanes were for crowded buses and boxy sedans with dark-tinted back windows, chauffeured for the government's many officials. What a contrast with colorful Hong Kong! No neon signs, no shops, no advertising, no skyscrapers, no miniskirts, no imported luxury cars. The tallest building was the Beijing Hotel, its eighteen-story east wing visible from blocks away.

This day, I had arranged a meeting at the Beijing Hotel's famous lobby bar, really just a set of tables in its high-ceilinged lobby, where foreign businesspeople were known to congregate. This bar had earned a nickname: the Hall of Broken Dreams. In 1978, during the first rush of excitement over China business, it had attracted hundreds of American and European traders, hungry to sell to a newly opened China. But suddenly, in 1979, China had backtracked, suspending contracts and restricting imports. The foreigners drowned their sorrows at this bar. Now, four years later, China was opening its doors again, and businesspeople were back to test the market, this time skeptical and cautious.

I was there to meet Ron Redmond, Beijing bureau chief for United Press International. Ron was a key contact for me. I didn't have a story to file from Beijing this time, but if I ever did in the future, I would need access to a telex machine. As UPI was a wire service, its reporters filed all their stories by telex, and they also had a Xinhua "ticker" that featured up-to-date news day and night.

A tall, confident American, Ron had no trouble finding me. "If you don't mind, let's go straight to the bureau. Our cook serves dinner at six on the button. My wife is out of town, but my colleague, Paul, is at the bureau. You'll join us?"

Pleased at his warmth, I felt my anxiety melt. And I was curious to see the UPI bureau. If *BusinessWeek* decided to open a bureau in Beijing in the future, my life would be like Ron's. The bureau was in a diplomatic residential compound. Only foreign diplomats and journalists lived in these apartment complexes, and Chinese guards prevented anyone from entering unless they lived or had official business there. Our taxi dropped us off at the front entrance, where a barrier blocked entry by outside vehicles. Several military guards stood at attention. Ron flashed his pass and told the guard I was his guest.

"They're short on space, so I have to live and work in the same apartment," he told me, striding across the courtyard to his doorway. "It's cramped, but it's actually pretty convenient. If anything happens in the middle of the night, I can check on it."

The UPI bureau looked like a typical Chinese flat, with a dimly lit entryway and several rooms off a hallway. I could hear the ticker clicking away.

"Paul, look lively! We have a visitor!" In one office, tapping away at a typewriter, was Ron's colleague. He stood up.

"Hey there. Great to meet ya." Paul had a Chinese face but spoke fluent English. "I'll be done in a minute."

"Better hurry, Paul," Ron said, as he led me to the dining room. "It's 6:02. Cook is probably fuming."

As we passed the small kitchen, I caught sight of the cook, a man in an apron, brandishing a pair of cooking chopsticks and grumbling about how the food was getting cold.

"He's assigned to us by the Diplomatic Service Bureau," Ron told me, as if that explained his rudeness. "We got rid of the last cook because he spat in the sink."

The dinner was not cold at all and looked delicious. Three big platters of Chinese food: chicken with mushrooms, thin slices of sautéed beef, and a heaping dish of green veggies. A cold bottle of local beer awaited each of us. I wished I had a cook, grumbling or not.

As we ate, I told them of my difficulty getting a visa as a Hong Kong–based reporter.

"I'd try the All-China Journalists Association," said Ron. "They can set up a tour for you. But you have to plan it out in advance and give them a list of exactly who you want to see."

"Ha!" Paul harrumphed as he reached for a morsel of chicken. "Those people say they're a nongovernmental group, but their job is to spy on you. They always send someone with you. They listen to everything you say and write reports to the Communist Party."

"Still," Ron countered, "that's the only way to gain access to provincial leaders who would never respond directly to a foreign reporter."

"It gets old quick, this spying crap," said Paul, lifting his beer. "Especially living here, in this compound. Everything is monitored. Our conversations, our mail, our phones, our telexes. Welcome to life in the complete grip of totalitarianism!"

Suddenly paranoid, I looked around. The cook slammed the door as he left.

"No kidding," said Ron. "See that lightbulb hanging over the table?" he asked. It was a single bulb on a long cord. "We assume that's where they hide the mic. Last night, I asked for more beef in our diet, and look!" He pointed to the plate of sliced beef.

They both laughed. Stunned, I stood up to inspect the lightbulb.

"Oh, the mic is too small to see. But there's a whole office in the back of the compound where the monitors work. Hordes of them come every day on bicycles."

I was appalled. "What if you need to discuss something privately?"

"We just go outside somewhere and take a long walk."

"Just to leave the city, we have to do battle with four bureaucracies!" Paul grumbled. "And we have to give them ten days' notice. Ten days! How can we cover the news that way?"

"When I was in Manchuria," I told them tentatively, "I noticed that people are living better now. They're working hard for themselves, and they seem to have more hope."

"You just go on believing that," said Paul, laughing. "All these reforms under Deng could be just a flash in the pan. The whole thing could fall apart in a minute. Remember Democracy Wall? Everyone was so full of hope, thinking they could say whatever they wanted. But then the government tore down all the posters and tossed the leaders into jail."

"I don't know," I said, starting to wonder about my own observations. "I talked to a lot of people on the streets. They love the new freedoms."

"Of course they love them. But the government will let it go only so far before it cracks down. Everybody knows that."

These journalists had a dark sense of humor, a grim paranoia, and a pessimistic view of the country. Later, I would learn that this was typical of Beijing-based reporters I met: they hated China. One reason was the difficulty of getting their visas renewed every year. Another was the stress of knowing that their translators, cooks, and drivers were all writing reports about them every day.

Before this dinner, I had been envious of the journalists based in Beijing, but now I wondered. Covering China from the comfort of Hong Kong, I was more upbeat about the country and its future. I wondered who was more objective.

⚜⚜⚜

I arrived back in Hong Kong with a massive tangle of impressions and details. That evening, I sat down on my couch to go through my notebooks and sort out my thoughts.

In two weeks, I had visited five cities in China's industrial heartland. Overall, it was still the Old China, dominated by inefficient state-owned factories, grimy with smokestacks and scrap metal, crowded with Soviet-style trucks and peasants carrying loads on poles. Modernization seemed as unlikely as a group of wobbly Chinese bicyclists setting out to win the Tour de France.

Still, I had seen many examples of Deng Xiaoping's economic reforms and how attitudes were starting to morph. I wanted to make sense of the contradictions I had witnessed and yet convey the sense of hopefulness I felt.

By Monday evening, I finished writing a long story, studded with quotes from my on-the-ground reporting from inside China. Those Beijing-based reporters had trouble getting out to the provinces, but I had done so. I typed the story on my typewriter, edited it by hand, and then spent an hour typing it into the telex machine. I took a taxi home and fell asleep immediately.

On Tuesday morning, I arrived early at my office, around 8:00 a.m. That was 8:00 p.m. in New York, so I knew I would have the edited version of my story to review that day. During my eighteen months in New York, I knew the drill: reporter sends in story; three editors and the copy desk revise it, then send it back to the reporter in the field. There it was, on the telex machine. I tore it off and sat at my desk, pen in hand, expecting to make a few corrections.

From the first sentence, bile rose in my throat. This version bore no resemblance to my story. The basic premise was there, but the heart had been ripped out. All my quotes had been purged. The variety and complexity I had observed was gone, replaced by newspaper quotes from Chinese leaders, as well as quotes from US-based China professors.

One thing I had learned in New York: because *BusinessWeek* was a weekly magazine, group journalism was in our DNA. No one got a byline. The articles reflected input from a range of people. New York had the final say. Insisting that New York editors throw out their version and go back to mine was not an option. I had one day to make revisions, corrections of fact, not style or theme. I worked that whole day, suggesting examples from my reporting that supported the new theme.

On Wednesday morning, I got back the final version of the story. Someone in New York had added two short quotes from my reporting, plus another paragraph mentioning Manchuria. Otherwise, the story ran as rewritten in New York.

I gave myself a day to cool off; then I called Bruce in New York, despite the huge expense of long-distance calls.

"Why did you even bother to send me out here?" I protested. "I go to China and see five cities with my own eyes, and you run a story that was basically written from New York."

"I get it, I get it," he said. "But don't forget who our audience is. We need a story that is easy for American readers to understand."

"What? Are American professors more believable than eyewitness reports?"

"Dori, calm down. You know what I mean. Americans don't know shit about China. They need context. A clear, concise story line."

Bruce's affable, sensible voice mollified me. He promised to run a sidebar I had written about a Western-style business school in Dalian.

As glamorous as it seemed to be a foreign correspondent, my stories were not my own. It wasn't lost on me that while Beijing journalists railed against the Communist bureaucracy, my biggest frustration was with my editors in New York.

I wanted to reflect, in my writing, the everyday realities of life in China—the real China, not the government in Beijing—but my magazine would not allow for such nuances and perspectives. I could not write the full, complex story I was seeing but had to simplify in ways my readers would understand. I wondered: Didn't this create a distortion of the news Americans were reading about China?

"Actually, I think the article is pretty damn good," Bruce added. "It does more to explain China's economic reforms than anything I've read."

He was right. The headline was "China Walks the Edge of the Capitalist Road"—a good quip for what I had seen. And I liked the illustration: a long Chinese New Year dragon with many human feet underneath—half of them going ahead and half going backward. But it wasn't my article. It didn't reflect the flesh-and-blood stories I had heard on the ground, how complex and multilayered China was.

I tried to be philosophical. After all, I was the one who got to travel throughout China. Bruce and the other editors were stuck in desk jobs in Manhattan.

CHAPTER SEVEN:

A Whiff of Panic

⋐⋑⋐⋑⋐⋑

自信心, *zì xìn xīn: self-confidence. Literally, trust in your own heart.*

*H*istoric news was breaking all around me.

While I was in Beijing, British Prime Minister Margaret Thatcher was there, too, on her first visit to China, holding private meetings with Chinese premier Zhao Ziyang and his boss, Deng Xiaoping. By the time I returned to Hong Kong, the colony was in panic mode.

An outspoken anti-Communist nicknamed the "Iron Lady," Thatcher had just won a war with Argentina to keep the Falkland Islands. She seemed determined to convince the Chinese to agree to continued British administration after 1997—with some face-saving mumbo-jumbo about Chinese sovereignty. Anything less, the British believed, would trigger a massive flight of people and capital. Most of us Westerners hoped she would succeed, though it seemed unlikely.

But Deng would have none of that. He wouldn't budge on his insistence that China would take back Hong Kong. To offer reassurance, though, he said China would wait until 1997 and make it a Special Administrative Region, with no changes in its way of life.

Despite the unbridgeable gap in their views, China and Britain announced they would begin formal negotiations over Hong Kong's future immediately, with the common aim of maintaining its "stability and prosperity." That wording would prove to be a key to understanding China's priorities.

But Hong Kong people weren't buying it. Lacking confidence in both Beijing and London, many began making plans to leave. Real estate and stock prices took a nosedive.

During this market mayhem, I was given a new task, crucial to my own future: to arrange interviews for Lew Young, the big boss in New York who had chosen me for this plum job. Lew planned to visit Hong Kong in late October, just four months after my arrival. Still a newbie, I wanted to impress him and bolster his confidence in me.

As editor-in-chief of the major business magazine in the most powerful country in the world, Lew Young expected to be treated like royalty. He sent me a telex letting me know that he wanted to talk to the "movers and shakers" in Hong Kong, and that it was my job to set up the meetings. Still wrestling with my meek self-image, I had been hesitant to contact important men, but Lew's order gave me an excuse to call and a deadline for action.

The centerpiece of his visit was to be a reception introducing me. Our advertising partners at Seavex had booked the Hong Kong Club, a posh private dining club for the colony's rich and powerful British merchants and officials. Only recently had Chinese men been allowed to join; women were still not admitted as members. I loved the irony that I would be honored there.

To get ready for the reception, I bought my first-ever designer dress. Hong Kong–based Diane Freis, with her colorful polyester georgette prints, had recently captivated the fashion industry. I paid what seemed an exorbitant price for a dress in blue and maroon, with a swishy skirt and tassel ties. Wearing it, I felt glamorous, but I wondered how well I would hold up at the reception. Chitchat was not my forte.

❦❦❦

The day Lew Young arrived, I met him in the lobby of the Mandarin Hotel. He was sprawled in a big chair, reading the *South China Morning Post*, and looked up as I rounded the corner. Tucking the newspaper under his arm, he bounded across the carpet to greet me with a firm handshake. The fringe of thinning blond hair behind his ears was wet, and his head gleamed like a pearly bowling ball. He smelled of shower soap.

"This place is falling apart!" he exclaimed, his blue eyes blazing.

I looked around the lobby, as meticulous as ever.

"The stock market! It's going bonkers! They all think the Reds are gonna take over."

Oh, right. "It's more than that, actually," I began, switching to *BusinessWeek* speak. "The property market is tanking, and some banks are collapsing."

As we walked to the Peking Garden restaurant for dinner, he quizzed me more.

"Real estate values started dropping the minute Thatcher shook hands with Deng in Beijing," I continued, trying to sound like an old pro. "Land values in Hong Kong are down by eighty percent. The big banks lent a lot of money on some risky property deals, and now they're underwater." Already, I had learned to sum up complex situations in a few slangy sentences.

Our advertising "guys," including Cindy, were at the table when we arrived, and Lew greeted them effusively.

"So, you and Dori have met!" Lew said, hanging on to Cindy's hand after shaking it. "You should be roommates!"

Cindy and I exchanged startled glances. We had been hanging out together a bit. But she had her own apartment, and we both assumed that being too close would cross the firewall between business and editorial. Apparently, it didn't bother Lew.

"You ordered Peking duck, of course?" Lew asked Cindy's boss, Francis Powers, who had. After some chitchat with them, the cold-appetizer platter arrived, and Lew turned his laser eyes on me. "So—who have you got lined up for me?"

He nodded thoughtfully as I told him about three days of interviews with many of the top men in Hong Kong. The biggest names were Trevor Bedford, taipan of Hong Kong Land, which owned most of the skyscrapers in Central, and Hong Kong Financial Secretary John Bremridge, formerly taipan of Swire Pacific.

"Good, good." Lew nodded in approval.

Then he turned to Francis. "What about the governor? And that new guy, the young taipan at Jardines?"

""I tried," I interjected. "But you know the Brits."

"Yeah. They think they're God Almighty," Lew said, with a wide gesture. "Colonial types. Do you know how much trade Hong Kong does with the US?"

None of us could answer.

"Around ten billion dollars. Now, that's nearly twice as much as US trade with all of China. That's why we sent Dori here to Hong Kong and not to Beijing. But we do six times as much trade with Taiwan. But you know how much trade we do with Britain? Less than half our trade with Taiwan. Asia is rising and Britain is falling. Yet these guys act like they're still ruling the world."

I sat in silence, drinking it in. So this was how he measured the importance of countries, by the size of American trade with them. I would need to plan a reporting trip to Taiwan. Soon.

The following week, Lew and I went from office to office together, and I learned a lot—not just about Hong Kong, but about reporting. For me, Lew's visit produced a mix of anxiety (would anything go wrong?) and heady exhilaration (was I really meeting these bigwigs?). I prepared good questions for him to ask. He opened each interview with some schmoozing. Then he leaned in and asked hard-hitting questions, but he never stopped exuding respect for the men he was interviewing. Each time we walked out of an interview, Lew gushed with enthusiasm. The financial crisis was terrible for Hong Kong but great for us as business reporters. We were a good team. Plus, we got some vivid quotes.

Our best quote came from the financial secretary: "There's been a whiff of panic in the air"—a classic British understatement!

After we finished the interviews, it was time for the cocktail reception. Nervous, I put on a touch of lipstick and donned my designer dress. Lew wore a fine suit custom-made by a Hong Kong tailor. He and I stood by the door and greeted everyone who entered. As head of

Seavex's office, Francis Powers introduced all the guests, mostly people he had invited. While I smiled and shook hands, I realized that many of the invited guests were in public relations or advertising; few were the kind of top-level executives Lew and I had interviewed. Although I knew I would need the help of these PR folks, I was disappointed.

As we greeted guests, Lew showed me off. Not only did he want to demonstrate that he was upgrading *BusinessWeek*'s coverage of Asia, he wanted to flaunt that he had promoted a bright young woman to a prestigious job.

"You know, she went to Princeton," he told several people in front of me. "She speaks fluent Chinese."

I was a little embarrassed; I almost never told people I went to Princeton, to avoid being judged arrogant or snobby. But I was also pleased at his pride. I was to be the eyes and ears of *BusinessWeek* in Hong Kong and China, and Lew wanted to ensure that the British and Chinese business communities treated me with respect.

Still, I was unproven, and I knew it. Those British PR guys, many of them former journalists, probably thought I was as likely to succeed as a woman on the Welsh rugby team.

"Are you in Hong Kong by yourself?" asked one flabby Brit, sipping a fragrant scotch.

"Yes, it's a one-person bureau," I answered.

"No, I mean, did you come with a husband?"

I was taken aback. "No."

"Really?" He looked me up and down, taking in my dress and figure. "Well, maybe you'll write a nice love story, like Han Suyin."

Half of me felt complimented. I adored the writing of Eurasian author Han Suyin and had read all her books, not just her best-selling *A Many-Splendoured Thing*, in which she fictionalized her affair with an Australian journalist. But I was repelled by this idiot's assumption that I, a business reporter covering China, could at best write a love story.

To the Brits and the Aussies, journalism was a scrum, meant for high school leavers or hungry young graduates of third-rate universities. Men in their twenties, yes, might come to Hong Kong, aggressive and competitive, to make a name for themselves. But they assumed that women just weren't assertive or determined enough to make it.

In my case, I suspected they were right. I was getting better at picking up the phone and asking to speak to chief executives, but I knew I would never develop the bluster of Lew Young.

Unlike the Brits, American "papers" had a habit of hiring and promoting graduates with advanced degrees from major universities. When China first opened its doors to US journalists, the *New York Times*, *Washington Post*, and *Los Angeles Times* all sent Harvard graduates to Beijing, including Fox Butterfield, who had a PhD in Chinese history. All three wrote books afterward. Clearly, I was second string. I had only a master's, not a doctorate, and I had majored in European history, not East Asian studies. I had a lot to prove.

After the last guests left the Hong Kong Club, the Seavex crew and I gathered around Lew to hear what he thought about the evening. Lew was exuberant, repeating many of the compliments he had heard. As an introvert, I was relieved but drained and ready to go home.

"Are you tired?" Francis asked Lew. "What do you want to do now?"

Lew looked at me with a mischievous twinkle. "I'm not tired. How about going dancing?"

My body stiffened, on high alert. *Dancing?* I had never been dancing in Hong Kong. Was he flirting with me? Was this part of my duties? I stared at him with my mouth open.

"Do you know any good dance clubs?" He was asking me, not the Seavex men.

"No, not really," I stumbled. "I'm . . . a little tired."

"Okay. Maybe some other time," he said, as if this had been a simple, standard request.

I got into a cab and went home, and Lew went off with the Seavex guys. Watching the windshield wipers, I felt confused and deflated. Dancing? Was that how Lew Young viewed me?

In the 1980s, women were so rare in jobs like foreign correspondent that there were no rules. What struck me as an inappropriate advance may have been Lew's idea of what young women enjoyed, far from home in foreign locales. I'll never know.

Two days later, the night before he left town, Lew Young and I met for a simple dinner at his hotel. I dressed extra modestly and tried to act businesslike. He surprised me with another question. "So, how long do you want to stay in Hong Kong?"

I wasn't sure how to answer. This was my dream job, and I had been here only four months. "I don't know. I love it here."

"Well, let me tell you the pattern I've seen in the bureaus," he said, laying down his chopsticks so he could jab the air. "In the first year, the reporter is just trying to figure things out. The second year, he's getting better. By the third and fourth year, he's hit his stride, writing good stuff, very productive. By the fifth year, he's getting lazy. He knows all the answers to most questions, so he doesn't bother doing much reporting. By the sixth year, it's time to move on."

I sat back, absorbing this startling perspective. Would I ever get lazy like that? It was hard to imagine. But Lew had been in the business long enough to see patterns.

Before he left, he gave me the go-ahead to write an article based on our interviews. Within a week, I submitted "A 'Whiff of Panic' in Hong Kong," and this time Bruce made sure that very little was rewritten. It was a good length, but it ran deep inside the magazine, on page 172. The real estate collapse that shook Hong Kong to its core barely made a ripple in New York.

Lew's acknowledgment of me, his reception in my honor, and those interviews gave me recognition and validity I needed to be more than just Dori Jones from Ohio. But I knew it would take time to overcome my insecurities and grow into the journalist Lew was projecting me to be.

CHAPTER EIGHT:

Barriers

ᙄᙄᙄᙄ

謙虛, *qiānxū: modest or self-effacing. To Chinese, an admirable, Confucius-like trait. Its opposite is* 吹牛, *chuīniú, to exaggerate or brag, literally meaning "blow cow." (Don't ask!)*

The next six months passed in a blur. Cindy and I cohosted a Thanksgiving dinner for our American friends at my apartment on Shiu Fai Terrace. Our ovens were small—Chinese people typically don't use them—so we each roasted a ten-pound turkey and Cindy brought hers over by taxi. Only one store in town even sold turkeys—all imported from the United States. Our party included six women and four men; it was a success. My community was coalescing.

But a week later, my friend Kevinne was laid off from her job as a copy editor at the *Asian Wall Street Journal*. She had confided in me about criticisms she had heard from her bosses, but I knew her to be smart and capable, so I was surprised. Then another American girlfriend of mine was fired from her job as a paralegal after only a few months on the job.

In January 1983, Cindy's job evaporated, too. Seavex wanted her to return to New York, although she loved living in Hong Kong. I felt like putting a placard around my neck saying WARNING: BEFRIENDING THIS PERSON MAY BE HAZARDOUS TO YOUR CAREER.

It didn't occur to me, at that time, that no young men I knew had been laid off. If they floundered in their jobs, they were given more training and a second chance. The women were sent home with their tail between their legs, certain that it was their fault they had failed.

But, unlike my other two friends, Cindy found a way to stay. She got a job with a small publisher who specialized in in-flight magazines and coffee-table books. Without a housing allowance, she could no longer afford her own apartment, so she moved in with me. In February, we became roommates. Whatever happened in Cindy's office, however badly my editors mangled my carefully crafted prose, we could rant and commiserate with someone who was 100 percent in our corner.

Still, I forced myself to come out of my shell and network. Through the Princeton Club of Hong Kong, an alumni group where I fit in, I developed connections with a few influential men. The biggest was Gordon Wu, a wealthy property developer who had built Hong Kong's Hopewell Center—a distinctive, round tower with sixty-four stories in Wanchai, then the tallest building in Hong Kong. Gordon Wu's office was on the top floor, with a commanding view of the harbor.

In an exclusive interview, he gave me details of a bold plan: to build a six-lane toll road in southern China's Pearl River Delta region, connecting Hong Kong to Guangzhou and other cities in the province. In China, a toll road was a novel idea, and no private company had ever earned a return on such an investment. I wrote a story called "A 'Class Enemy' Bets on China."

As the months passed, I found plenty of other good topics for articles, including a commentary about China's foreign policy, an in-depth look at opportunities in China's oil exploration, and an analysis of China's coal production. When US Secretary of State George

Shultz visited Beijing and Xi'an, I managed to get credentials and tag along as part of the press pool. I developed a dislike for the show-offy preening of reporters at press conferences; I always sat in the back and listened.

Remembering what Lew had said about focusing on countries that did a lot of trade with the United States, I turned my attention to writing about the "four tigers"—the dynamic economies of Hong Kong, Singapore, Taiwan, and South Korea. In April, I planned a big trip to the Philippines, my first, to conduct interviews in Manila and to visit the southern island of Mindanao. As a former US colony, the Philippines interested my readers more than other countries in Southeast Asia.

Still, I beat myself up about my shortcomings. I had been inside China twice but had no good sources there. Some articles I wrote were subpar—including one single-source story about a third-tier American computer maker trying to break into the Asian market. I still railed and raged when my editors rewrote my stories. Some weeks, my morale was low. Once, in a letter to my cousin, I complained bitterly, and she wrote back, mystified, saying, "I thought you loved your job!" Yes, I did. But even the best job has annoyances. I was young and green and alone, trying to re-create myself in my image of a great foreign correspondent, like Martha Gellhorn.

My biggest barrier to success, I believed, was my personality. Especially that self-effacing, self-destructive part I called Little Me.

✿✿✿✿✿

One evening in March, bright light blazed out of cylindrical chandeliers dangling over a Hong Kong hotel ballroom. Cheerful chatter and hearty laughter rose like steam as uniformed servers circulated with platters of delicacies. I tasted a savory bite of shrimp wrapped in bacon and glanced around. Half the faces were Chinese, half Caucasian, and most were men.

My shoulders tightened. Cocktail receptions were torture. I didn't see a soul I knew.

Wait. Wasn't that Michael Sandberg, chairman of the Hong-kong and Shanghai Banking Corporation, surrounded by admirers?

Midfifties, with dramatic dark eyebrows and a full head of white hair, he stood out from the blander-looking executives. And there beside him was Li Ka-shing, the billionaire who had bought a big British conglomerate with the bank's help. I recognized his large glasses and receding hairline from countless newspaper photos.

I ducked behind a column but edged closer.

Sandberg was the head of the biggest bank, and Li was the wealthiest Chinese businessman in Hong Kong. Both would have good reason to talk to *BusinessWeek*'s correspondent, right? I knew I needed to learn to schmooze. If I had been naturally bubbly and sociable, I would have sashayed right over to them and broken in with my brilliant smile.

But I headed the other way, straight to the bar. I asked for a glass of wine to break down my resistance. My back to the bigwigs, I gulped down half of it in three swallows.

"Better get out of here," Little Me warned. "They'll never talk to you anyway."

The nagging voice had dogged me ever since I became a journalist, freezing my hand as I dialed the number of someone I needed to interview. Conscious of my inexperience, I didn't want to say anything dumb or take up someone's time. These men had more important people to talk to than a nobody like me. Maybe this attitude came from my mother, who had taught me good manners, modesty, and deference to older people.

One New York editor had noticed this reticence. "You're right. Those men don't want to talk to *you*. But they do want to talk to *BusinessWeek*." That advice helped me overcome my fear of phoning people. After all, I wasn't asking them for a favor; I was offering them a chance to speak to a large audience. But approaching a powerful man in public? That was different.

I wasn't exactly shy, but I was definitely introverted. Also, like my mother, reserved, diffident, self-effacing, and quiet. For a reporter—in the age of investigative journalism—this personality was a serious flaw.

Just as I stared across the ballroom at the two men I most wanted to meet, trying to screw up my courage, a young Brit in a suit came on to me. "Well, hello there. Have we met?"

I began chatting with him, and by the time I looked for Sandberg and Li, they had left. Failed again! This Little Me idiocy was sabotaging my career. But I was relieved to slink out the door and go home.

Back in my bedroom that evening, though, I read up on Li Ka-shing. Doing extra research was the best defense against appearing dumb. Born in Chaozhou, Li had lost his father at age fifteen and fled to Hong Kong. In the 1950s, he became wealthy manufacturing plastic flowers. When the colony's economy crashed in 1967, he had the foresight—and the cash—to buy real estate at bargain prices. By 1979, his fortune was fat enough to buy control of a colonial powerhouse, Hutchison Whampoa. He sounded like just the kind of self-made billionaire who would appeal to *BusinessWeek* readers.

Landing an interview with Li Ka-shing would be a coup. The problem was, he hated the press. Specifically, he hated foreign journalists, who, unlike locals, could not be bought with bribes. Reporter friends had tried and failed to reach him. Why had I passed up the chance to chat him up at the reception? What a nitwit.

One morning a week later, I noticed a small article in the *South China Morning Post*. Li Ka-shing would attend a ceremony to celebrate the completion of a building his company had developed. I noted the time and place. When the day came, I locked up Little Me in my file cabinet and headed out.

Misty rain kept away most other reporters. Only twenty people attended the ceremony, on a rooftop not far from my office. I was highly visible, the only non-Chinese person. Also the sole woman. The rain let up as the ceremony began.

The tycoon wore a tailored business suit with a striped tie. As he cut the ribbon, his eyes wandered in my direction. I smiled and nodded, clutching my reporter's notebook.

After the formalities, that inner nag, never one to be left behind, began nibbling at my confidence. "He'll never talk to you. He hates reporters," she whined. But this might be my only chance to reach him. I dropped her on the cement floor, quashed her like a cigarette butt under my sandal, and stepped toward Li Ka-shing.

He looked at me with a friendly smile. It was too late to say nothing.

"Mr. Li, I've longed to meet you," I said, using a polite phrase I had practiced in Mandarin. "I am the Hong Kong bureau chief for American *BusinessWeek*." I handed him my name card, Chinese side up, with both hands. This was Chinese courtesy, but I was drawing on something deeper—the manners my mother had instilled. Respectful. Dignified. Ladylike.

He accepted my card and flipped it to the English side. "Miss Jones," he said. Then he switched to Mandarin. "You speak Chinese! Are you visiting Hong Kong?"

"I live in Hong Kong," I said. "I've read about your achievements. *BusinessWeek* would like me to write an article about you. Please, may I interview you sometime, at your convenience?" My Mandarin tones were just right. My Chinese teacher would have been proud.

Like a Confucian gentleman, he nodded in a slight bow. He glanced at a subordinate, who quickly produced Li's name card. "Call my secretary, and she will arrange it."

As I took his card, the tycoon swept out with his entourage.

An unspoken shout reverberated from my gut to the clouds above. Could it be that easy? Perhaps I underestimated my appeal as a fresh-faced, twenty-eight-year-old American woman—and the lure of an article in an influential global business magazine. As an Asian man, Li saw me not as a mere woman but as the personification of *BusinessWeek*. But I suspect he was also responding to my manner—polite and modest, not confrontational or entitled.

I was gaining wisdom that would serve me well: with some people, courtesy and respect work better than brashness. Maybe Little Me could be an ally. Instead of silencing her, I could co-opt her. Your personality type doesn't have to stop you from doing what you want.

If this exclusive interview came about, I vowed to ask some tough questions—while remaining respectful. Could I do that? Like an iron fist in a velvet glove? Would Li be more open with me once I gained his trust? I was in unexplored territory.

෧෧෧

Each article, each interview, each reporting trip added to my courage and self-assurance. Confidence grows with knowing what you're doing—and from doing it well a few times.

As I waited to hear back from Li Ka-shing's secretary, I packed my suitcase for my first "home leave." *BusinessWeek* had asked me to fly back for an all-staff conference in May 1983 in the Poconos of Pennsylvania. All reporters and editors would attend, from bureaus all over the United States and the world. I was eager to compare notes with my editors and colleagues.

One rainy morning a few days before leaving, I stayed home a little later than usual and took stock of my first ten months in Hong Kong. I wrote this in my journal:

"Thinking back on all the self-doubt I had three years ago makes me realize how much I have changed. I wanted so badly to live abroad, to be a reporter, to feel a sense of accomplishment as I saw story after story of mine appear in print. And I have all that now. . . . No matter what else happens in the rest of my life, I know that I was able to rise from a doubt-wracked nobody to a successful foreign correspondent."

I had what I called my Ideal Job in my Ideal City.

Life was peaceful, stable, calm, and orderly. About to be disrupted.

CHAPTER NINE:

Serendipity

☙☙☙☙☙

缘分, *yuánfèn: fate or chance that brings people together.*

On April 28, 1983, I checked in for my Pan Am flight to America. I had stuffed my carry-on bag with magazines to read on the plane. My mind was on my work.

As I boarded my flight, I caught sight of Li Ka-shing. What a lucky coincidence! He was flying to San Francisco on the same plane—in first class, of course, while I was in economy. His secretary had returned my call the day before, promising an interview in mid-May.

An idea popped into my head. Hong Kong people were agonizing about the future. Many wondered: Did Li Ka-shing have a foreign passport? If he did, it meant he lacked confidence in the future of Hong Kong. I decided that I would, upon arriving in San Francisco, try to go through customs right after Li Ka-shing, to see what kind of passport he had. A scoop!

Preoccupied with the proximity of the fat cat, I buckled my seat belt and stared out at the run-down apartment blocks of Hong Kong, so close to the airport I could see each sleeveless T-shirt that the residents hung out to dry on bamboo poles sticking out from their balconies like prayer flags.

Just as I was settling in, a minor commotion in the aisle diverted my attention. A Chinese man was holding a boarding pass and pointing to the middle seat next to me. He was addressing an old woman in the aisle seat.

"May I put that package into the overhead compartment for you?" he asked her, in clear Mandarin. After one frustrating year trying to pick up Cantonese, I was delighted to hear Mandarin spoken in the pure northern accent I had studied for seven years. This man's voice was calm and polite, and his smooth vowels soothed my ears.

Now I watched with interest as the woman responded in Cantonese. In front of her legs was a huge, overstuffed bag, the kind Mrs. Ng disparaged as a "refugee bag." Square, striped, and zippered, it was made of lightweight plastic and blocked access to our row. She looked like a fisherman's wife, yet this man addressed her like a revered grandmother. He smiled at her, picked up the bulky bag, and placed it in the bin as if it had breakable dishes in it. A gentleman.

Nice-looking, too, I thought, as I watched him raise his muscled arms. He had pleasing round cheeks, a genial smile, generous eyebrows, and a hunk of black hair that fell over his forehead in a fetching way. I sat up straighter. His diction and glasses hinted that he was an educated man. And he was kind. Probably in his thirties. He slipped into the middle seat, nodded at me, and fastened his seat belt. Self-conscious, I tucked a strand of hair behind my ear and slipped my *Far Eastern Economic Review* under the edge of my skirt.

As I listened to the flight attendant during takeoff, I formulated in my mind the Mandarin words of a question to ask him. I had a habit of mulling over what I wanted to say before opening my mouth—especially when speaking a foreign language. Maybe this guy and I could have a good conversation in Mandarin. I was always looking for such opportunities.

My mind was not on my love life. Like most of my girlfriends, I was leery of traditional men who might, like those of my father's generation, assume I would give up my career for marriage and children. Most of my girlfriends felt scorn for women who jumped off the professional track and trailed after their husbands.

But I was pushing twenty-nine and had proved I could make it on my own. Before leaving New York, I had walked away from my long-time college boyfriend, eager to fly solo. Now I was starting to think it might be nice to have a man in my life again. Not at the expense of my career! But someone to have fun with. Both Cindy and I had noticed that in Hong Kong the pickin's were not great. Most American men were married, and my buddy Robert—who had seemed promising—had found himself another girlfriend, an American journalist older and more accomplished than I was. Only recently had I begun to consider dating a Chinese man—definitely a step into the unknown. Most of those I met were conventional—bankers or lawyers.

"*Ni zhu zai Xiang Gang ma?*" I finally asked the man. Do you live in Hong Kong?

He turned to me and examined my face: my round nose, blue-gray eyes, wavy brown hair. He answered in fluent American English, "You speak good Chinese!"

"*Wo zhu zai Xiang Gang*," I persisted, "*danshi wo buhui jiang Guangdonghua.*" I live in Hong Kong but don't speak Cantonese.

"Very good!" he persevered in English. "How did you learn Mandarin?"

Very good, but apparently not good enough for him to converse with me in Mandarin. Mildly annoyed, I switched to English.

"It's too bad you have a middle seat," I said, after explaining that I had studied Chinese for two years in Singapore after college.

He sighed and shook his head just as the flight attendant asked what he wanted to drink.

"Actually," he continued, after taking his tea, "I didn't ask for middle seat. I booked aisle seat. But when I get to the airport, Pan Am can't find my name."

"Oh no," I said, smiling at his funky grammar—and sympathizing with his predicament. Being squeezed between two strangers for fourteen hours can be torture, even if you don't have extra-long legs. "What happened?"

"I tell the woman my name, Paul Yang. He looked and looked. Finally he found my reservation—under Paul Wang. They spell it wrong! And gave my aisle seat to someone else." He told the tale with a wry smile and seemed unperturbed. His English was clearly American, fluent but with a charming accent and typical Chinese grammar mistakes—mixing up "he" and "she" and mangling verb tenses. I guessed he was not American-born but had lived many years in the States, where he had picked up the English name Paul.

"That's terrible!" I smiled, glad for my window seat. "You were visiting Hong Kong?"

"Well, I live here now, work here. But home is Portland, Oregon. I go there now—for a short visit." He seemed relaxed and friendly, open to conversation.

Something about him sparked my curiosity. "How long have you lived in the States?"

He examined my eyes, as if deciding how much to tell a young woman like me. "Oh, long time. I came here for grad school."

"Where did you grow up?" My mind was spinning. Obviously, he was not from mainland China. Beijing had only recently started to allow its citizens to go to the United States for grad school. "Taiwan?" I guessed. A lot of northern Chinese had fled to Taiwan in 1949, when the Communists took over, and the schools there used Mandarin.

"Right! Good guess," he said. "What about you? Why were you in Hong Kong?"

I was eager to learn more about his background, but I figured I had to answer some questions about myself first. I told him about my job with *BusinessWeek*. I jabbered about Li Ka-shing, revealing that he was on the same flight. Paul knew all about Li. Clearly, this man was up on all the latest news in Hong Kong.

"I'm a news junkie," he admitted. That did it. We were insiders in the same club. "Well, see, I used to work as a city planner in New Jersey. I got to know lots of reporters from the Bergen *Record*. They interviewed me."

"You're a city planner?" I asked, astonished. Most Chinese Americans I knew were in academics, engineering, or business. His choice was certainly unconventional.

By coincidence, he had moved to Hong Kong in June 1982, the same month I had. His job now was to sell US condos to jittery Hong Kong investors who were eager to find an escape route to America in case China really did take over Hong Kong in 1997.

We talked on, through the first meal and after they darkened the cabin to show the movie. We both disliked the smell of cigarettes that wafted over from the plane's smoking section. We both liked Beijing-style *shui-jiao*, boiled dumplings stuffed with juicy pork.

"So, your parents came from northern China?" I asked.

He nodded. "I was born there. We escaped to Taiwan in 1949, on one of the last flights out of Shanghai."

My mental calculator clicked. He was at least thirty-four. "I like northern Chinese food better than Cantonese food," I said, although in fact I liked both. "I don't know any good northern Chinese restaurants in Hong Kong. Do you?"

"Oh, yeah," he said. "I know a place in Kowloon with great *shui-jiao*."

After the meal, he pulled out his bag and I noticed an ET doll. "For my daughter."

Oh, I thought. *Married*. "How old is she?" I asked.

"She's eleven. My son is thirteen," he said.

Ah. He was probably older than I realized. In his forties?

"They live in Portland with my ex-wife," he added, watching my face for my reaction. "We're separated."

I nodded, pretending it didn't matter. Separated. So, he was available. When had I begun to think of him this way? And why did it matter?

He smiled gamely, with a hopeful look. "That's an interesting dress you're wearing."

I looked down. This particular dress was comfortable on long flights and had a flowy skirt made of eight panels. The seams connecting them were visible outside the skirt. It was one of my favorites. I blushed that he had noticed.

Encouraged, earnest, he continued. "It looks like it's on backwards."

What? I checked his face to see if he was joking. He wasn't. He was just making an observation. I decided not to take offense. Clearly, he meant none. He was just honest. And maybe a little clumsy. Anyway, not skilled in the art of picking up pretty women on planes. Not skilled enough to hide that he had kids. Certainly not out to entice me. That was endearing.

"It's designed that way," I said gently.

After several hours, we finally stopped talking. I closed my eyes and slept, conscious of how close this man was. He was appealing, agreeable, attractive, available. He was Chinese, yet open and easy to talk to. We had common interests. And he lived in Hong Kong. Not like anyone I had dated before, but different in an intriguing way. Surprising. Unexpected. Thoughtful. Besides, most of the men I had ever dated were unconventional.

Usually when I slept on a plane, I leaned up against the window. But it's possible that on that day, my head lolled the other way and landed on Paul Yang's shoulder. That's what he would claim years later, against my protests to the contrary.

After we woke up to eat breakfast, an hour before landing, Paul Yang and I began talking again, groggily, over coffee (for me) and tea (for him).

"You said you liked *shui-jiao*," he began hesitantly. "I could take you to that Kowloon restaurant, if you'd like. When do you get back to Hong Kong?"

My heartbeat sped up. "Sure. In two weeks."

"Here's my name card," he said, handing me a card he had long ago pulled out of his wallet. I received his card with two hands, thumbs on top. In Hong Kong, more than anywhere else I'd ever been, you *are* your name card. What you do is who you are.

I wasn't as prepared as he was. I fumbled in my purse for my cards and handed him one, half turning to face him, using two hands, with a slight bow of the head. He received it with two hands and a slight smile. A formal exchange, but with a frisson of something under the surface.

"I get back in ten days. I'll give you a call."

I nodded. "I'd like that." He probably wouldn't call. If he did, it would mean a nice meal, at least. I wouldn't say no to good dumplings.

When our flight landed in San Francisco, Paul Yang said goodbye, his chocolate eyes warm and easygoing. "Hope to see you again."

"Yes. *Zaijian*," I said. The Chinese word for goodbye means "till we meet again."

Once inside the airport, I rushed and wrangled myself a spot in the customs line just behind Li Ka-shing. He didn't recognize me, and I saw him pull out a Hong Kong passport. So the rich businessman had confidence in the future of Hong Kong. I had seen proof.

I danced through the airport to my connecting gate. It had been a valuable flight: a news scoop, a name card, a dumpling date.

Months later, I would learn the Chinese term *yuanfen*. It means "fate"—a chance occurrence that is meant to happen. If Pan Am had not misspelled Paul Yang's name, I would never have met the man who became my husband.

CHAPTER TEN:

Mango Milk Shakes

∽∽∽∽∽

浪漫, *làngmàn: romantic. The Chinese had no word for
"romantic," a European concept dating from the Middle
Ages, so they created this word, borrowing the sounds.
"Langman" literally means "a flood of waves," implying
"swept off your feet."*

Paul Yang was not a romantic man. In fact, he was a highly unlikely
match. Not at all a man my girlfriends expected me to date. Let
alone my parents. Maybe that's why I dropped my guard.

On a Friday evening a week after I returned to Hong Kong, I
walked into the familiar luxury of the Mandarin Hotel lobby. The
pink veins in its black marble walls winked at me. Chandeliers of
hanging crystal beads made everything glow. Outside the windows,
traffic surged past, but inside I heard only muffled, cheery voices and
the clinking of cups and spoons.

A Chinese man stood up from one of the rosewood sofas and
walked toward me with an uncertain smile.

Yes, it was Paul Yang, the man I had met on the plane. Two days earlier, when he had phoned me at the office, I had needed a few beats to remember who he was. I had answered the call in confident business mode, pen in hand, expecting to take notes. When he told me his name and reminded me of his promise to take me to a good restaurant for northern Chinese food, my shoulders relaxed. Yes, I had enjoyed that meandering plane conversation over the Pacific Ocean. Yes, dinner would be nice.

But now that I saw him in the lobby, meeting me for a date, my doubts kicked in. Who was this guy, really? He dressed simply, in a short-sleeved collared shirt, light blue. No tie. And sneakers. He didn't look like a challenge to my career.

"Dori?" he said, reaching out for a handshake. His smile lit up his face. His teeth were a little crooked. Nothing intimidating about him. Kinda cute, actually.

Suddenly, I felt shy. Our first conversation had lasted fourteen hours, but he was still a stranger. "Have I kept you waiting?" I asked, keeping it formal.

"Oh, no. You wanna have a drink here or go right to the restaurant? It's in Kowloon."

I tried to read his preference in his face, but he was leaving it up to me. "Let's go straight to the restaurant. *Wo hen jiu meiyou chi shui-jiao.*" (I haven't had dumplings in ages.)

We headed for the Star Ferry, talking as we dodged the rush-hour throngs in the warm evening air. "So, you got your interview with Li Ka-shing?" he asked in English.

"Yes! Just a few days after I got back to Hong Kong. His office is pretty plain for a billionaire." Nice of Paul to care about my work.

"Wow. Great! Did you learn any secrets?"

I laughed. "Not really. I asked some pointed questions, but he told me only what he wanted to. He's kinda low-key, actually. Soft-spoken. But he said he could raise three hundred million dollars in twenty-four hours if he needed to."

Paul hummed softly in admiration.

We reached the Central Pier and put our copper twenty-cent coins in the turnstiles. Worth about three US cents, they got us a seat on the air-conditioned upper deck. We followed the crowds up a ramp to the waiting area, where large open windows faced the harbor.

"I can never get enough of this view," I said, feeling oddly nervous about this man. Side by side, we gazed at the barges, junks, and sampans motoring along the narrow harbor between Hong Kong Island and Kowloon, the peninsula on the other side. The sun was sinking, and a breeze rippled the water. A boat horn moaned.

"Yeah. Really nice." The late-afternoon sun was glinting on Paul's glasses. He seemed comfortable in his own skin. I decided to get him talking by asking how his business was going.

"Great! We almost sold out." He told me an amusing story about a group of Hong Kong investors he took to Portland, where they bought condos with cash—at $45,000 a pop. They had no intention of moving there but wanted to own a piece of America, in case Hong Kong crashed.

A bell rang, a metal gate swung open, and the crowd began to shuffle down the ramp and onto the ferry. Paul pushed ahead toward the bow, where the seats had a better view. With a gesture familiar to anyone who has ridden the Star Ferry, he flipped the chair backs so that we could sit facing forward. He offered me the window seat. I liked his easygoing good manners.

We were sitting even closer now than we had on the plane, with no armrest between us. His bare arm was only inches from mine.

"Is that what happened with your family?" I asked. "Did the Communists take your land away?"

He laughed. "Well, no, not really. My dad wasn't a landowner. He worked for the government, though, so he had to get out of there. When we left, paper money was worthless. Have you heard about that? The only thing worth anything was gold."

"Gold?" I asked. "You mean gold coins?"

"Gold bars. About this big." His hands formed a rectangular shape approximately six inches long and two inches wide. "When we left Shanghai, my parents strapped five of them around my waist. They thought children were less likely to be searched. They put the gold bars in a cloth and wrapped it around me, under my clothes. Same for my sister. She was eight."

The image shook me. Two little children, carrying their family's entire savings, strapped to their waists, fleeing their country. "How old were you?"

"About ten."

I quickly did the math. If he was ten in 1949, he was now forty-four. I had just turned twenty-nine. That was a big age gap, fifteen years.

Paul Yang had been watching my eyes as I calculated, and his brimmed with humor. "Yeah. I'm an old guy."

This time, I laughed. "You look young!"

His smile was warm and natural. "That's what they tell me."

With a lurch, the ferry docked in Kowloon. A sailor tossed a thick rope to his coworker onshore, who secured it to the pier. Then we streamed off the boat and out onto a bustling square. Paul lightly touched the small of my back to guide me, sending a tingle up my spine. We flowed along to the main drag, Nathan Road, and walked up a few blocks, then turned onto a side street. Looking at the cacophony of Chinese signs, I suddenly felt very foreign and wondered what the heck I was doing on this strange street with this unknown man.

"There it is." He pointed up to a sign that said SPRING DEER in English and Chinese.

"*Lu Ming Chun*," I read the Chinese, using my best tones. "*Jing Cai*"—Beijing food.

"Good accent," he said—in English. "The door is hard to find. I think it's over there."

Long years of living in America, I realized, had accustomed Paul Yang to speaking more English than Chinese. I set aside any last-ditch hopes of a long conversation in Mandarin.

Paul led me into a tiny souvenir shop selling jade elephants, cloisonné pens, and painted paper fans. In a musty hallway beyond, we climbed a flight of stairs. Many well-known restaurants were hidden away in such unlikely places. It was as if the owners didn't want you to come unless you heard about the fine cuisine from your friends. Great decor and a visible location were irrelevant. It was all about the food.

The restaurant was simple but clean, an airy room with a well-mopped linoleum floor and cloth-covered tables. No candles or wineglasses. Just a tempting aroma of pork, ginger, and scallions and the hiss of oil in a wok somewhere.

Paul ordered us each a beer and scanned the menu. "How many *shui-jiao* can you eat? Fifteen? Twenty?"

"Oh, maybe ten."

"Ten is not enough! Let's get forty for the two of us. I'll order some other dishes, too."

Forty! It seemed like a lot, but I wasn't about to object. I loved those dumplings.

When he ordered, I recognized the words for stir-fried pea shoots and thick corn soup, as well as cold dishes: vegetarian goose and drunk chicken. Not at all like the Chinese food in New York. No General Tso's chicken.

When the waiter left, I turned back to the conversation. "So, your mother is from northern China?" When feeling uncertain, I always liked to get other people talking.

"Yep. She grew up in Hebei, not far from Beijing. Everybody loves *shui-jiao* there."

The beer arrived, and I took a sip, eager for the liquid amber to soften the edge of my nervousness.

"So, finish the story," I continued, forcing a smile. "What do you remember from that day when you left China?"

He cocked his head, as if connecting to the memory. "My father says it was the last plane out of Shanghai. When we got to the airport, we heard gunshots. The Red Army was that close."

"Gunshots? Really? You must have been scared."

"Yep. Everyone was rushing to get out. It was really hard to buy plane tickets. Somehow, my dad got four: two tickets on an earlier flight, and two on the later flight the same day. We didn't know if the second flight would take off. So my parents had to decide who would go first."

I leaned forward. "Like *Sophie's Choice*! Who went first?"

"Well, my dad was in the most danger. If he didn't escape, he would be killed for sure."

I sat back, trying to imagine the dread. "Nothing like that ever happened in my family."

"Oh, lots of Chinese families have a story like this. Most American lives are boring compared to Chinese lives."

The plate of *shui-jiao* arrived. Each boiled dumpling was shaped like a crescent, with a pleated edge around a plump core of juicy minced pork. Steam rose from the plate. Paul poured dark vinegar onto his plate and mine. "Here. It tastes better with this."

With his chopsticks, he picked up a dumpling and dunked it in the vinegar. Then he held it a moment, to let it cool a bit, before popping it into his mouth. His thick eyebrows rose as he chewed it with pleasure. I nabbed one with my chopsticks, too, and blew on it first.

The waiter brought two small cold dishes: drunk chicken and vegetarian goose. The flavors danced lovely swirls in my mouth.

"So, tell me. Who went with your father on that first flight?" I asked at last.

Paul finished a mouthful of leafy pea shoots. "My sister. My parents decided I should stay in Shanghai with my mother. If the second plane didn't take off, I would take care of her."

"At age ten?" I shook my head. Imagine. A ten-year-old boy, holding his mother's hand, waving goodbye to his father, not sure if he would see him later that day or never again. "My God. Did you understand what was happening?"

Paul nodded. "I think so. But the second plane did take off. And my father and sister were waiting for us in Taiwan. The next day, the Communists captured the Shanghai airport."

"Amazing!" I put down my beer glass and stared at him. When I was ten, my family moved across town and I had to go to a new school where nobody liked me. When he was ten, his country shattered apart. "You were lucky."

He nodded. "We thought we'd go back in a few years. My parents didn't realize we would never see our relatives again."

"Those relatives you left behind in China—did they suffer?"

I knew about the "literature of the wounded," grim tales of ordinary people who were beaten or imprisoned or persecuted in the 1950s and '60s. These stories had shocked many American scholars, some of whom had sympathized with Mao Zedong and believed the rosy reports that came out of China through official sources and carefully orchestrated visits.

In reality, tens of millions of people starved to death in the early 1960s during the so-called Great Leap Forward—when Mao tried to restructure the farming sector into communes just as a drought hit. And during the misnamed Great Proletarian Cultural Revolution, millions more were jailed and persecuted in the name of continuing revolution. It wasn't until after Mao died in 1976 that the world learned some of the true stories.

"Oh, yeah, they suffered, of course," Paul said, heaping pea shoots on my plate. "People with relatives in Taiwan were accused of being spies. For thirty years we couldn't communicate with them at all. But I found some of them when I went back for the first time, in 1981."

I thought of my own close-knit family and couldn't imagine losing touch with relatives for thirty-two years. "How did you ever find them?"

He told me how he had contacted his uncle in Nanjing and visited him briefly, during that first trip back to China. Then he dropped another bombshell: an older sister, left behind. She had stayed in China with her fiancé—and suffered badly after his parents left for Taiwan.

As he spoke of her, Paul's voice wavered. He drew a line on his cool beer glass and paused to regroup. "I called her Jie-Jie, Older Sister. She was a schoolteacher, so she eventually got her job back. But when her children were teenagers, they were forced to go to the countryside. They were not allowed to finish high school. Her son became a tractor driver."

My mind was spinning, and it wasn't from the beer. Wave after wave of stunning stories.

"How did it feel when you first saw your sister after so many years apart?"

His eyes glistened as they locked with mine. "Sad, of course. But also happy. She cried." He gathered up the emotions he had spilled like peanuts on the table. "You eat the last *shui-jiao.*"

That evening, we also discussed the latest US news and found that we held similar opinions about President Reagan—and hopes that he would be unseated. Paul had strong views yet wanted to hear my opinion. I liked the feeling of equality and frankness between us.

What I found in this man was something I had not thought to look for: a window on a Chinese mind, life, family, and history. Someone who understood the Chinese language and culture well enough to interpret it for me. Someone I could talk to, with no barriers of language or culture, about my life and his, about America and China. Besides, I liked his smile.

෨෨෨

After dinner, he offered to show me the glorious view of the Hong Kong harbor from behind the tall, plate-glass windows of what was then the Regent Hotel.

"Let's go there for a drink," he had suggested. In the lobby bar, we marveled at the panorama on the other side of the harbor—a parade of skyscrapers, each with a neon sign advertising some company or consumer brand.

But when we scanned the drinks menu, Paul surprised me. "I recommend the mango milk shake. So good."

Hearing that, I decided not to order a glass of port. "I'll have one, too."

The milk shake, made with fresh Philippine mangoes, was awesome, blending the familiar Western taste of ice cream with a startling tang of Asian fruit. Sip after sip, it struck me as a modern mixture of East and West. So were we, Paul and Dori. We were products of China and America, yet both of us had immersed ourselves in the language and life of the other's country. Both of us loved *shui-jiao* and milk shakes.

As he laughed and relaxed, with no need for liquor, I noted that Paul was attractive and thought-provoking yet confident and ingenuous enough to order a mango milk shake on a first date. He approached me as an equal, with respect, but didn't think to compliment me. He didn't try to be someone he wasn't.

Still, I didn't choose him deliberately. It felt a lot more like a tidal wave, out of my control. I was ready to be knocked over but didn't sense the strength of the underlying currents.

CHAPTER ELEVEN:

Tidal Wave

⋯⋯⋯

君子, *jūnzǐ: an old-fashioned word for a gentleman scholar. Confucius used this term to describe a superior person, noble-minded, educated, cultivated—the ideal man.*

What makes us fall in love with one person and not another? Sometimes it defies logic.

I had a date the next night with a man who should have been perfect for me. A relative of mine gave my name to her brother-in-law, who often traveled to Hong Kong on business.

Ryan came from Southern California and was single, about my age, and good-looking, with curly hair and a short-cropped beard. He had moved to Hong Kong the previous year to take a good job with Bank of America. He had learned to ski before he was five, loved classic cars, and had once assembled his own microcomputer. He was pleasant and talkative.

In all ways, he was a good match for me. A much better match than Paul Yang, who was fifteen years older, separated from his wife, the father of two children, and from a different race and culture. But I found Ryan boring. He seemed young and green. Almost everything he discussed with gusto, I found dull. With Paul, I felt just the opposite. Despite his openness, there was something unexpected, unlikely, unpredictable about him.

At this stage of my life, I didn't need a man to validate me, or support me, or shore me up, or take care of me. I certainly didn't want a man who would tie me down or prevent me from living out my dreams. I was independent and proud of it.

So why—after years of pushing away more suitable men who were devoted to me—did I let this man into my heart? Something about him, unpretentious and artless, caused me to fling wide the door, heedless of the consequences.

✻✻✻

The day after my date with Ryan, Paul and I followed through on a plan we had made over mango milk shakes: to go hiking on Lamma, one of Hong Kong's outlying islands.

Paul came dressed for it, in blue jeans, a polo shirt, and a sturdy pair of Nikes. I wore white shorts and sandals, with a blue handbag slung over my shoulder.

"You didn't wear sneakers?" he asked me, half worried, half scandalized.

"Oh, these are pretty comfortable," I said, looking at my sandals, hoping they would hold up for this hike. I didn't like the look of sneakers on my feet.

The ferry ride to Lamma took almost half an hour, and we stood on the deck and surveyed the cityscape of Hong Kong. We were lucky it was partly cloudy. Just enough sun poked through to light up the lush green mountain behind the crowded city and the choppy water of the harbor.

On the ferry, I took a closer look at Paul Yang. What did I find so attractive about him?

He looked much younger than forty-four, with a head of thick black hair and smooth cheeks. As a northern Chinese man, he was taller than most Cantonese men, and his skin was as light as mine. His gestures, his mannerisms, his way of speaking—all bespoke a man of experience and confidence. Yet he did not seem arrogant or domineering. He struck me as a gentleman, even-tempered and mannerly.

I asked him about the American period of his life. He had studied in North Carolina and worked in New Jersey and often went into New York on weekends to meet friends for dim sum. I asked about his work as a city planner.

"In the sixties, urban redevelopment was a hot topic," he said, leading us to a nearby bench.

I remembered big empty lots in downtown cities in Ohio, and my dad's scorn for urban redevelopment. "How did it work out?"

He detected the skepticism behind my question. "Well, you probably know, in a lot of cities, it failed. They tore down buildings and moved people out and never got the money to rebuild. But in Englewood, it was different. Actually, one of the most successful programs. We cleared out the slum area and built over four hundred units of new housing. We relocated three hundred families and even thirty businesses, including a funeral home and a junkyard."

Clearly, Paul Yang was not your average Chinese immigrant—the kind who shied away from jobs that required a lot of speaking and reading in English. He had plunged deeply into American life. At some point, I stopped noticing his garbled grammar.

When we reached Lamma Island, Paul was amazed that it was quiet and rural—just the opposite of the urban clamor of Hong Kong. With only a few thousand residents, mostly fishing families, Lamma did not allow any cars, so its only roads were for bikes and walkers. We followed our fellow passengers through the sleepy streets of the village to a paved path through verdant hills.

We clambered up a hillside, down and across a beach, and up a steep slope to a rocky ledge high on a cliff. After half an hour in the hot sunshine, I was ready for a rest. We sat on the ledge, and he took out two water bottles. I slipped off my sandals and rubbed my feet.

He commented on the fine vista overlooking the sea, dotted with Chinese sailing junks, just beyond a large power station. As we sat,

I asked him how the slums of New York compared to low-income housing in Hong Kong. Both were subsidized housing built by the government, but the colony's high-rise public housing projects, where about half the population lived, seemed cleaner and safer than those in American cities. He analyzed the differences for me.

"There was a lot of racial tension in American cities in the sixties," I said. "How did that affect you?"

He nodded glumly. "It was rough, to be honest. In Plainfield, they had a huge riot and two policemen were killed. We were on the national news every night. The governor called in the National Guard. It was like a shooting war."

"And you were right in the heart of it?"

"Yeah. But for my job, I made friends with the leaders of the Black community. So I went to their homes with a six-pack of beer and talked to them. Or they'd come to my office and chat. Sometimes we would argue. I told them I was trying to find a way the city could help them."

I nodded in respect, certain that I would never have had the gumption to knock on strangers' doors with a six-pack of beer. I couldn't imagine the young banker Ryan doing it, either.

"After the riots, I held meetings in the Black neighborhoods. One time, in a school auditorium, I was up front, leading a public meeting. Suddenly, this group of tough-looking guys walks into the auditorium. They close the door and lock it. I see that under their shirts, they all have guns. They were Black Panthers."

I remembered the fear of that era. When I was in eighth grade, riots broke out the day after Martin Luther King Jr. was shot. A rumor raced through my school saying that "all the Black kids are gonna beat up all the white kids." Some white kids did get roughed up.

"Those Black Panthers weren't local guys," Paul explained. "They came up to the podium and grabbed the microphone from me, disrupting the meeting. I let them talk. They talked about the importance of long-term struggle, saying 'We can't be quiet anymore. We have to stand up and demand our rights.' I just listened. They finally walked out, fists in the air."

"I would have been petrified. Were you?"

He smiled at me with appreciation, as if I had just formed a fan club for him. "Not really. I know lots of folks in that community. They wouldn't let anything bad happen to me."

"Plus, you were neither Black nor white," I added.

"Yeah. Maybe they were more open to me because I was Chinese."

His vivid stories transported me a long way from the tranquility of Lamma Island. His voice was matter-of-fact, but I could see how proud he was of his achievements.

"You know," I said, "you weren't even a US citizen then, yet you did far more to make America a better place than most people I've ever met."

He laughed and shook his head. "I didn't even know what city planning was when I applied to study it. I wasn't trying to change the world. I just wanted to get a good job."

This man in jeans and sneakers presented himself as a pragmatist, yet he obviously had a dollop of idealism and the passion to achieve those ideals. He put himself in unsafe situations and built bridges during a time of America's worst racial tension. He found a way to be part of the solution, using government funds to provide decent, affordable housing for slum dwellers. He loved my country as much as I did—maybe even more.

The sunshine glinting on the ocean faded from my view. All I could see were Paul's brown eyes, glowing with intensity and—I thought—with fondness for me, as if my admiration had blown fire back into the embers of his memories.

We both leaned in a little, but he pulled back, as if realizing the age gap. I had been in junior high school when he was rebuilding America's cities.

"Let's hike on. Do you want more water first?" He broke the spell and held out his water bottle. Mine was empty. I took the bottle that had touched his lips a few moments earlier, and I swear he knew what I was thinking as I drank from it.

If I ever decide I'm in love with this man, I thought, reverting my eyes to the distant view, *I'll pick this moment as the time I fell for him.*

❧❧❧

On the ferry ride home, after a supper of fresh seafood in a fishing village, we stood at the railing as the boat glided past the mist-enshrouded profile of the islands. The brilliant tropical greens and blues faded to gray, and a light sea breeze blew my hair back. Flavors of ginger and shrimp still echoed in my mouth, and the ferry engine vibrated in my body.

Shoulder to shoulder, our four hands on the railing, I commented on the strong muscles of his arms. "I did gymnastics in high school," he told me.

As the setting sun painted vivid orange lines around a cloud, I edged closer to him and he put his sturdy arm around me. I lifted my face, and this time our lips met for a long kiss.

I didn't notice the tide turning beneath us.

Paul Yang enchanted me—not just with his stories but with his whole being. His deep voice, his smooth arms, his light laugh—all drew me to him. In ways that other people saw, he was not a good match for me. He was a refugee, an immigrant, a foreigner, an alien—not my age, not white, not Christian, not Ivy League, not from some fine family my parents might admire. Not even, as I later would discover, as single and free as I assumed he was.

CHAPTER TWELVE:

Inside a Chinese Family

内人, *nèirén: wife. These two characters literally mean "inside person." In the old society, Chinese wives (of wealthy men) were shut up inside homes, unable to go out the gate into the streets. A man's nèirén was his wife. Chinese has no good translation for "insider" in the American sense.*

Our relationship progressed at jet speed. Three days later, Paul and I danced and kissed to throbbing music and flashing lights at the top of the Excelsior Hotel—on a weeknight. I drank just enough wine that it felt natural and easy to follow him back to his room. The following weekend, we explored the antique shops and art galleries on Hollywood Road and the Chinese market stalls on Cat Street. We hiked among the green hills and craggy peaks of another outlying island, Lantau, and visited its hilltop Buddhist monastery in the fog, where I first tasted the delights of Chinese vegetarian food.

We admired a *rongshu*—a beautiful variety of banyan tree with a thick trunk, glossy leaves, delicate scarlet flowers, and vine-like offshoots that connect it to soil far from its roots. We found it symbolic of us. Whenever we could, we spent days and nights together. We started taking photos of each other—and of us together. We spent hours in conversation, including sharing full revelations about our past love lives. From strangers to lovers in a flash.

Dori & Paul

Less than two weeks after our first date, I left for Indonesia for a one-week reporting trip. Paul took me to the airport to see me off. The parting was especially wrenching because we knew that just a few days after my return, Paul would leave on a six-week business trip to Taipei and then to North America.

"I wish I didn't have to go," I said at the airport, nuzzling my nose into his shoulder.

"Why don't you fly to Taipei with me next week? You can meet my parents."

I pulled back in surprise, examining his face. "You want *your parents* to meet me?"

"Sure! Why not?"

I certainly wasn't ready to tell *my* parents about *him*. "Well, for one, your divorce isn't final." He hadn't told me much about his home life, but I knew this.

He laughed. "Oh, they know that's over. They just want me to be happy. They know how miserable I've been. When they heard that she filed for divorce, they were relieved."

I paused, letting this sink in. It was the most he had said about his divorce. "Well, I've been meaning to get back to Taiwan for another story . . ."

"Great! Let's plan on it!" He kissed me with newfound familiarity, and I headed for the immigration checkpoint, a little unsteady.

The next Sunday, alone in Jakarta after two packed days of interviews, I spread out my notebooks and news clippings on my hotel bed, trying to collect my thoughts for the next day's meetings. Falling oil revenues were forcing Indonesia to postpone its dreams of growing into a heavy industrial powerhouse. A good *BusinessWeek* story.

But I just couldn't concentrate. I kept examining the stack of photos of Paul and me as if they showed ultrasound images of my life to come—blurry but enticing.

This man had a lot of fine qualities: he was open and friendly, instantly likable, intelligent, stable, sincere, and fun-loving. He liked to do most of the things I enjoyed. He had a steady self-confidence that I admired. Plus, he was crazy about me. I smiled as I recalled asking him, "Do you have any faults?" He had answered with a grin, "If I did, I wouldn't tell you!" Until I found any, I decided, I would conclude that I had found my Ideal Man.

It was wonderful, once again, to have someone to care about, someone who cared about me, someone to look after me, hold me, sleep with me. We were so perfectly suited to each other. Separation from him was a jolt to my system. My empty arms felt as if I had been hugging a full moon for twelve days and suddenly it had floated away like a balloon.

But what would it mean? Could I really imagine marrying him?

I sat back in alarm. When had that idea germinated? Why was I even thinking of marriage? Before I met Paul, I was set on flying solo, putting my career first. Why risk messing that up? Then again, why couldn't I have both: a career and a man? In the modern world of the 1980s, attitudes were changing.

But what would my parents think of Paul Yang? My mom assumed her children knew that we should stick to our own kind. My dad disapproved of divorce and volubly criticized his own sister for hers. I shuddered to think of what he would say if I married a divorced man.

And fifteen years, that was a big age gap. *When I'm sixty-five*, I thought, *he will be eighty—if he lives that long.* And what would his children think of me? Could I function as a stepmother? I definitely wanted to have children, someday. But would Paul want any more kids?

As a strong-minded, independent woman, eager for equality in a relationship, I wondered if it made sense to fall for a man from a culture that demeaned women. I knew about foot binding, about the Chinese preference for sons, and more recently about baby girls being abandoned because of China's one-child policy. But Paul didn't have those attitudes. Toward me, he was polite, respectful, and caring. He met me at the airport. He treated me to dinner. I liked that. I didn't find it belittling, because he knew I could take care of myself.

I wanted mutual respect. I wanted a man whose work was in a different field, not competitive with or comparable to mine. And I wanted a man who was equally proud of his own accomplishments and eager to achieve more.

And, face it, I was attracted to the idea of doing something different just because it was different. Of going outside—and far beyond—any cultural or family expectations. That had been true of me all along. Embracing the unknown was part of leading an extraordinary life.

Still, falling in love with Paul was definitely going off the map. I could not see what cliffs and crevasses might lie ahead.

That night at eleven thirty, long after I had turned off the lights, the phone rang. I grabbed the receiver, desperately glad to hear his voice. He sounded gentle and lonely and longing—just what I felt. I talked as long as I could, but international calls were expensive.

After I hung up, my body began shaking. Delirium tremens. I needed a fix.

⁂

A week later, Paul and I were sitting together on a plane again—this time flying to Taiwan.

During the intervening days in Hong Kong, Paul and I had made the first tentative moves to take our relationship public. I introduced Paul to Cindy (eager to meet my Ideal Man), and I took him to dinner at the gossipy Foreign Correspondents' Club. Interracial couples were not uncommon there, but most included a Chinese woman and a Western man; I enjoyed reversing this stereotype. Paul and I went hiking with his colleague, Denny, to yet another outlying island, where we spent another magical day outdoors, climbing along the rocky seacoast and exploring a pirate's cave. We had even gone shopping together; he insisted I buy a sturdy pair of sneakers.

But now, traveling with Paul Yang on purpose, getting ready to meet his parents, felt like a giant step forward.

"What will they think of me?" I asked after my first sip of tea. I knew that his first wife was Chinese, also born on the mainland and raised in Taiwan. His own kind.

"They'll love you."

My face must have reflected my doubts.

"You'll like my father. He's a writer, too."

"Really! What does he write?"

"He wrote a lot of short stories for magazines. Mostly romantic."

"Whoa! Romantic?"

A wicked grin. "Yeah. He has an interesting life story. I'll tell you sometime."

"But he doesn't speak English, right?"

"Right. You'll have to speak Chinese with them."

"Hmm." Normally, I loved long conversations in Mandarin with people. It was like exercising my muscles after months of sitting at a desk. But now I worried. A lot was at stake. Good intentions can be lost in verbal miscues and cultural faux pas.

I took his hand, and he squeezed mine. We weren't planning to stay with his parents. Instead, he had booked a room at the Hotel Regency, where we could spend hours alone.

As we rode in a taxi from Chiang Kai-Shek International Airport to Taipei, I remembered my first visit to Taiwan, in 1977. That had been my first time in a truly Mandarin-speaking place, and it felt much more authentically Chinese than Singapore or Hong Kong.

Now in 1983, Taiwan was modernizing quickly. It exported tons of low-cost clothing and shoes and watches to the United States and was trying to move "up the ladder" by producing computer monitors and semiconductors. It was brimming with good business stories.

Outside the taxi window, I observed motorcycle repair shops, plastic buckets of live fish, piles of dried herbs, rickety tables on the sidewalks for noodle sellers. High school boys with shaved heads wore military-style uniforms. Paul told me that "dancing parties" were illegal.

Taiwan was still reeling from Jimmy Carter's decision in 1979 to close our embassy in Taipei and open an embassy in Beijing, recognizing the People's Republic as the legitimate government of China. Technically, Taiwan was still under martial law, although no shooting had occurred for more than twenty years. No one was allowed to visit mainland China or even write letters to relatives there. I wondered how that affected his parents.

Before I met them, though, Paul took me on a tour of his childhood. We savored his favorite breakfast: a big bowl of *doujiang*, hot soy milk, with flaky flatbread and deep-fried crullers. We visited the National Revolutionary Martyrs' Shrine, which honored his grandfather, who had died defending China against the Japanese. In the seaside town of Danshui, he showed me the old Japanese-style house his family had shared with relatives, and his tree-shaded middle school.

Holding hands, we sat on a bench overlooking the Taiwan Strait. The late-afternoon sunlight shimmered on the sea, and a light breeze softened the harsh humidity.

"I'll miss you while you're traveling," I said.

He took my hand and held it on his knee, touching my knee. "I'll write every day."

"Will you?" This surprised me. "You'll definitely come back, right?"

"Oh, yeah. Don't worry about that." His reassuring smile failed to loosen the tension in my chest.

"Do you think . . . ," I stammered.

"What?" he asked, gently, as if he knew what I wanted.

"Do you think we could ever make a life together?" I couldn't believe my own words.

"I've been thinking about that, too," he admitted. "After two years of being single and seeing a lot of women, I realize now that what I want is . . ."

"What?" I could barely wait to hear.

"To love and be loved." Each word carved itself into my memory.

"I think we could do that," I said, choosing my words carefully. "But it's a little frightening as well."

"Yes, it is." Waves lapped against the concrete bulkhead.

"Because you feel so vulnerable," I said, thinking of myself.

"Do you feel vulnerable?"

"More so every day."

He had my heart in his hands and could feed it or break it.

❈❈❈

The next night, we went to the home of Paul's parents. I had been alternately dreading it and looking forward to it. It felt like a privilege, a welcome chance to get behind the wall of politeness that made me feel like an outsider. Chinese are known to be clannish, and the whole country had hidden behind walls for centuries. Just as the Great Wall was built to protect China from invaders, decades of isolation had built barriers of distrust toward "outside-country people" like me.

Paul had assured me his parents were nice folks—his mom loving and warm, his dad thoughtful and deep. Still, I worried they might have trouble understanding me. Chinese tones are notoriously difficult, and I wondered if Paul would have to jump in frequently to correct my pronunciation. Plus, they had a right to be skeptical of my relationship with their son.

"You'll do fine," Paul said after we got into the taxi. I squeezed his hand but wasn't reassured. He had been speaking to me almost entirely in English; how did he know how I would fare?

The taxi drove across the river to a district called Yonghe. It was even more of a warren of tiny streets than central Taipei. A hodgepodge of tiny shops stretched along the avenues. Alleys jutted off at crazy angles. Motorbikes whizzed along sidewalks, beeping their horns.

"My mother and I found the house they live in," Paul told me. "I was in college, riding my bike, and I saw a FOR SALE sign. I took my mother to see it, and we negotiated for it."

Paul directed the driver onto a side street, and we stopped in a tiny alley. "This area used to be rice paddies," he said as we got out. "Look at it now!"

All the buildings, even on this one-way alley, had gray walls blocking them from the street. Everything was crammed and dusty. No green yards or flowerbeds. A few scraggly trees yearned for sunlight. It was the polar opposite of the leafy yards of my childhood neighborhood in Ohio.

Sharp doubt pierced my insides: *What am I doing here?* I had not expected Paul's parents' home to feel so alien.

Eager to see them, Paul didn't notice. He strode to a metal gate in one of the long walls and pounded on it, ringing the bell and shouting, "*Huilaile!*" (I've come back!)

I heard an echoing shout from behind the gate and footsteps scurrying toward us. With a *clunk*, the gate swung open and two smiling faces greeted us. His mother was short and round, wearing a classic Chinese dress with knot buttons along the shoulder. His father stood tall, with thin gray hair, an unusually sculpted face, and a large, wide smile.

"*Qing jin, qing jin,*" Paul's mother said to me, polite for "please come in."

"This is Dori, Zhong Derui," Paul said in Chinese. He had recently given me this Chinese name because he thought the one my Chinese teachers had assigned me was not sophisticated. The surname Zhong stood in for Jones. Derui suggests high moral standing and a bright future.

"Mr. Yang, Mrs. Yang," I began in Chinese, adding, "I've longed to meet you." The back of my neck felt tight.

"Miss Zhong, come in," his father said in Mandarin, stepping aside to let me enter a narrow, stone-paved courtyard. Potted plants bloomed with ruby hibiscus and amethyst bougainvillea.

The building had four stories, but the Yangs occupied only the first floor. As I stepped through the front door, delicious smells of steaming rice and stir-fried onions piqued my nose. Paul sat on a bench to take off his shoes. I did the same and slid my feet into a pair of black soft-soled slippers with embroidered pink flowers that his mother offered. I noticed that her feet were tiny, a remnant of the bound feet of her childhood.

The living room was large and open, neat and spare, with a sitting area on one side and a "moon gate" entrance into the dining room, which had a round table set with chopsticks and bowls. Paul's parents showed us over to the sofa, where his mother poured us each a cup of tea, placing a lid on each cup. Bowls of snacks graced the table: pumpkin seeds, hard candy in wrappers, and almonds.

"Please, help yourself," his father said. "You speak Chinese very well."

"*Guojiang, guojiang*," I answered. (You honor me by exaggerating.) Chinese good manners require humility. Saying "thank you" to a compliment sounds not grateful but boastful.

"Yang Bao says you're a journalist." His father spoke slowly.

"Right. I work for *BusinessWeek*." I knew that Paul's family and close friends called him Yang Bao, the nickname his parents had given him as a baby. He had chosen the English name Paul because he thought it sounded like Bao.

His father, taking the lead, asked the usual questions: How long have you lived in Hong Kong? Do you like it there? How long have you worked as a journalist? His mother folded her hands and listened closely. I answered smoothly and easily, taking care to make sure I pronounced my tones correctly. Paul's father didn't embarrass me with the most obvious questions: How did you meet our son? Why is he staying with you at the hotel and not with us?

Sipping tea as they asked Paul a few questions, I relaxed into the scene. Their attitude was one of curiosity and welcome toward me, affection and care toward Paul. Mrs. Yang encouraged me with tea refills and a friendly smile whenever she caught my eye. Mr. Yang, whom Paul called Baba, had the distinguished air of an intellectual and smiled humbly when Paul showed me his framed calligraphy on the wall.

"His calligraphy is really great," Paul told me in English as we stood to admire it. "He writes in grass style."

"What does it say?" I asked, recognizing only a few of the stylized brushstrokes.

"It's a poem, a famous one from the Tang dynasty," Paul answered. He turned to his father and asked him to recite it aloud.

Mr. Yang did so, standing tall, with poetic expression to his voice. "The moon sets, a crow caws, frost fills the sky . . ."

Paul translated and explained it.

"It's beautiful!" I told Paul's father. "Will you write it down so I can memorize it?"

"With pleasure!" He nodded. "Is this your first trip to Taiwan?"

"No. I came here last January, to interview your economic affairs minister."

His father raised his thick eyebrows at Paul. "You didn't bring her to meet us then?"

"I didn't know her then," Paul answered, grinning at me.

"How long have you known each other?"

Paul hesitated, then answered, with a sly smile, "*Lao pengyou*"— old friends.

I blushed. We had met less than two months earlier. They didn't push for specifics.

Soon they invited us into the dining room for a home-cooked meal, which included a fine fish called *guiyu*, quick fried to seal in flavor, then steamed and served with ginger and scallions. Their live-in cook and housekeeper, a retired soldier they called Old Wang, brought in dish after dish. I could hear him stir-frying in the kitchen between courses.

"Do you hope to go back to visit the mainland someday?" I asked Paul's father.

His face darkened. "Oh, no. It wouldn't be safe."

To me, China was safe, but as long as the Communist Party ruled the mainland, Paul's father would not trust it with his life. I decided to steer clear of anything political.

Old Wang brought in a final dish, spare ribs, and sat down to eat with us. Home-cooked Chinese food is not the same as restaurant

Chinese food. It's as different as Mom's meat loaf is from a McDonald's cheeseburger. Paul's parents expressed surprise I could use chopsticks—a common reaction of many Chinese who know about Americans only from the movies.

"It's so convenient that you speak Chinese," his mother told me.

"Do you know many foreigners?" I asked.

"Well"—his mother looked at his father—"the second daughter of the Wang family married a man from Switzerland. He couldn't speak Chinese at all."

Paul's father laughed merrily. "He couldn't communicate with us, so he just got on the floor and *fan gentou*!" His mother shook her head in amazement.

For the first time, I had to ask Paul for a translation: somersaults. Apparently, that foreigner had opted for action when words failed him. I guess Paul's parents were relieved that I didn't do anything outrageous.

During dinner, I asked them the names of vegetables and dishes, where they'd bought the food, whose favorite it was, what Paul liked most. I asked his mother about the house. Paul didn't jump in to correct my Chinese. If I mispronounced words, they figured out what I meant. They seemed to forget I was foreign and just talked to us about their life and concerns, about their health and Paul's, speaking at a normal pace. I missed a few words but, to my relief, understood the gist.

As the evening progressed, my sense of foreignness slipped away. I began to think of them as Baba and Mama. It didn't matter to them that I had blue eyes and a "high" nose. I had unlocked a small door and slipped behind the Great Wall to mingle with the family of China.

I had already fallen in love with Paul; that was the prerequisite. But that night I fell in love again—with the heady feeling of being *inside China*. Yes, it was Taiwan and not mainland China. And I would always be a *waiguoren*—an "outside-country person." But I was inside a Chinese family, accepted as one of them, communicating smoothly. It felt like magic—as if I had stepped into some fantasy world. I had sipped the elixir of this feeling and wanted more.

Why should any of us look behind the next hill, or across the border, or across the ocean, into the warm living rooms of people who don't look or think or talk as we do? It makes more sense to stay home and deal with pressing issues inside our families, our towns, our borders. But what if we all—or at least some of us—crossed those thresholds and listened in the language of people we too often misunderstand? What if we opened our minds and tried to see the world through their eyes?

When I sat down with Paul's parents, I already had a master's degree in international affairs. But my education about the possibilities of cross-cultural understanding had just begun.

⚭⚭⚭

Later, in the backseat of a cab, I asked, "Well? Did I pass?"

Paul grinned and put his arm around my shoulder. "A-plus."

A warm wave washed over me. Life was good.

That night, after Paul fell asleep, I lay awake, staring at the ceiling of the hotel room, reliving the evening and the past few weeks. I decided that, yes, I did want to live the rest of my life with this man. Not just because he gave me an insight into China and made me feel at home within a Chinese family, but because he trusted me with his heart. Now he was heading back to North America, and I would not see him for six weeks.

At the Taipei airport the next day, I hugged him tightly, reluctant to say goodbye. Six weeks without touching him seemed like torture. I could see, in his manner, his words, the way he treated me, that he felt the same about me.

I would trust my heart with him, too. By the time he returned, surely, his divorce would be final.

CHAPTER THIRTEEN:

Gale-Force Winds

∽෧෧෧෧∽

台风（颱風）, *táifēng: typhoon. Asian term for hurricane or tropical cyclone. When caught in a typhoon, tape your windows, stay indoors, and wait out the storm.*

At the age of twenty-nine, I had found the man I wanted to marry. I had been in love before, but I had never felt such certainty. Now that I had found him, I wanted to shout the glad tidings from the tops of Hong Kong's skyscrapers. I wanted to set a date, figure out how to break the news to my parents, invite all my friends to a banquet to celebrate with us. But I couldn't, not yet.

That summer, while Paul was away for six weeks, seemed endless. He and I wrote each other every day and talked by phone once a week. I accumulated a hoard of postcards and letters, which I treasured. His English spelling made me smile fondly. In one of them, he called me "dear sweatheart." I could never have written half so well in Chinese. I consoled myself with the stack of photos we had taken on excursions to Lantau, Cheung Chau, and Taiwan, plus five well-thumbed pictures of Paul I kept with me at all times.

To get through his long absence, I threw myself into my work with renewed vigor. Now in my second year on the job, I began developing a better sense of what news would interest my editors. They accepted more of my story pitches, and I started writing for different sections of the magazine. And I was learning how to shape stories for American readers who cared about business but were not immersed in Asia. I never heard from readers, but my editors didn't rewrite as heavily as before. Encouraged, I became more productive, finishing four articles in six weeks: on Indonesia's economy; a rich Taiwan plastics maker; high-tech pioneers in Taiwan; and Hutchison Whampoa, the formerly British Hong Kong company now owned by Li Ka-shing. My understanding of the Asian business climate was growing.

Still, during quiet evenings, I brooded about Paul. I thought deeply about what had caused me to break up with my previous boyfriend and whether I could make this new relationship work. Five years earlier, at age twenty-four, I had felt tormented by self-doubt and driven to prove that I could achieve as much in my career as a man my age. Success seemed ephemeral, likely to flit away like a butterfly. Now that I had the confidence of knowing I could make it on my own, success was more like a bird in a cage. Whenever my mind came back to it, it was there, undeniable, chirping or scattering seeds. I was ready for a man to share my life with.

I saw no reason to hesitate. I was ready to jump in feetfirst, to make a lifelong commitment to this man. "There are no barriers whatsoever," I wrote in my journal in mid-July.

When Paul returned from his trip, my own naiveté slapped me in the face.

I went to Kai Tak Airport to meet him, eager to grab and hug him and begin planning for our future together. When he walked down the ramp in the greeting area, he suddenly looked like a stranger. Our time apart, six weeks, had been longer than our time together.

Then he saw me and a huge grin lit up his face. I steadied myself on a barrier post. When he reached me, I embraced him as if he were bringing salvation. He melted into my arms as if I had rescued him from drowning.

For the first few hours, I didn't mention the one issue that had been nagging at me.

Finally, late that night, my chin on his shoulder, I dared to ask, "So, what's the status of your divorce?"

He sighed. "It's more complicated than I would like, but don't worry. It's not a problem."

My heart shrank. That wasn't the answer I had hoped for.

"What happened?" My voice came out tiny.

He looked away. "She lost her job. A real blow. It was a good one."

"But what does that . . ."

"She withdrew the divorce petition."

This wasn't a problem? "Because?"

"She's very upset. Going through a tough time."

"But you can file for divorce now, right?"

"Not right now. I don't want to make things worse. I worry about the kids."

The air in the room seemed too thin to breathe. Very upset? So was I. "You could bring them here," I said, my voice wavering. What did I know of parenting?

"No way she would let me do that. Anyway, they're better off living at home. They wouldn't want to leave their school, their friends."

That made sense. "But . . ."

"Besides," he continued, "you wouldn't want me if I was the kind of man who could easily walk away from my kids."

I shut my mouth. That was true.

"So it will take longer than I thought," he concluded. "Can you be patient?"

My jaw tightened. All that joy, the delight, the discovery of the ideal man. I had trusted him with my heart. And now . . . he wanted me to be *patient*?

Paul held me and reassured me that he loved me. "Believe me, there's no way I could go back to her. Things will work out. Trust me."

In a few heartbeats, I dropped from ecstasy to despair. I was now the "other woman."

Long after he fell asleep, I lay awake, thinking. My choices were limited. I could break it off. That would be the wisest course. Maybe just until the divorce was final. But my heart screamed out against the idea. Or I could wait, as he asked. But I hated that prospect, too. Wait how long? I could take the high ground and possibly lose Paul forever—or compromise my principles and suffer the indignity of being, in effect, his mistress. My thoughts ricocheted miserably between one bad option and the other.

Fate had brought us together. Now it was conspiring against us.

"Legally separated," I learned the hard way, did not mean "almost divorced." It meant "still married."

My friend Mrs. Ng, at lunch a few days later, bluntly pointed this out to me. "If he is not willing to get a divorce, he is just cheating on his wife."

I felt like a fool. Angry. Disappointed. Sorry for myself. But after four weeks together, what had I expected? That he would upend the life he had created over fifteen years with his wife and children? To me, Paul had a clear choice: me or her. If he loved her, he should go back. If he loved me, he should finalize that divorce.

Years later, I would recognize this reaction as self-absorbed. At twenty-nine, I was used to getting my own way. I felt no compassion at all for his wife—or his kids. He had shown me a few pictures of his son and daughter, but I could not imagine their perspective. I never put myself in the shoes of that bewildered girl, aged twelve, whose dad had disappeared from her life, or the boy on the cusp of manhood, with no man to show him the way. I should have known better, but I lived only inside my own head. And I wanted this man. Now.

A true dilemma is not a choice between right and wrong. It's between two options that are equally compelling—or equally hazardous. Heart-stopping dilemmas have high stakes and outcomes that will change your life forever. It's easy to point out the growth and opportunities that come from grappling with a dilemma. But in the moment, such a choice is excruciating. The stress of it can make you literally sick.

✤✤✤✤

Hong Kong's agony over its future felt more personal now that my own was in doubt. Like Paul and his wife, the governments of China and Britain were locking horns in a struggle of wills that had no obvious solution. The people of Hong Kong were caught in the middle, with no good options. I knew that feeling.

By the end of summer, it was clear that the second round of Sino-British talks, begun in July 1983, had broken down. Stock prices, which had perked up on feeble hopes, were once again tumbling. Local banks were raising interest rates in a desperate measure to stanch an outflow of money. The whiff of panic of the previous autumn was now gusting into a storm.

All this was spiraling into one of the biggest stories I would ever cover: the negotiations over the future of Hong Kong. Although no journalists were allowed in the Beijing rooms where the talks were held, the choices that the governments of Britain and China made, we all knew, would have historic impact: on the demise of the British Empire, the rise of China, the future of Communism.

Like me, Margaret Thatcher, the Conservative prime minister of Britain, had to consider whether to compromise her principles. She had started negotiations in September 1982 with a strong assertion: she would work out some deal wherein China could save face on "sovereignty" but permit continued British administration. After all, China benefited from having this dynamic financial center at its doorstep. Why would it want to kill the goose that laid the golden eggs? Confidence in Hong Kong, in its future as a financial and trade center, would collapse if Thatcher agreed to give it back in 1997. That was the British view—and the American one, too.

But China's leaders, especially Deng Xiaoping, wanted Hong Kong back—as badly as I wanted Paul. In their view, Britain had grabbed Hong Kong and Kowloon in "unfair treaties" that weak emperors were forced to sign at gunpoint after losing two wars to Britain, then an aggressive colonial power peddling opium. China's leaders would not budge on their sovereign right to take Hong Kong back "at an opportune moment." But they also worried about how to make sure Hong Kong did not implode—just as Paul did not want to harm his children.

Deng proposed a creative but implausible solution. The previous December, China adopted a new constitution that gave a legal basis to his newest brainchild: "one country, two systems." Hong Kong could become a Special Administrative Region, a capitalist enclave within a socialist country, keeping its laissez-faire economy, its legal system, and personal freedoms, long after 1997. It defied logic.

Thatcher didn't buy it. Yes, China had pragmatic leaders now, but the Communist Party was known for radical swings in policy. Deng Xiaoping may have had good intentions, but some future leader might renege on his promises. Thatcher didn't want to preside over another postcolonial disaster. That said, Britain really didn't have much leverage. If it pulled out of the talks with Beijing, China could send its army to take back Hong Kong in a day—or just cut off its water supply.

The people of Hong Kong were vulnerable. Two leaders who had never even visited Hong Kong were deciding their future. They were pulled in two equally compelling directions. As ethnic Chinese, they felt pride in their heritage and identified culturally with China. Britain, as colonial overlord, had offered them a stable place to live and thrive in freedom, but it had no allegiance to them. It issued them second-class passports and no right to move to Britain. Despite Britain's long history with democracy, it had never allowed colonial subjects the right to choose their own rulers. Hong Kong had freedom but not democracy.

But most Hong Kong people had good reason to distrust China's Communist government. Many remembered bitterly how their fathers and grandfathers lost it all in Shanghai or Tianjin in 1949—as Paul's parents had. Others were refugees from China's disasters: the years of starvation, the brutal political campaigns, the persecution even of anyone who dared to question Chairman Mao. As one Hong Kong Chinese stock broker said to me, "Everybody's afraid."

Like me, Hong Kong Chinese faced a hard dilemma. They could stay and hope things would work out. Or, if they had money, they could flee—or at least find safe havens for their money, as Paul's clients had done in buying a piece of America. Most chose to stay for the time being, to enjoy their traditional way of life, but many were making contingency plans. More than twenty thousand left permanently every year in the early 1980s.

Although I possessed a passport that ensured I could return to a stable country, I felt in my bones the same spasms of frustration that many in Hong Kong felt. My future was uncertain. Someone was bound to be hurt. There were no easy answers.

❦❦❦

After just a few weeks of tense togetherness, Paul had to go back to Portland for business, both professional and personal. His job in Hong Kong had begun to look shaky, and his family was in crisis mode. I was begging him to find a way to stay in Hong Kong with me, and he had lined up a job interview that might provide a way. He bought a round-trip ticket and promised to return in two weeks. But as I said goodbye at the airport, fear rose in my throat.

I could smell the storm about to break, but it came first from an unexpected direction: Typhoon Ellen.

Just days after Paul left, I was at my office when I heard the news: typhoon signal number 10, the highest danger alert. Gale-force winds expected. The eye of the storm was to pass directly through our city. Schools and government offices closed. So did the airport, the stock market, shops, and restaurants. Urgent voices on the radio told everyone to go home or shelter in place.

In the rising wind, I rushed home. Cindy had arrived before me. The biggest danger was that the wind would break windows. Cindy's boss had said to put masking tape on our windows in big X's, to minimize shattering. But we didn't have masking tape.

So we cowered in our apartment hallway, far from any windows, huddling under blankets, munching crackers and listening to the English-language news on a portable radio as the wind whipped against the building. Neither of us had ever lived through a typhoon before, but both of us had read James Clavell's *Noble House*, with its disaster scene of an entire apartment building sliding down a hill in a typhoon mudslide. Our building perched on the edge of a steep slope. Who knew how well it was constructed?

The wind howled, louder and louder. The rain lashed against our windows. The radio announcers' voices got shriller as they reported gusts as high as 134 knots. Our twelve-story building shuddered and swayed. We grabbed and held each other. Suddenly, the wind stopped. The eye of the hurricane hovered over us for five, ten minutes. Then the fierce rushing sound began again, as suddenly as it had ceased.

Crack! Somewhere in our apartment, a window broke. We didn't dare leave the hallway to investigate. We trembled, waiting for the wind to calm down. Finally, the radio reported that the storm had moved on, crashing into the coast of Guangdong Province.

The wind was still howling when we went to investigate. The small window over my bathtub had blown in, and rain was pelting through—going harmlessly down the drain. My shower curtain was twisted in agony, but no further damage. Just one window to replace.

We lived through the storm. But eight people were killed, more than three hundred injured. Twenty-two ships ran aground in the harbor. More than fifty thousand people lost power. Two thousand people were left homeless.

Typhoon Ellen symbolized all the storms lashing through my life and my world. The calm confidence I had felt about the direction my life was heading, just five months earlier, now lay shattered in my bathtub.

✿✿✿✿

After that jolt of vulnerability, my fears kept rolling in like dark clouds. Maybe Paul would not return this time. The life he had built, over decades, was in Portland. What did I have to offer that could compare? A promise that his life would be happier in the future? No guarantees, that was for sure. If I were in Paul's shoes, would I return to Hong Kong? Breaking it off from a distance would the easiest path. He wouldn't have to face me. I braced myself every time he called.

Our prospects for building a life together looked grim. During one call, Paul told me that his boss in Oregon was enticing him to return and had offered him his old job, as vice president of project development. Hong Kong buyers had scooped up all the condos his company had for sale, so his job here was finished. And demand for housing in Portland was starting to pick up. The offer was tempting, but Paul assured me he would return.

"I can't wait to get back to you." His vehemence was palpable. I wanted to believe him.

Once I hung up, I collapsed. Clearly, it was possible that I would lose him.

What a cruel twist of fate. My ideal man was about to slip out of my grasp. If Paul moved back to Portland, our relationship would end. As much as I loved him, there was no way I would give up my dream job for him—especially when he was still married to someone else.

I wept and wept, gnashed my teeth, and burned through pages in my journal. The tears squeezed my heart into a dry ball that shrank in my chest like the black stone in a lychee. My whole body shriveled in pain around it. In the past, I had always been able to take action to solve problems. I hated feeling helpless.

Paul did come back to Hong Kong. Again, I met him at the airport. I tried to smile, but my heart was throbbing. In the taxi, he told me about a Texas company that was looking for people like him, salesmen who could attract Hong Kong buyers for US properties. Here was the nugget of hope I had been praying for.

Within days, Paul applied for the job—and got it. The position was temporary, and pay was commission based, with a small salary. To save money, he moved out of his hotel and into a flat shared with a friend. My hopes rekindled.

This new employer invested in a huge advertising campaign, taking out three full pages in five local papers, touting low-priced condos in Dallas and promising a guaranteed 7 percent annual return. But on the day the ads ran, only fifty-eight people called. It was a disaster—for the company, for Paul's job prospects, for the future of our relationship.

After the phones stopped ringing, Paul came over to my apartment. He was glum when he arrived. I gave him a hug and a glass of wine. "You know," he said, shaking his head, "I'm not used to setbacks. Up to now, everything I've tried has gone so well."

I did know. Ever since he'd met me, his career had been going downhill. Just as with those girlfriends of mine. But I wouldn't say that. "Maybe you could switch fields. A lot of American companies are scrambling to get into the China market. Could you take advantage of that?"

"You think so? I wouldn't know where to start."

"Of course! It's your homeland. There have to be opportunities."

He sniffed, and I glanced at his eyes to see if he was crying. "Just a cold," he said, wiping his nose. "Maybe. But, you know, my old boss is talking about building some new projects in Seattle. Seattle has two newspapers. You'd like it there."

I thunked my wineglass down. "Seattle?" I hadn't seen this coming. Seattle was hardly a step up after I'd been a foreign correspondent in China. "*BusinessWeek* doesn't even have a bureau there. We have bureaus in ten other cities, but Seattle isn't . . ."

He shook his head, looking forlorn.

"Well, it's bigger than Portland," I said, trying to make him feel better. The idea that he thought I might move back to America with him riled me. My career was just lifting off. Yes, I loved him beyond all reason, but how could I cut short this amazing opportunity I had been given? If this was a test of how much I loved him, I was failing.

China was just starting to open up and change. Couldn't he see that?

CHAPTER FOURTEEN:

The Big Prize

⚈⚈⚈⚈⚈

命, *ming: life; destiny. Traditional Chinese wisdom held that an individual should resign himself to destiny and submit to the will of heaven. As an American, I rebelled against this notion.*

Amid this distress, my job was hurtling off in unexpected directions. Thanks to an eager tech editor who couldn't get enough of my work, I immersed myself in the world of technology as I wrote about how Hong Kong, Taiwan, and Korea were churning out new kinds of electronics.

It was the early age of personal computers, and I had to learn new lingo: motherboards and chips, modems and floppies, RAM and ROM. Computer monitors were thick and bulky, housing glass cathode-ray tubes. Tiny Asian producers, flouting potential prosecution, began producing clones of IBM's popular desktop computer with pirated software. A whole industry, attuned to US demand, was taking off in Asia—although not yet in China.

I went back to Taiwan and donned a white clean-room "bunny" suit to see how tiny integrated circuits were made. Even a mote of dust could ruin a semiconductor, so all visitors had to wear full-body scrubs, including booties. I also traveled to both Singapore and the Philippines on reporting trips, working with our stringers who were based there. Jetting around Asia was the life of travel I loved.

Still, the big prize eluded me: a cover story. Some of my stories had been long, but none was important enough to reach the cover. If I could write a piece big enough to get on the front of *BusinessWeek*, that would be the moment of triumph.

I talked frequently with my editor, Bruce, as well his boss, Bob Dowling, about what story would qualify. As always, we had to look for the business angle. (My fellow reporters joked about this constraint; if we were sent to cover the crucifixion, one quipped, we would have to interview the peanut seller.) A cover topic needed to appeal to most of our readers, whether they did business in Asia or not. What happened in a Communist country mattered to *Business-Week* readers only as it affected the capitalist West.

Hong Kong was where those two systems met, and I knew I was living at the epicenter of a massive shake in the world order. Fortunately for me, economics and trade were at the heart of China's transformation. But how could I frame the story for my readers?

China was astounding everyone with its reforms and opportunities, and American companies were opening offices and testing the waters, although none had made money there yet. But Hong Kong was freaking out, sure it would be sacrificed along the way. Deng's changes inside China would determine its destiny, but how—and at what cost? No one could imagine what Hong Kong might look like under Chinese rule. What might that mean for the United States—and for American business? The whole thing felt huge and complex.

When you are witnessing history close up, it's easy to get distracted by the details. The journalist's challenge is to call out the big trends. A cover story was my opportunity to do that.

In the meantime, signals out of China had taken an ominous tone. Deng's open-door policy was moving ahead, but conservative rivals were sniping at him. In October, the Chinese Communist Party

National Congress held a crucial meeting where Deng called for a campaign to combat "spiritual pollution." Nobody knew quite what that meant, but Deng defined it as "the spreading of various decadent and declining ideologies of the bourgeoisie and other exploiting classes." It sounded a lot like a return to the bad old days.

His speech set off a rash of articles in China's press denouncing such "Western" offenses as fashion models, obsession with money, and excessive individualism. Liberal intellectuals and artists, they said, were encouraging frivolous and depraved drama and literature, which were un-Marxist and led youth astray. In one city, vigilantes in the streets cut off long hair and bell-bottom trousers. One office in Beijing banned makeup and jewelry. To the people of Hong Kong, this seemed like yet another omen that they would not be able to keep their way of life, as Beijing promised. Many worried it might signal a reversal of the fragile experiments Deng had begun in China. Was this the beginning of the end?

I decided to make another trip to China, this time to Guangzhou (Canton), to take the temperature there. Maybe I would get some ideas for a cover story. I began setting up interviews.

Right then, Paul's not-quite-ex-wife found out about me. Suddenly, she wanted Paul back. Frantic after losing her job and worried about life as a single parent, she flew to Hong Kong to pressure him to return to Portland. Her strong-arm tactics pushed Paul closer to me—but also quashed any hope I had for a quick divorce. Our lives fell into a different sort of spiritual pollution, a depraved drama more alarming to me than anything China's leaders faced. A deep murk descended on us, and I couldn't see any way forward.

"Someday, the two of you will be best friends," Paul predicted. Talk about far-fetched!

My vision of a happy marriage to Paul seemed like stupid, wishful thinking. But the more impossible it seemed, the more I clung to it. The longer I had to wait for him, the more I treasured him. Some days I slipped into despair. But I didn't want to give up. Someday, he would be mine. Paul and I were fated to spend the rest of our lives together.

By the time I set off for Guangzhou by hovercraft, I needed an escape from my personal crises. An American from San Diego sitting next to me chatted the whole trip. He was on his way to another Chinese city to set up production facilities for satellite receivers and fiber optics. Another guy, a young Scot, joined the conversation; he was in the oil consulting business. Both were jazzed about the China market, the possibilities for doing business there.

Their enthusiasm was infectious. It was just what I needed to calm my nerves and shift my focus to the reporting.

During my three days in Guangzhou, I discovered that American and European businessmen were swarming into the city, mostly dreaming of selling to the China market—especially consumer goods. Officially, China's stated policy was that it would import only essential goods it could not produce for itself: raw materials, advanced machinery, and technical equipment. But some consumer-products manufacturers had managed to slip in. Beatrice Foods of Chicago was one of the best known; it had set up a joint venture in Canton to produce food. I interviewed the Beatrice project manager and arranged a tour of its factory.

Guangzhou was also preparing to become the Houston of China, a base for the twenty-five foreign oil companies that had signed contracts to explore for oil in the South China Sea. They were all scrambling to find space, equipment, and subcontractors to prepare to start drilling as soon as possible. Several hundred British and American oil specialists had already moved to Guangzhou, and they were expecting hundreds more. The Chinese were planning to build a $75 million foreign-style neighborhood about fifteen minutes outside the city, with low-rise garden houses, schools, a chapel, a supermarket, bars, a disco, a sauna, and a putting green.

Guangzhou was brimming with optimism, open for business. Such a contrast with the stormy seas of Paul's business. Surely there would be job opportunities for him there.

Back in Hong Kong after my trip, I discovered that Paul's sniffles had exploded into a major head cold. He was miserable, with a stuffed nose, a sore throat, aches and pains, and general fatigue. Too much stress. I made him hot cups of ginseng tea, and he curled up on my couch under a blanket while I worked on my "Letter from Guangzhou."

I told him about the excitement I had found in Canton, especially the oil companies that were staffing up there. "You can write letters to all of them and apply. It can't hurt!"

He took another tissue. "I don know anyding aboud oil."

"You're totally fluent in English and Mandarin. You lived and worked in the States for years, so you know how American businesses work. Think how many American companies are eager to get into the China market! There's got to be something."

"Like what?"

"Well, all the big oil companies are there: Exxon, Shell, Chevron, Arco. They're planning to spend millions of dollars to drill for oil in the South China Sea. They've got to be hiring."

He looked skeptical. "But I've never worked inside China. People are different there."

"Yeah, neither has anybody else. You could figure it out faster than most people."

He blew his nose and wiped it. "Ya think?"

"It's worth a shot, right?"

The next day, at my office, I got to work on my Paul Yang Employment Project. In a slim brown reporter's notebook, I listed all the companies I knew that were eager to enter the China market. Surely all of them needed bilingual, bicultural people like Paul Yang. He could take the initiative and write to them. As a business reporter, I had access to information that most job seekers would kill for. As he tried to beat back his cold, I made fresh copies of his résumé. With his permission, I drafted a cover letter, using language he supplied, leaving a spot where he could sign. I checked in with everyone I knew in the China trade. It felt good to take action after months of passive frustration.

The more I talked it up, the more eager Paul became to take this new path. Many of his Taiwan classmates had made fortunes when Taiwan's economy took off in the 1970s. During those same years, Paul had been working for American city governments, hardly high-paying jobs. He believed he had missed one wave, and he didn't want to miss another. Of course, he also wanted to stay close to me. It could be, I thought, a win-win.

I had no power to make decisions for Paul. I couldn't dictate the timing of his divorce. And I couldn't make him healthy again. But I did have choices about how I reacted.

Together, we could do this. We could find a great job—perhaps even a great new career—that would make it worthwhile for him to stay in Hong Kong with me.

It was Bruce who came up with an idea for a cover story. China's biggest company, Bank of China, had just started constructing a skyscraper in the heart of Hong Kong. Meanwhile, the colony's biggest British company, Hongkong and Shanghai Bank, had torn down its iconic headquarters and was building a competing skyscraper. Bank of China's tower, set to be the tallest building in all of Asia, was designed by noted Chinese American architect I. M. Pei; Hongkong Bank's corporate headquarters, the most expensive in the world, was designed by British architect Norman Foster. They were like two young men strutting in a boxing ring.

Both of these ultramodern skyscrapers would overshadow the old British seat of power, centered in nearby Statue Square, a quaint colonial park, with its two-story, neoclassical Supreme Court building. And they would symbolize the two competing powers in Hong Kong: Chinese state-owned commerce and British global finance.

"How will the Brits cope with Red Capitalism?" Bruce asked me in a telex.

The term "Red Capitalism" made me squirm; using the word "red" to describe Communists seemed out of date, from the 1950s obsession with the "red scare." But it was true that Chinese state-owned companies were beginning to flex their muscles in Hong Kong, none more so than Bank of China, which financed most of China's overseas business and printed the national currency, with Mao's face on the bills. Hongkong Bank, though private, was so closely tied with Britain that it issued most of the local currency, featuring the Queen's face. As China ascended and Britain's colonial empire crumbled, the locus of power was about to shift—not just in politics but in business. The competing banks created a perfect metaphor.

In long phone calls with Bruce in New York, we hashed out a story line and I made lists of people to interview. The most important would be the chairman of Hongkong and Shanghai Bank, Michael Sandberg. This time, I was sure, he would talk to me.

Just as my reporting shifted into high gear, the future of Hong Kong was decided. In December 1983, after months of stalled talks, Britain and China reached a breakthrough. Although the talks were secret—and by no means finished—the news leaked out. Thatcher agreed to give the colony back to China in 1997 and trust Deng's promise of "one country, two systems." She caved. Deng won.

Many details remained to be worked out before a Sino-British Joint Declaration would be signed, a year later, but this was the moment.

This news gave us the hook we needed. The Beijing breakthrough might propel my Hongkong Bank story onto the cover. Bruce promised to lobby for it.

Fortunately, I had already decided not to go home for Christmas that year. I stayed in town, working like crazy on my cover story. That distracted me only a bit from Paul, who had returned to Portland to spend the holiday with his kids. He was getting sicker, but he still promised to return to Hong Kong. I hoped so. In the meantime, I collected his mail.

When he came back in January, Paul had almost completely lost his voice to laryngitis. He was desperate and unhappy and torn. His Christmas in Portland had been one of tension and worry about his kids.

Within days of his return, Paul followed up by calling Esso and Chevron. Both told him they had a job opening—not in Hong Kong but in Guangzhou. That was three hours away by train or hovercraft. Still, it was closer than Portland.

The following week, on the same day I submitted the first draft of my cover story, Paul took the train to Guangzhou for interviews. His voice was so hoarse, it was barely audible.

Still, Esso offered him a job, as "liaison director" for Esso China in Canton. That meant Paul would get to know the local Chinese officials, keep track of what they were thinking, and help head off potential disputes. It was a managerial position, with six people reporting to him. The job paid well, with benefits. He would have to sign a two-year contract. He would be working for a big corporation, with lots of promotional opportunities, and getting to know high Chinese officials in the oil industry. As a US citizen, he would be safe inside China.

Chevron came up with a similar job offer the next day, so Paul had a choice. He selected Esso, a subsidiary of Exxon, then the largest company in the world.

Paul and I fell into each other's arms, collapsing with relief. The eye of the typhoon had blown over. The wind and waves were still high, but we could manage.

This job, with its two-year commitment, would give us both time. Paul would have a steady income and time to settle his family issues. And I would have time to break the news to my parents, get them used to the idea that, one of these days, their daughter would marry a divorced Chinese man, fifteen years older, with two children. I knew they wouldn't be pleased.

Within weeks, Paul moved to Guangzhou and my first *Business-Week* cover story came out. It ran more than seven full pages, including sidebars on the political situation in Beijing and China's investments in Hong Kong. The cover showed Michael Sandberg, the chairman of Hongkong Bank, in a British derby hat, holding an umbrella, wearing a Mao suit and a bright red flower, under the words "The Future of Hong Kong: Can Michael Sandberg's Hongkong & Shanghai Bank Live with 'Red Capitalism'?"

Holding it in my hands was a thrill. It took three months of work and countless interviews. Although *BusinessWeek* still did not normally grant bylines, the magazine ran a "publisher's memo" with a photo of me posing next to the Bank of China stone lions, looking serious and journalistic. The memo, written by Lew Young, said *BusinessWeek* was among the first to realize that "Asia's influence in the world's business affairs is here to stay." Although the memo spoke of a "team" of reporters, I had done 90 percent of the work myself.

After a year and a half on the job, this was my crowning glory. I had the cover image enlarged and mounted. I proudly hung one copy in my office and donated another to the Foreign Correspondents' Club. Now, *BusinessWeek*'s cover—my cover—joined the work of other Hong Kong–based reporters on the venerated walls of the FCC.

CHAPTER FIFTEEN:

Distrust

⁄⁄⁄⁄⁄

宣傳, *xuānchuán: can be translated as either "propaganda" or "public relations." To Chinese, those are the same.*

In mid-March 1984, just two days after Paul began his new job at
Esso China in Guangzhou, I took the train up to visit him. Paul
met me at the Guangzhou train station; now that he was with Esso,
he had the use of a car and driver. It was nice to sink into his arms in
the backseat as the chauffeur took us to the fancy new hotel where
Esso China employees were staying.

That evening, the city seemed gloomy. Only a few buildings
topped five stories, and those were wrapped in fog. On side streets,
stores and night markets hummed with buyers and sellers under light-
bulbs, but the main streets were deserted. This city's population was
similar to Hong Kong's, yet it seemed dull and gray by comparison.
Guangzhou had only a few dozen neon signs. It was like going back
in time thirty years.

The White Swan Hotel was one spark of modernity—easily the most luxurious in all of China. As we drove up its long driveway, the hotel, lit up at night, shone like a white sail over the muddy Pearl River. At twenty-eight stories, it was by far the tallest building in the city.

Its lobby took my breath away. A four-story atrium beckoned like a lush tropical garden in paradise. Ferns hung from the ceiling, and greenery draped over the balcony walls. A red-pillared pagoda with a curved tile roof perched high on a rough-surfaced rock, and a waterfall cascaded in tiers into a lovely palm-lined pool. Large carp swam lazily.

I drank in the soothing sound of the waterfall. Here was a refuge of tranquility in the midst of our crisis.

The next morning, we walked around the hotel's neighborhood, Shamian Island. It was one of those places where history pulls you in. In the mid–nineteenth century, it had been the home of the small but influential European community. In those days, Guangzhou was called Canton (by foreigners), and it was the city where all of China's foreign trade was conducted. European-style stone mansions with verandas still graced tree-lined avenues. In the old days, only foreigners could live on this island, and the European trading companies, including Jardine Matheson, had warehouses along the riverfront. Wearing my blue Chinese padded jacket, called a *mian'ao*, I walked arm in arm with Paul along the storied streets of tiny Shamian. Many of the imposing houses were in disrepair. The last of the foreigners moved out after the Communist victory in 1949, and the state took over the foreigners' warehouses. Trade with the West stopped almost completely.

The saddest site was an elegant little yellow church, with a four-story steeple and arched doorways. Paul and I peered into the windows and could see that it had been used as a factory—probably during the Cultural Revolution. The Communists had expelled all foreign missionaries and shut down churches to eliminate any competition for loyalty.

The sight of the church brought up different memories for Paul. "Did I tell you?" he said. "I was brought into this world by a Catholic priest."

"You're kidding!" I said. "I thought you were born in Luoyang." His birthplace was deep in the heart of China. During wartime, when Paul was born, most foreigners left such areas.

"Yeah. My parents were on a train, and my mother went into labor. After they got off in Luoyang, my father rushed out of the station, looking for a hospital. Someone directed him to a Catholic mission, where a few priests doubled as doctors. An Italian priest delivered me."

I shook my head in disbelief; his family stories had unimaginable twists and turns. "Did he baptize you?"

He seemed surprised at the question. "I don't know. Do they usually do that?"

"I think so. Maybe you're a Catholic!"

He laughed. "Would that help when I meet your parents?"

I laughed but hid my anxiety. My parents disapproved of marriages that crossed social or religious lines. Chinese did not fit into any category because none of us knew any. Still, it was hard to imagine Paul Yang walking into the Youngstown Country Club or the First Presbyterian Church. I had written to my parents about a man called Paul but had not yet mentioned his last name. I knew it would shock them.

Paul and I continued walking, hand in hand, on Shamian Island, the ultimate symbol of the traumatic meeting of East and West. Canton. This was the place where the British and Chinese merchants worked together most closely. It was also here that violent clashes first occurred.

At first, the Chinese emperors scorned foreign trade. In 1793, Emperor Qianlong told Britain's king that he saw "no need to import the manufactures of outside barbarians." William Jardine and his competitors built up trade anyway. They wanted to buy Chinese tea and silk and porcelain but couldn't afford to keep paying in silver, so they started selling opium. China banned it, but smugglers brought it in, and gradually many millions of Chinese became addicted. In 1839, the emperor sent an official to crack down on the trade; he seized more than a thousand tons of opium from British warehouses and ships and burned it.

Walking the tranquil streets of Shamian in 1984, Paul in his jeans and I in my padded jacket, we seemed to bridge that ugly divide that had once ripped his people from mine.

❀❀❀❀

The depth of China's distrust of foreigners came home to me one weekend when Paul was in Hong Kong for a visit. He suggested we go see a movie, one of our favorite pastimes. This time, he made an unusual choice: a film produced in the People's Republic of China in 1958, called *Lin Zexu*. That name alone—which means nothing to most Americans—stirs up righteous resentment in many Chinese hearts, including Paul's. Naively, I went to the movie just because it was a good chance to learn new words in Mandarin.

Lin Zexu was the famous official whom the emperor sent to Canton to wipe out the opium trade. The movie portrayed him as an honorable, heroic figure who took the moral high ground.

Although I knew this movie could classify as propaganda, I was still appalled to see the behavior of the British. As an American of British ancestry, I had always admired the British—who, I had been taught, paved the way for democracy with the Magna Carta and for the modern world with the Industrial Revolution. To me, "Victorian ideals" meant restraint and high standards of behavior. So it was a shock to see, depicted on the big screen from the Chinese perspective, how British merchants, citing the noble cause of "free trade," had pushed China to import highly addictive illegal drugs.

The movie's biggest scenes were toward the end of the movie. During the burning-of-the-opium scene, people around me started booing the foreigners. In the movie, some of the British forces took up arms and attacked. Patriotic Chinese fishermen and farmers gathered up primitive weapons and rushed against the British soldiers in the rain. "Never allow the foreign devils to fight their way to Guangzhou!" one brave Chinese man shouted.

The moviegoers cheered as the foreigners ran away like scared dogs. I squirmed in my seat, leaning into Paul's shoulder and looking around me. I did not see a single foreign face in the audience. At the end of the film, a victorious throng massed on a hillside and brandished their weapons. The moviegoers applauded.

I tried to sit still, half wondering if someone might attack me—even though I personally had nothing to do with the bad British merchants in the movie. It was the only time I felt even mildly unsafe in Hong Kong. I urged Paul to leave the movie theater quickly.

Assuming I understood Chinese history, Paul was surprised at my reaction. Later, he explained. Yes, this movie was propaganda. Almost certainly, Beijing had rereleased it at this moment, hoping that the nonpolitical, non-Communist Chinese people living in British Hong Kong could be whipped up into patriotism by remembering that humiliation. They were right.

In real life, of course, the British responded by invading China and badly defeated it in the First Opium War. Their reward for their bad behavior: the emperor granted them the right to rule Hong Kong Island. Now, 145 years later, China was about to take back its territory. And Hong Kong people—who the previous year had been eager to emigrate—were now cheering. I was seeing contradictions and layers of complexity I had never thought of before.

Watching that movie was the first time I truly understood how deeply it wounded the Chinese to be humiliated by foreigners in their own land. At China's weakest point, when its economy and military were backward, the Europeans had trampled all over it. And the Americans had, too. This resentment—understandable, really—underlies all interactions between China and the West. At a gut level, I finally got it.

The movie opened my eyes to a truth most foreign correspondents see, eventually: our home countries, however beloved, don't look so benevolent when we view them through the lenses of people around the world. We easily recognize propaganda in other countries but are blind to it at home. What strikes us as natural—educating our children in the superiority of American values while leaving out inconvenient truths—can look to foreigners like whitewashing. The journalist needs to recognize both "propaganda" and "public relations" and determine what is true and what is hot air.

As a reporter, I decided, I needed to convey both the Chinese and the American points of view and to make sure my readers understood the deep implications of the different perspectives. Often those paragraphs got cut out of my stories, but I put them back in wherever I could. Just as I was learning to see the world through Paul's eyes,

I wanted my readers to dig beneath superficial, red-white-and-blue explanations of China. We Americans needed to understand our own biases before passing judgment on others. Deng was breaking through old stereotypes to create something new in China; good reporting required me to be equally bold.

✿✿✿✿

The distrust went both ways. To Americans in business, Chinese were slippery and unreliable. In a negotiation, the Chinese kept a blank face, not giving away their true reactions. The real deal was often unwritten, a back-door agreement based on a handshake, with payments given along the way. To the Chinese, Americans were naive—unable to hide their intentions. Americans were legalistic, insisting on spelling out everything in a contract and following the letter of the law.

"Sleeping in the same bed, dreaming different dreams." This Chinese adage best describes what I saw on my reporting trips to China in 1984. As a *BusinessWeek* reporter, I talked to a lot of Americans doing business in China, and their goal was clear: they wanted to sell to the huge Chinese market. But China's leaders had a different intention: they wanted to modernize by using advanced foreign technology. In effect, the Americans were shouting, "Give us access to your market!" while the Chinese were shouting, "Give us your technology!"

Those two goals clashed most sharply when Americans invested in China. The Chinese wanted foreign companies to bring their best technology to China to modernize Chinese factories, but they didn't want to give up control. So Beijing refused to allow wholly foreign-owned factories but encouraged fifty-fifty joint ventures with Chinese partners. Most American companies didn't really want to invest in China, but a few did so when the Chinese insisted it was the only way to sell into their market. With open eyes, they agreed to give away their technology, starting with outdated versions, assuming that China was so backward it could never catch up. Business in China was changing so rapidly that the country had no clear laws or ground rules to protect either foreign investors or Chinese who dared to try something new.

The Americans wanted to make money. But the Chinese considered "profits" a dirty word. If foreigners made money, in Communist thinking, that meant they were exploiting China and its workers—just like the opium smugglers. To Chinese, foreign investment meant an inflow of free money, technology, and equipment. They were looking to improve heavy industry. By contrast, the foreign companies that arrived were more interested in selling beer, soft drinks, crackers, cigarettes, and shampoo.

That conflict made for a good story. So, in late March, I headed for northern China again, this time planning a long trip to four cities to find out how American investors were faring.

After a year of avoiding it, I finally gave in: I asked for help from the All-China Journalists Association to arrange my trip. A "nongovernment" entity set up to host visiting foreign journalists, the ACJA was known to be a tool of the Communist Party, part of the government's attempt to control coverage of China by the world's free press.

I didn't trust them but believed I had no choice. Booking air tickets in China was notoriously difficult, and setting up interviews with government officials was impossible without permission. Airline tickets were sold only in the departure city, one-way, and had to be bought in person with cash—a time suck that involved hours waiting in line.

ACJA agreed to arrange these logistics—but it also sent along a bilingual minder to translate. I knew this handler would submit reports about me—about my attitudes and activities. My challenge would be to make use of the help while keeping vigilant if my minder tried to hide or distort the truth.

One cool morning in late March, I took the elevator down to the lobby of the Beijing Hotel. The moment to meet my minder had come.

The elevator doors opened, and I stepped into the high-ceilinged lobby of the hotel's tower—an eighteen-story building that was the city's only modern high-rise.

A Chinese woman rose from a sofa to greet me. About my age, she wore a unisex Mao jacket and had thick glasses and a short, unattractive haircut—remarkably like Honey in the *Doonesbury* cartoons. She waited for me to approach her and then shook my hand, speaking quietly in clear English.

"Welcome to Beijing. My name is Tian Bin." She handed me a name card.

I accepted the card with two hands and introduced myself. It wasn't a mystery how she recognized me. We were the only two women in the lobby. No Chinese citizens were permitted entry into this hotel unless they were on official business.

"Shall we sit? I will explain our itinerary." Her manner was efficient, calm, pragmatic, and no-nonsense, but not unfriendly. I towered over her, but she matched me in dignity. I had imagined a constant frown and a total lack of humor. Would I spend the next two weeks trying to escape her scrutiny? Would she refuse to translate certain questions?

Her itinerary was typed neatly in English and included exact times of flights and interviews for the next two weeks, as well as some interviews not yet arranged. As I'd requested by telex, she had set up two days of meetings in Beijing, followed by a trip to Shanghai, Wuxi, and Guangzhou. Speaking British-accented English, she was all business.

My goal was to visit factories to find out how American investors were faring. With some difficulty, I might have found the phone numbers of the American managers and interviewed them long-distance, but phone connections were poor and I wanted to see the factories in person. Despite the minder by my side, I hoped the Americans I interviewed would be candid—although I knew that businesspeople, like Communists, had their own agendas.

My article was timed for publication just before a six-day visit by President Ronald Reagan to China in late April 1984, a watershed in US-China relations. This was the first time an American president would come to China since Richard Nixon's groundbreaking trip in 1972.

"I still have to confirm a few details. In our office, we have been busy planning for your president's visit next month," Tian Bin said, after answering my questions about the itinerary. "Six hundred foreign journalists will visit then. Will you come back for that?"

I shook my head somberly. "No. My magazine prefers to write an article in advance of his visit." In classic weekly-magazine journalism style, my editors wanted me not to travel to China with Reagan's entourage but instead to make an in-depth trip in advance and write a "curtain raiser." Their logic: the dailies, wire services, and television would cover anything that happened during his trip. Our piece had to come out beforehand and provide depth and perspective. While I was disappointed to miss out on the chance to hang out with White House correspondents, I didn't mind leaving coverage of government-to-government news to others. My style of reporting, I believed, got closer to the heart of the real story of China.

"Your English is excellent," I said, interrupting Tian Bin just as she was about to go back to our plans. "How did you learn to speak so well?"

She nodded in a matter-of-fact manner. "I studied in England for one year."

"Really?" I pulled my head back in surprise. "When?"

"In 1974, when I was at university." Her tone was straightforward, but I guessed that her life had been anything but. She had left China two years before Mao died—and returned. Obviously a reliable, loyal Communist. During the Cultural Revolution, all universities had closed, and when they reopened, the only students admitted were either children of high officials or from poor families—workers, peasants, or soldiers.

"Very few Chinese studied abroad at that time," I said carefully.

"That's right. Now, on Saturday morning, you will need to be ready at . . ."

Her abrupt change of subject made me think I had reached the limits of any personal discussion. She probably had orders not to get too chummy with the foreign devils.

Later that day, as we rode in a private car with a driver arranged by Tian Bin, I was still thinking about my minder and her life. I wondered if I would ever get behind that austere shell.

"I'm curious," I said to her in the car, gently but directly. "How did you get chosen to study in England?"

Her smile contained two dimples. She seemed a tad more relaxed now that we were no longer in a busy hotel lobby, where other Chinese might overhear her. "I had no connections," she said, as if understanding the question beneath my question. "I came from a very poor family in Yangzhou. I was lucky to be chosen to attend university in 1972."

Aha. So she was not a high official's daughter. In years when college admission was decided based on political purity and targeted the children of workers and peasants, she was lifted from poverty and trained to be a true believer. Only the reddest of the red were allowed out of the country.

"So, you were *gongnongbing*, right?" I asked, using the jargon for the "good" family categories of "workers, peasants, and soldiers."

She tilted her head, as if surprised that a foreigner would know such an insider term.

I tossed her a mischievous smile. "Definitely not one of the *heiwulei*!" That was the term for the "five black categories" of political undesirables: landlords, rich peasants, counterrevolutionaries, bad elements, and rightists. At the height of the Cultural Revolution, Chinese from those categories were scorned and persecuted, but those days were over now.

She nodded once, still wary and unsure how to react to me.

"Myself, I come from a petit bourgeois family in Ohio." I switched to Mandarin in a low voice, as if confiding a secret. "My father was a capitalist. He owned a bookstore."

She let out a small laugh, as if appreciating my honesty and my understanding of China's obsession with class background. "Well, then!" she said, switching back to English. "We shall get along well."

Yes, I had a Communist minder. But she had a sense of humor. Could two young women, working for different teams, circumvent Cold War stereotypes?

CHAPTER SIXTEEN:

Dreaming
Different Dreams

ೞೞೞೞ

同床异梦, *tóngchuáng yìmèng: sleeping in the same bed,
dreaming different dreams.*

Decades later, it would be hard to imagine how backward China was in the early 1980s. Only a few foreign-built hotels had opened, and most of them fell into disrepair after Chinese managers took over. The beds were lumpy, the decor was old-fashioned, rugs were tattered at the edges, toilets often broke, the hot water and air-conditioning were unpredictable, and telephone service was maddening. To make an international call, you had to connect to the hotel operator and wait. The connection was scratchy and often broke down. The minute you hung up, a hotel attendant would come to your door, demanding you pay for the call in cash.

Fortunately, Tian Bin ran interference for me. She also set up my interviews with both Chinese officials and American businessmen. Good as her English was, I discovered that I could conduct the Chinese-language interviews directly, without stopping to wait for her interpretation, so she just listened. I took notes half in English, half in pinyin, the Chinese spelling system. If I didn't understand a word, I would ask her. When I interviewed Americans, she listened but didn't interrupt. She didn't hinder me at all, and we developed an easy rapport.

Tian Bin was not permitted to share meals with me, but in our many hours of car rides and airport waits, we got to know each other. Neither of us tried to convert the other, but we both listened and learned, the Communist stalwart and the capitalist roader. We laughed a lot.

The Americans told tales of endless negotiations, worker apathy, and bureaucratic turf battles. Everyone had a variation on a common tale of this culture gap. The biggest US manufacturing investment in China was the Beijing Jeep factory. After five frustrating years of negotiation, American Motors was about to start assembling Jeep Cherokees at a Chinese factory. But it had been rough going, with a surfeit of ten thousand workers and a hodgepodge of aging machinery. Workers still used iron hammers to smooth out rough spots. It was like going from the Stone Age to the Jet Age.

"Westerners are deceived. When they see Chinese carrying heavy loads on bicycles, they marvel at how hard the Chinese work," Corning Glass's China manager told me. "The contractors who built this plant worked hard—but they only worked three and a half to four hours a day. If they work or don't work, they get paid the same."

The biggest problem, by far, was how to make profits—and how to get them out of the country. China had rules that made it impossible to convert salaries, let alone profits, into hard currency.

Still, those who had invested early had a pioneer's pride, and many more were eager to get in China's open door. By the end of 1983, American manufacturers had invested only $85 million in twenty equity joint ventures, not counting Big Oil, and I visited most of them on that trip. China was issuing a steady stream of new laws and regulations to protect foreign investors and loosen restrictions on converting profits into US dollars. They sounded great on paper, but investors said the new rules weren't always followed.

During the whole trip, I found only one joint venture that was profitable. At Beijing Air Catering, three Hong Kong companies had secured a monopoly on providing food to airlines flying out of the capital. The day I visited, hundreds of white-uniformed workers were chopping chicken and preparing salads for up to five hundred meals a day in a pristine kitchen that looked nothing like the dirty factories I had visited. China's airlines had once offered only preserved plums, candy, and lukewarm tea. In less than three years, I learned, the Hong Kong partners had already managed to get their total investment back—in hard currency. That was rare.

After the trip, I wrote a five-page piece called "The Problems of Doing Business in China." It sounded like a litany of complaints. "The fabled work ethic of the Orient is lost in China," one American industrial expert told me.

In June, I wrote a second piece based on this same visit, called "Can China Become a High-Tech Powerhouse?" Ironically, it began, "China. The name evokes a multitude of strong images—but hardly one of high technology. Yet the People's Republic of China is determined to become a commercial powerhouse, if not a world leader in high tech."

China was in the infant stage of development, and its goal was to ramp up its ability for large-scale production of computers, semiconductors, communications equipment, and consumer electronics. Chinese were very open about their goal of leapfrogging the normal learning process by getting advanced manufacturing know-how from the United States and Japan. Some experts, whom my colleagues back in the States interviewed, predicted that China could catch up to Taiwan, Korea, or Japan within ten years, but the Americans I met in China doubted it. Only a psychic could have predicted that China might one day surpass the United States in any cutting-edge technology.

Still, the US government had strict controls on high-tech sales to Communist countries. I visited a semiconductor factory near the willow-lined Grand Canal in the city of Wuxi, seventy miles west of Shanghai. It had ordered $1.7 billion worth of equipment from US companies in 1981–82, but Washington had delayed the shipments. I peered into their "clean rooms" and saw yellowing paper signs taped on the floor, marking the spots where the delayed American equipment was to be installed.

Many American business leaders vociferously objected to these strict controls, which dated from Cold War suspicions of China and the Soviet Union. They objected to government restrictions, wanted to shift production to low-wage countries, and viewed China as a fast-growing, untapped market. Many were as eager to transfer technology—of course, yesterday's technology—as the Chinese were to receive it.

To me, my prediction to Lew Young seemed to be proving true. After thirty years under Communism, China could never transform itself into an industrial powerhouse. Like almost every observer at the time, I would prove dead wrong.

❧❧❧

Paul and I, too, were sometimes sleeping in the same bed, dreaming different dreams. Although we both dreamed of a day when we could live together in the same city openly, as a couple, we had separate views on what that future might look like.

Turning thirty was a big deal for me. It felt like a major milestone, the end of my adventurous twenties and time to reevaluate my priorities for the next phase of life.

On May 14, my thirtieth birthday, I worked in my office from 7:30 a.m. to 11:30 p.m. to meet a deadline. "Work comes first"—that was a concept both Paul and I agreed on. I celebrated a few days later, when Paul came down from Guangzhou to spend the weekend with me.

That Sunday, Paul and I were zipping along on bikes on a smooth, paved trail to the High Island Reservoir. It had taken us more than an hour by subway and bus to get to this remote peninsula. This was how I had chosen to celebrate my birthday—exploring "the middle of nowhere." Typical of me, both then and later.

I pushed my legs to go faster on the three-speed bicycle we had rented in the fishing village of Sai Kung. The semitropical hills around us glistened emerald on this glorious, sunny day, but the trail was not steep. After a few miles, we came to the reservoir. I pulled over to enjoy the view. We parked our bikes, pulled out our water bottles, and plopped down on a bench. I seldom got such intense exercise and felt exhilarated. Paul was panting. For a moment, I felt very young.

"Whew." Paul wiped a tissue over his forehead. "Not bad for a guy my age, right?"

I smiled. "And not bad for me, over the hill at thirty."

He laughed. "Ha! I wish I was thirty again."

My breathing slowed down. The reservoir glimmered in the sunshine like sequins spread out below us. "It's funny. I used to think thirty was really old. What were you doing at thirty?"

"I was, well . . ." He looked at me as if asking if I really wanted to know.

"In December 1969," I prompted, remembering his birth date.

"I was married, and Steven was a baby. We had just bought a house."

A cloud moved over the sun. He stared out over the water, as if thinking of how that idyllic life had gone wrong, battered in storms of acrimony.

But to me, marriage and a baby sounded like a Shangri-la I might never reach. There was no way we could set up a household together anytime soon.

The cloud made me shiver. "Do you think we'll ever get married?"

He grinned. "If I married you, would I have to eat hamburgers the rest of my life?"

Shocked, I was about to protest that my family almost never ate hamburgers, but he quickly took my hand, on my knee. "Of course we will. Just be patient. Besides," he added, "you're focusing on your career now."

This was true. And I certainly had no cause for complaint.

And yet as I turned thirty, I felt frustrated. I had found the man I wanted, and I knew he loved me, but we couldn't get married and start a family. My former self would have been glad that Paul was not pressuring me. But I had left her behind with my twenties. A pang of sadness hit me like a dart.

An unexpected sob blocked my throat. I tried to swallow it.

Paul's eyes widened with worry. "What's wrong?"

I looked away, feeling stupid about my rush of self-pity. Finally, the words stumbled out. "It just doesn't seem like enough anymore."

"It's not enough to be a foreign correspondent in China for a major magazine?"

"You know something? It's not fair. Men can have careers and families. Women should be able to, too. What if I get to the age of forty and never have a kid?"

"You really want a kid?" He seemed alarmed.

How could I explain? Somewhere, somehow, my priorities had shifted. Or had they? I stared off at the reservoir, whose surface had gone dull.

In my early twenties, I had scoffed at the idea of getting married right out of college and having babies. I knew that motherhood required compromises. Still, I had never decided against having children. I had friends who didn't want kids, and I was not one of them. To me, it was a matter of timing. If I had been married with kids at the age of twenty-seven, when Lew Young offered me this job, I would have had to turn it down. I would have stayed at home and seethed.

In the early 1980s, social attitudes were changing. My sister Trudy had quit her job as a schoolteacher after the birth of her first baby and become a full-time mother. My other sister, Trish, had pursued a high-powered consulting career and had no husband or kids. The message to me: it was either-or. It wasn't possible to have both a baby and a serious career. Yet my high school friend Sara had had a baby at twenty-four and then managed to get her PhD and teach plant biology at the college level while raising her daughter. Maybe it could be both.

I still wanted to "be somebody." I wasn't sure what that meant, but it involved being recognized as an expert—in my case, on China at this pivotal moment of change. This burning desire was a strong motivator for me, but it didn't mean no children. I just wanted to wait until I had secured my place on my chosen path so I could continue working and also raise a baby. I didn't want to leave the fast track. I wanted to have it all.

Hong Kong seemed perfect for that. Almost every American expat with a job and a family in Hong Kong had a live-in amah, usually from the Philippines, and it would not be hard to hire one who excelled at childcare. Economic opportunities in the Philippines were limited, so sometimes Filipinas with college degrees or other experience took jobs in domestic service. In America, only the super-rich could pay for live-in childcare. In Hong Kong, it was affordable. I really would be able to have it both ways.

But of course I could not, would not, have a baby until Paul and I were married and living together. As long as his job was in Guangzhou and mine in Hong Kong, this vision was a mirage.

The breeze whipped up, and Paul broke my silence. "I thought you didn't want children."

"I never said that! It's just that . . ." I stopped to try to articulate my mental jumble. In recent months, I had been admiring darling Eurasian toddlers I saw on the streets. I just hadn't discussed it with Paul. "Well, I can feel my childbearing years draining away from me."

"You want kids? I'll give you two. No diapers."

I shook my head. "You know what I mean. I can't wait to meet your kids, but I want a baby of my own. To experience motherhood."

"Motherhood and apple pie." He shook his head. I didn't care for this cliché. "Your job is so demanding. How would you combine kids with that?"

"Oh, in Hong Kong, it's easy. We can hire a Filipina amah."

"What's the point of having kids if you don't raise them yourself?"

"That's so old-fashioned! A mother doesn't have to be there every minute of every day. Lots of women these days are raising babies while continuing their careers."

His eyes looked troubled as he gazed at the view. I was so caught up in my own dreams that I couldn't fathom his. His experience with marriage and kids had torn him to shreds, and now he was finally free to pursue an exciting second career. "Kids are a big responsibility."

"Of course. I know that!" I said, though I really didn't.

"How many do you want?"

"Two. That's all."

"Two? How about one?"

I locked eyes with him. "One? Really?"

He looked at his hands. "I didn't tell you, but in Taipei I visited a palm reader."

I didn't believe in such things, but I listened raptly.

"See this line?" Paul pointed to a crease on the side of his palm. "She said this means I will have a child when I'm fifty."

"You're kidding!" I laughed out loud. I was delighted and hopeful—although I didn't want to wait five years. "So . . ."

"Well, maybe we could have one."

Perhaps I imagined it, but the sun broke out from behind the cloud and shone down on us, like two angels in a Renaissance painting. Between us I envisioned a cherubic child—with pretty, dark hair. A union of East and West. The best of both worlds. Could it happen?

CHAPTER SEVENTEEN:

Capitalism and China

～～～～～

摸着石头过河, *mōzhe shítou guòhé: crossing the river by feeling one stone at a time. A saying often used to describe Deng Xiaoping's pragmatic policy of trial and error. When you're doing something that hasn't been done before, take it step by step.*

*D*eng Xiaoping also had a big birthday in 1984: he turned eighty in August. Years later, pundits would declare that 1984 was his most glorious year. China became self-sufficient in food, a major milestone. In January, Deng toured the Special Economic Zones he had set up in 1979 in the South, areas allowed to experiment with private ownership and offer more flexible terms for investors. In April, he expanded the idea to fourteen other coastal cities. He also expanded his private-sector reforms from farms to urban areas throughout the country. The opposition's scary campaign against spiritual pollution fizzled. Instead of confirming George Orwell's *1984* nightmare of thought police and a stifling Party, China under Deng was becoming more open.

Nobody had ever imagined that any Communist party would choose to turn its state-run socialist economy into a prosperous one by using capitalist methods. Marxists were aghast, and the West was skeptical. Deng had already been purged twice for trying. There was no blueprint. He called it "socialism with Chinese characteristics," but to American eyes it sure looked like an injection of capitalism. Deng's approach was the ultimate in pragmatism: Try it, and if problems crop up, make adjustments. If you've never crossed this river before, just keep moving ahead, testing out each stone under each foot.

A lot more than the future of China was at stake. China would become a case study, a testing ground for those who believed self-interest, free markets, and private enterprise were keys to unlock people's energy and lift them out of poverty. Beyond that, many in the West believed that any people, once free to live and think as they chose, would choose democracy. The world was watching.

Lew Young was watching, too. Japan had long been important to *BusinessWeek*, but the rest of Asia was an afterthought. Now that I had begun to produce interesting stories, he decided to staff up in Asia. He was ready to add a second journalist to the Hong Kong bureau to help me cover China and Southeast Asia. He asked me to look for one.

Although my title was bureau manager, I had never managed anyone. Now I would have to learn how. By trial and error.

First, though, I had to find a bigger office. Away from the men's public toilet! My office assistant, Janita Tam, helped me find a perfect space on the twentieth floor of a respectable building on Queen's Road East, still in Wanchai but within walking distance of Central. The office had three rooms and was five times the size of the tiny space Hal had found. Every day I would enjoy a panoramic view of Hong Kong's business district.

I looked around Asia for bright young American reporters who spoke Chinese. The *Asian Wall Street Journal*, a daily published out of Hong Kong, had many of them, and I chose Dorinda Elliott. Dorinda was twenty-six—four years younger than I was—and an East Asian studies graduate of Harvard, fluent in Mandarin. She was fairly green, with experience mainly as a copy editor, but she was whip-smart. She had a great laugh and was fun to talk to. It was a funny coincidence that our names were similar; fortunately, her nickname was Dinda.

For her first story, I assigned her a short piece about advertising in China. With no one to teach me how to manage, I just followed what I had learned from Bruce Nussbaum in New York. I talked over story ideas with her, helped her to get the go-ahead from New York, and suggested contacts for interviews. I hoped to be the mentor for her that I had so sorely needed.

Her first draft needed help. She was a good writer, but *Business-Week* had its own preferred style, so I had to rewrite it. I knew how painful that would feel, but it was the only way I knew to show her. Then I explained, paragraph by paragraph, why this new version worked better. "We're a weekly. We can't do things the same as the dailies," I said.

Her face turned red. "Sorry," she said, her face crumpling. "I feel terrible."

"Don't! It took me more than a year of working in New York to figure out what the magazine wanted. Even now, they almost always rewrite my lede. Drives me nuts, but that's the way it is." She listened carefully and learned quickly. I wanted her to succeed.

Her second story was much better, and I let her submit it as written. As usual, the New York editors changed the opening paragraph, but nothing else. I felt gratified to see her do well.

One morning a few weeks after she started work, I arrived at my office a little early. Dorinda was sitting at my desk, a pen in her mouth, looking through my box of name cards—Hong Kong's version of a Rolodex.

"Hey! Morning!" I said. She flashed me a wide smile. I loved having a colleague at last, especially one as cheerful as Dinda. I raised my eyebrows, wondering why she was at my desk.

She took out the pen but kept a finger in the "C" section. "Looking for some sources."

I dropped my purse and looked over her shoulder. She had written a few names and phone numbers on a notepad. "No problem. What story is this for? Maybe I can suggest a few."

"It's about yesterday's drop in the stock market. I'm looking for securities analysts."

I was confused. "Actually, we don't cover day-to-day fluctuations in the market. As a weekly, we can't, really. Did someone in New York ask for that?"

"Well, no. Actually, it's for Adi. They finally assigned him a story!"

My heart turned into a brick that threatened to drop on my toes. Adi, her boyfriend, worked for the *Asian Wall Street Journal*, our chief competitor. "What? They have dozens of people there who could help him!"

"I know." She smiled gamely. "I just wanted to help with a few names to get him started." Her face shone with love.

Normally slow to anger, I struggled to keep control of my voice. "Dinda," I began, snatching my name-card box out of her hand and snapping shut the clear plastic lid. "I . . ."

She jumped out of my chair and backed off, as if I had turned into a wolf.

I hated confrontation. But this had hit me where it hurt. "Listen." I had to pause to keep my voice from going shrill. "When I came to Hong Kong two years ago, I had no contacts. None. I had to develop every single source on my own."

She nodded but kept her mouth in a firm line, eyes still wide.

"So many times, I wished I had colleagues like they have over at the *Journal*. They have a whole office full of people! And every one has a Rolodex. They've been cultivating contacts for years. And I'm just one person. I'm happy to help you with any contacts you need for your *BusinessWeek* stories. But Adi? Really? You're helping the *Wall Street Journal*?"

"I'm sorry," she said. "It's just that Adi is new and he doesn't . . . Sorry. I won't do it again." She slunk back to her desk.

After that outburst, I sat at my desk, staring at my name-card box, tapping my pen.

It came flooding back to me, that feeling I had in the early days. I had started out by circling names of experts quoted in the local newspaper and looking up their numbers in the phone book. As much as I dreaded talking to strangers, I had called them, one by one. Some, I had met for lunch or coffee. For an introvert, it was agonizing.

I adored Dinda. Her mistake was understandable. I needed time to calm down.

Sometimes you don't realize how important your harvest is until someone pilfers it. That name-card file contained the food I had gathered to survive on my own—and to feed Dinda. Afterward, though, I wondered if I had been too harsh. Had I let my own insecurities blind me to someone else's? Or was I creating appropriate boundaries? I could have used some good mentoring in people management.

❧❧❧

The 1980s were a great time for China to jump into the swirling waters of capitalism. And Hong Kong, as it turned out, was at the center of the vortex. Under Ronald Reagan, the US economy was growing again, and East Asia was booming by selling to us. Japan's economic miracle was wowing everyone, sparking American fears that Japan was out to overtake us in high tech. Much as it would do against China thirty years later, the US government slapped tariffs on imports from Japan and pressured Tokyo to stop what it considered unfair trade policies.

China, most of us assumed, needed to follow Japan's model of economic development, which had worked well for South Korea and Taiwan. Starting in the 1950s, Japan had modernized by flooding the United States with cheap trinkets. Earnings from those exports helped Japan transition "up the development ladder" to more high-end, profitable production, including steel, autos, and consumer electronics. Taiwan and South Korea were thriving by following Japan's example. With lower labor costs, they eagerly picked up the export industries that Japan was outgrowing: clothing, toys, watches. Now they were starting to move beyond those cheap goods and invest in assembly of more complex products.

The hot new industry was electronics, especially computers. As American consumer demand grew, Asian companies were scrambling to produce televisions, watches, cameras, and personal computers.

Backstreet startups in Hong Kong and Taiwan sold cheap copies, called knockoffs, of popular "microcomputers" designed by Apple and IBM. Hong Kong had a market devoted to such copycats, and I admit I purchased a knockoff of an Apple IIe, the coolest new computer, and flouted US customs laws by taking it back to the United States in pieces for my brother's family. I captured this craze in a long article from Taiwan called "The King of Knockoffs Rushes to Go from Imitation to Innovation."

By chance, that article provided my first byline on a news story, shared with Otis Port, tech editor in New York. The reason: in August 1984, Lew Young surprised us all by suddenly stepping down as editor-in-chief. He had chosen his successor, Steve Shepard, but tension arose between them during the transition. After fifteen years at the helm, Lew wasn't willing to make the changes Steve suggested, so one day he just announced he was leaving. When Steve took over, one of his first moves was to allow bylines for all articles. This elated all of us reporters, who had been writing news articles anonymously.

But producing computers, even knockoffs, for the US market required agility and risk-taking that China clearly lacked. Chinese people in Taiwan, Hong Kong, and Southeast Asia were some of the best entrepreneurs in the world. Moneymaking seemed to be in their genetic makeup. But across the border, Chinese manufacturers seemed stodgy. After years of central planning, they were saddled with a huge bureaucracy and old-style factories that supported thousands of workers and social programs. How could China be nimble enough to follow Japan's export-oriented model to prosperity?

By chance, I was sitting on the answer: Hong Kong. For decades, its small manufacturers made money by figuring out how to meet the mercurial needs of the huge American market and producing stuff cheaply and efficiently. Thousands of tiny Hong Kong companies had names no one in New York could recognize or pronounce, but these Chinese entrepreneurs had skills unlike anyone in Beijing. For decades, they had been churning out clothing, shoes, watches, and toys for export. Many produced American-label products under contract. Soviet Russia had no such swarm of entrepreneurs on its doorstep to help it modernize.

Now in the 1980s, behind the scenes, many of these little guys on the backstreets of Wanchai and Kwun Tong figured out that they could make stuff even more inexpensively—by opening factories in southern China. Deng Xiaoping's policies had suddenly made that possible.

One by one, then by the dozens, they started manufacturing in southern China, across the border from Hong Kong, where labor was cheaper. They were not taking over massive state-run factories. They were hiring young Chinese and training them to do assembly work and simple sewing and soldering in bare-bones new factories, built on farmland.

I missed this story at first. We at *BusinessWeek* had a bias toward big corporations with household names, so I focused initially on US companies that were investing directly in China. For them, the China experience was a tough slog. Like many American journalists, I assumed the important China stories all originated in Beijing. But the best story was outside my window.

In October 1984, I did turn my attention to this trend, reporting a story called "How Hong Kong's Entrepreneurs Are Hedging Their Bets." Many of the dozens of businessmen I interviewed came from families that had fled Shanghai when the Communists confiscated their assets. One, Dennis Ting, posed with armfuls of Cabbage Patch dolls, among the many popular toys he made in Hong Kong. But instead of spotting cross-border investment by small manufacturers as key to China's future, my story focused on the worries of the Hong Kong businessmen. Ting had transferred much of his personal wealth to North American real estate, and his son was studying in Canada. Like many in Hong Kong, he did not trust Communist promises.

The surge of low-cost exports started as a trickle, almost entirely in the south, near Hong Kong. A pocket of low-cost manufacturing popped up just over Hong Kong's northern border, in a former fishing village called Shenzhen, which Deng had chosen to be a Special Economic Zone. The Japanese discovered it quickly: Sanyo Electric made videotape recorders and transistors there, and Hitachi and Toshiba competed to build a plant that would produce color-TV tubes. But the only Americans who paid much attention were importers.

Skeptics still thought that workers in Communist China would never show the same work ethic as those in capitalist economies, but Ting and his peers found out otherwise. Their workers were mostly local farm girls who had never developed bad factory habits or socialist expectations. They were compliant and eager to earn their own money. Under managers from Hong Kong and later Taiwan, hardworking Chinese laborers quickly defied their country's reputation for shoddy inefficiency and began producing reliable, decent-quality products for the American consumer. Hong Kong became China's training ground and window on the world.

Few of us could imagine that Walmart stores would one day be filled with affordable goods made in China—least of all Deng Xiaoping, who planned for China to fund its modernization by exporting oil.

Meanwhile, Paul and I were also crossing the river by feeling one stone at a time. Together but apart, a couple in two cities, we kept seeing each other every weekend. We were determined to create a future together, but the way forward was shrouded in fog.

Paul liked his job with Exxon, made good friends, and was gaining valuable experience dealing with a new type of Chinese bureaucrat, open and eager to cooperate with foreign companies. But he still believed it was the wrong time to file for divorce. His not-quite-ex-wife got a new job, which involved importing from China, so she flew to Guangzhou several times and once even brought the kids as pawns to help convince Paul to go back. I did not witness any of the painful scenes, so that is not my story to write. But I saw the wrenching effects on Paul.

I didn't make it easier. I pressured him repeatedly to file for divorce—or else. But I found I had no stomach for "or else." I did not want to be patient, but pressure didn't work. Month after month, some new twist would leave me weeping through the night. So much for my rosy vision of a happy marriage and cherubic baby.

Fortunately, I had close friends who could commiserate. Cindy was going through a torturous time with her boyfriend, and we spent hours talking over our heartaches. My best friend, Katy, from my days in Washington and New York, moved to Hong Kong that year to take a new job. She knew all my history and offered advice and sympathy. We brilliant, accomplished women all had trouble finding a good match. Exciting careers, it seemed, were not compatible with mating. Still, great girlfriends were a refuge from the storms.

No way would I tell my parents about my frustrations with Paul. They would be shocked to know I was seeing a married man. Still, I wanted them to know more about him. I mentioned that he and I had traveled together to Thailand. Finally, I casually mentioned that his last name was Yang.

My dad called up my sister Trish to break the news: Dori's new boyfriend was Chinese. One step ahead of him, I had already told my sister—and even sent her a photo of Paul.

"I guess it was bound to happen," my dad told her. "She has a taste for the exotic."

Dad's word choice made me laugh. Attractive as he was, I viewed Paul as more pragmatic than "exotic." What a silly word to apply to more than one billion people!

"Well," my sister told Dad, "I don't see how it makes any difference, as long as he's a good man and she likes him." Mom, ever the quiet one, usually took her cues from Dad.

In early October, Paul and I visited his parents again in Taiwan. He told them we planned to get married—someday. They didn't mind that I was a foreigner; Paul's first wife was Chinese, and that match had failed. At his stage of life, they just wanted Paul to find happiness. Paul's mother herself was a second wife; his father had divorced his first. But they never mentioned that.

Paul had to leave Taiwan early, and I stayed on to do some reporting. One night I went over to have dinner with his parents again—by myself. By then, they had questions. Baba asked me if it would be hard to move, in my kind of work, and wanted to know how long Paul would stay in Guangzhou. I told them Paul wanted to go back to America eventually and that I would be willing to move back someday, too.

"Will you obey him, or will you make him obey you?" Paul's mother asked.

I squirmed. It sure wasn't the language of feminism, but I tried to think of their intent. They liked me and wanted to see us get married.

"I will listen to him, and he will also listen to me," I answered. In Chinese, "obey" and "listen to" are the same word, *ting*.

"If you get married and move to America," Paul's father asked hesitantly, "could we come and visit sometime?" This was a loaded question, I knew.

"Of course!" My enthusiasm was honest. "You have welcomed me here so many times!"

They smiled at each other.

"Good," said Paul's father. "If I can, I will attend your wedding, wherever it is."

Just a few weeks later, my mother and Trish came to visit me in Hong Kong—their first time in Asia. I took them to the Peak by tram, to Kowloon by subway, and to Macau by jet foil. Trish loved shopping in Stanley Village, where she bought a cloisonné cigarette lighter for herself and kung-fu pajamas for Trudy's little sons.

Seeing Hong Kong through their fresh eyes was fun. They had not been able to imagine my life in this foreign environment. Just seeing everyday things at my home (a plastic dish rack, grilled cheese sandwiches, Corelle ware) amid unfamiliar ones (my funky gas stove, the water heaters in my bathrooms, my Chinese cleaning woman) gave them a way to relate. Now they could picture me living in Hong Kong: taking taxis around town, speaking simple Cantonese to the drivers; riding a double-decker bus to Stanley; rushing through crowded streets to my office. They were both far outside their comfort zone.

Trish described their first encounter with culture shock, on the airplane ride across the Pacific. The flight attendant gave them each a bowl of Chinese noodles, and they stared at it and each other. They had no idea how to eat it. Across the aisle, a Chinese passenger picked up his bowl of noodles, held it close to his mouth, and scarfed it down with a few swipes of his chopsticks. To them, it looked like he had swallowed all the noodles in one gulp. We all laughed at my sister's vivid portrayal. But I knew that most Chinese ate noodles this way. It made me wonder: When had I first seen this? Had I found it funny? I could not remember.

Their perspective reminded me just how far I had come from my childhood home.

The big moment arrived when they met Paul, who traveled down from Guangzhou that weekend. He stayed at a hotel in Kowloon, and we met him in the lobby. Paul was not nervous, but I was. How foreign would he look through their eyes?

When I introduced him, Paul smiled with confidence. My mother regarded him with curiosity and had no trouble understanding his slight accent. He helped Trish buy a camera, haggling the price down. That evening, at my suggestion, Paul and I took them to dinner at the Jumbo Seafood floating restaurant.

My mother mostly listened and observed us as we interacted. Although I had learned as a child to read her minutest expressions, this time I couldn't.

"What do you think of Paul?" I asked her after he had gone back to Guangzhou.

"I can see that you like him very much" was her careful answer.

She showed no signs of disapproval—or enthusiasm. I wondered what she would report back to Dad. Probably, they hoped I would lose interest.

✻✻✻

Communist China looked less and less Communist by the month. One day that fall, I was astounded to read the news that China was considering opening a stock exchange. It was too early for a real market, but a few Chinese companies began raising money by issuing stocks and bonds. Even China's cadres began acting like capitalists, developing hotels and shopping centers on government-owned land.

All this capitalistic behavior in the world's biggest Communist country boggled my mind. China had changed so quickly from that street vendor selling eyeglasses that I had met in Manchuria two years earlier. Deng, it seemed, was willing to try anything to cross that river and modernize China. At age eighty, he was a man in a hurry.

On my frequent visits to Guangzhou, I found many Chinese citizens willing to talk to a foreign journalist. China brimmed with hope: that individuals would get more freedom to choose the work they preferred, that farmers could plant the crops they wanted and keep the profits, that workers could find jobs that paid better than the state.

Sentiment among American businessmen, too, had brightened. Convincing Chinese officials to agree to normal business terms remained tough, but the possibilities for the future seemed wide open. Although the oil drillers were starting to lose hope, other companies were flooding in, hoping to sell their products in China's huge consumer market. A deodorant marketer coined the memorable phrase "one billion people, two billion armpits."

Chinese women wearing lipstick shopped for scarves and earrings alongside workers in baggy trousers and black-rimmed glasses. Dance clubs popped up. Rock music was heard, and—gasp!—young couples were seen kissing in the streets. Even China's premier, Zhao Ziyang, regularly wore a coat and tie. Many Chinese now owned bicycles, radios, and watches. They next aspired to buy televisions, washing machines, and motorcycles.

Deng Xiaoping never actually said, "To get rich is glorious"— the slogan often attributed to him. That was the title of a new book by longtime China watcher Orville Schell that came out in December 1984. What Deng actually said was, "Socialism does not mean shared poverty."

Clearly, it was time for another cover story. Dinda and I spent hours planning it out, talking with Bruce in New York, analyzing the rapid changes in China and how we could capture them in words. I sent Dinda off on her first big reporting trip, to Beijing and Chongqing, with the help of a friendly minder from the All-China Journalists Association. As usual.

I chose to do my reporting in nearby Guangdong, where I had discovered a hotbed of private enterprise. A couple who ran a tiny noodle stand on a busy street corner told me that they, with their earnings, had bought a color TV, a refrigerator, a stereo cassette player, and a camera. In the countryside, a young veterinarian told me he raised chickens, ducks, and geese to supplement his income. "A decade ago," I wrote, "he could have been jailed for such daring."

We captured this fervor and nerve in a cover story called "Capitalism in China," published in January 1985. The subtitle: "Under

Deng Xiaoping, it's O.K. to get rich." Our photo department found a picture of a young Chinese woman wearing a stylish red hat and a fuzzy rabbit-fur coat—far from the still-prevalent uniform style of loose pants and white shirts.

Unlike my first cover story, this one was more typical of "group journalism." The byline listed six reporters, starting with me and Dorinda Elliott. I was learning to accept good reporting done in America, as long as it combined well with my on-the-ground observations.

To make sure we didn't get carried away, we mentioned fears of "a backlash" that could wipe out recent gains, as well as concern over inefficiencies. But opponents of reform, we noted, did not have a leader anywhere near as strong as reformer-in-chief Deng Xiaoping.

Still, our article fed into the exuberance of the time. "Imagine the energy and enterprise of Hong Kong multiplied by a population 200 times as large," we wrote. "Imagine the global balance of power if China matches Japan's success in high technology." Such words were considered hyperbole. After all, China's per capita annual income was only $300, less than that of Haiti—and tiny compared with Japan's, which was more than $10,000. Still, we predicted, "China could even become an economic superpower" by 2050. Imagine that.

A few friends ribbed me for going overboard with enthusiasm. But years later, as China rose to outperform even the most passionate prognosticators, our prediction would seem bland.

Just as we were finishing up that cover story, Britain and China finally announced they had signed a joint declaration: Britain would give Hong Kong back to China on the promise that it could retain its capitalist system and "a high degree of autonomy" for at least fifty years.

Yes, it was a glorious year for Deng Xiaoping.

CHAPTER EIGHTEEN:

Hurdles and Hazards

ဘဘဘ

伤脑筋, *shāng nǎojīn: Most people translate this term as "worrisome." But it literally means "to hurt the brain." I love that vivid imagery. Sometimes solutions seem impossible.*

For me personally, 1984 had been a year of nightmares, and I was glad to see it end. Just before 1985 began, I flew to New York, where I put the finishing touches on my cover story and had a private lunch with the new editor-in-chief, Steve Shepard. He was pleased with my work and happy with Dorinda. I encouraged him to visit China.

On January 1, 1985, on my journey back to Hong Kong, I saw "Capitalism in China" at an airport newsstand and bought a copy. Paul and I were sitting in an airport lounge in Los Angeles when he broke the news: he had filed for divorce. It would be final in three months. I expected a gush of relief, but it didn't come. The contentious split had stressed his kids, and he had no confidence that their lives would get better soon. It was not a moment to celebrate. Still, it lifted the cloud over our heads. Or promised to.

During January, I wrote four stories and traveled to Manila for reporting. Every once in a while, I let myself dream about marrying Paul and planning for a wedding. But the obstacles still seemed insurmountable. We lived in different cities.

Then, in early February, Paul got a phone call in the middle of the night. The kids' maternal grandmother, who had cared for them throughout their childhood, was dying. He rushed back to Portland and arrived a few hours too late. The kids were distraught. Their grandma had been their constant source of love and stability. After a few days at home, Paul called to tell me he had decided to postpone the divorce for another three months.

Alone again in Hong Kong, I sank into despair. Had I been asking too much of the universe? Was I being punished for coveting what was not mine?

China's flirtation with capitalism was not going smoothly, either. Not everyone was thrilled with it. Orville Schell, one of the few American writers allowed to visit China during the days of Mao, saw mostly the dark side of Deng's reforms. In his December 1984 book, *To Get Rich Is Glorious: China in the Eighties*, which I reviewed for *BusinessWeek*, Schell pointed out the rise of petty theft, black-market imports of jeans, and the dismantling of collectively built irrigation systems vital to farming. Once a left-leaning friend of socialism, he decried the crass materialism he saw in China's lavish French restaurants and lamented the lack of care for the poor. In China, people were now looking out for their own interests. No one cared for the common good.

In my view, Schell's book was a swan song for the Old China and for the type of idealistic, socialist view of China that it represented. My cover story celebrated the arrival of the New China, the start of a new era. Socialism was out. Capitalism was in. I felt no nostalgia for Mao-style Communism.

What appealed to me in the New China was not idealism but dynamism, a gung-ho desire to make up for lost time and grab for the high bar. I didn't accept the ethos of the 1980s, "greed is good," but I did share the breathless enthusiasm *BusinessWeek* showered on such successful innovators as Steve Jobs and Bill Gates. They were not just trying to get rich. They were thinking outside the box and creating something of value for all. Someday, maybe, China would produce entrepreneurs like that.

Change on a massive scale always produces heartache, with winners and losers. So does the individual pursuit of well-being, which breaks old molds in the hope of creating something better. Paul was moving in stark new directions, in the hope of a creating a new career, but the fault lines were breaking under his kids. In Deng's China, too, many who lived just fine under the old rules suffered when the system changed.

Still, my admiration for Deng Xiaoping was rising daily. What Deng was doing was so unlikely, so daring. How could he convince the Communist Party to trust the forces of capitalism? How could any centralized power voluntarily loosen its control? Deng was challenging a centuries-old attitude of fatalism. He was choosing to shape China's destiny.

As an American, I was riveted by the notion of defying the odds. The Chinese language doesn't even have a good translation for "defying the odds." The closest terms are those for "risk danger" or "disdain fate." Why would anybody do that? That's what I had been doing, too, in my personal and professional life.

When you defy the odds, though, you repeatedly risk failure. It's like crossing the ocean in a clipper ship, sailing through storms that might sink the ship and sacrifice all onboard. Deng was an unlikely captain, a modest man who rejected the grandiosity of Mao Zedong.

Throughout the 1980s, Deng steered China through smooth waters and storms, and whenever he hit a rough patch, internal critics seemed eager to grab the helm. They were a group of "old guard" leaders, aging revolutionaries who had brought Deng back to power after Mao's death. Chief among them was Chen Yun, an influential leader who tried to rein in Deng's most daring moves. Chen Yun supported market reforms but only within the firm limits of a Soviet-style central plan—like a bird in a birdcage. Starting in 1984, when the split became apparent, the Western press began calling Chen Yun and his allies "conservatives"—a foil to Deng's "reformers." In reality, they led China as a group, but when their differences surfaced, we China watchers got whiplash.

That spring of 1985, China hit rough seas. Its economy was over-heating—and in danger of spinning out of control. "Evil winds" were threatening to derail Deng's grand experiment. In late March, Deng's protégé, Premier Zhao Ziyang, laid out the problems in a blunt speech televised nationwide. Economic growth, in both agriculture and industry, was three times faster than expected. China's imports were surging so wildly that the country's foreign-exchange reserves dropped 30 percent in just six months. The economy was in runaway mode.

Unleashing the entrepreneurial spirit was like letting a dragon loose. Party and military officials were among the first to jump into the fray. They bought up steel at low prices and resold it. They imported trucks and color TVs, in short supply inside China, and resold them at higher prices. Horrified, the Party barred its members from starting their own businesses. Free enterprise was so new that China didn't have the laws or systems to prevent abuses. Instead of Adam Smith's invisible hand setting prices, the market was just distorted in new ways.

Zhao announced plans to tap the brakes. First, he tried monetary policy—restricting credit and raising interest rates—to curb inflation. That was foreign for Chinese leaders, used to more direct intervention. He also pulled back on some of the foreign-trade privileges recently granted to cities and factories. He tried to stem the flood of consumer-goods imports and cracked down on officials suspected of taking bribes and giving themselves pay raises. That wasn't the kind of personal wealth Deng meant.

We in the press were quick to call it a crackdown, but what Deng and Zhao were trying was really a calibration of free-market forces with central planning. They aimed to create a hybrid of capitalism and socialism. They wanted to free up the private sector and grow the economy, but they didn't want it to spin out of control. It was a balancing act, like a plate spinning atop a stick—done by an amateur.

Still, these measures shook up American business, as I wrote in early April. With the stroke of a pen, policy could change. Companies with investments in China worried they would have extra layers of trouble importing equipment or repatriating profits. Provincial enterprises began to delay payments, cancel orders, and suspend talks on big projects.

By then, it was becoming obvious that China's offshore oil bonanza was a bust. Almost all the wells drilled were dry. World oil prices, which hit a peak in 1980, were dropping steadily, making China exploration even less attractive. Four typhoons that interrupted drilling, plus a fatal supply-boat accident, made the whole enterprise seem cursed.

Paul's boss at Esso tried to remain optimistic, but the high tide of spending was over. Although he had a two-year contract, Paul could see the handwriting on the wall. I encouraged him to apply for jobs that would allow him to move back to Hong Kong—with me.

Finally! I thought. After a year of living in separate cities, Paul and I might be able to reunite in Hong Kong. Maybe this bad news for oil exploration would be good news for us.

🐟🐟🐟

In April 1985, just as Paul sent out his first queries for jobs in Hong Kong, I returned to the States for yet another *BusinessWeek* editorial conference.

It was time to tell my parents I planned to marry Paul. We could not set a date, but our marriage seemed likely—well, at least possible. Since my mother had already met him, I had reason to hope they would approve. Still, I was nervous. In their eyes, I was sure, Paul was the wrong guy. As in China, old values and unthinkable new ones were colliding, and I was not confident I could steer the ship of my life through these roiling waters.

That first night back in Youngstown, at nearly midnight, I started walking down the dark stairs of the home I had lived in since age ten. My hand gripped the wooden rail, and my bare toes scuffed the worn carpet. With each stairstep, I shored up my resolve. I had interviewed tycoons and taipans, but this time the risks were far higher. The downside was that I could alienate my parents and create a rift that wouldn't heal.

My parents had always been loving and supportive, although they had certainly never expected me to live in such a foreign country for so long. Cocooned in their country-club world with traditional values that had worked well for generations, they couldn't imagine the appeal of marrying a man from a different race and culture. My parents had no particular prejudice against Chinese people, but they had firm ideas about the traits I should look for in a husband: well-educated, well-off, from a fine family. And, obviously, white and Protestant. A product of his upbringing, Dad firmly believed that we should marry our own kind. Marrying outside the fold was asking for a life of conflict.

I had planned to talk to Mom earlier that evening, after Dad went to bed. But my nerves had failed me. Just five minutes earlier, I had said good night and gone up to my bedroom. I chastised myself for cowardice, then turned around and walked back down those stairs. Despite my dread of confrontation—inherited from Mom—I needed to tell her tonight, to pave the way for an even bigger talk with Dad the next day. Dad had a more forceful way of expressing his feelings, but I recalled that it was Mom, not Dad, who had sent me to Hong Kong with the advice "Just don't marry a Chinaman."

When I reached the dim, smoky lamplight of the living room, Mom was sitting on her couch with a paperback. Her feet were tucked under her. Surprised to see me again, she stubbed out a newly lit cigarette as I sat down in my great-grandmother's platform rocking chair, opposite her. I steadied myself by grabbing its wooden arms.

"I need to tell you something," I began. She was regarding me steadily and not unkindly. I leaned forward in the rocker, feet planted on the carpet, and spat out the words I had bottled up all evening: "Paul and I have decided to get married."

Her face registered neither surprise nor happiness. "I wondered about that."

I swallowed. "We haven't picked a date yet. Possibly this fall. In Hong Kong."

An endless pause. Was she reading my face? I didn't look like a girl rushing in with happy news. "Do you love him?" she asked at last.

"Oh, yes. Very much. He's responsible, warm, considerate, smart, good-natured . . . I wish I could be more like him." I leaned forward, willing her to understand the depth of my feelings. I wished I could be as articulate speaking as I was when writing in my journal.

Her second question surprised me: "What does he think about having a wife who works?" Typical of her generation, Mom had never had a career. The unhappiness of housewives that Betty Friedan called "the problem that has no name" meant nothing to my mom. She assumed that working and marriage were mutually exclusive.

I smiled. You never really know what objections others will raise. "He's very proud of me, and supportive. Things have changed, Mom. Lots of women have careers and also a husband and kids. But of course we have to think it through—where we'll move next, considering his career and mine."

Relief softened my anxiety as the conversation continued. Mom was hesitant yet curious, asking about the reason Paul's first marriage had broken up, his religious views, his age. She was surprised to learn that he was fifteen years older than I was.

"My grandmother once told me, 'Never marry a man who's a lot older because you might end up spending many years as a widow.' She lived more than twenty years alone."

"That's possible, I guess. But Paul is healthy and takes good care of himself."

"Are you planning to have children?"

"I would like to. We've talked about it, and he agreed to one more child."

"Is that enough for you?"

"I'd like to have two, but I'm pretty busy with my work, so one would be okay."

Mom raised questions but did not get upset. Thank God, I thought, for the *Rakehell Dynasty* novels, about a dashing New England clipper-ship master who married the love of his life, a beautiful, well-educated Chinese lady. Mom had told me about those books earlier.

"What do you think Dad will say?" My voice quavered.

"I don't know." She regarded me steadily. "You'll have to talk to him about it."

My fear gushed back. I wondered: Why is it so hard to talk to the people you love the most?

⁂

I didn't sleep much that night. After going over every detail of my conversation with Mom, I tried to imagine how it might go with Dad.

Dad's personality was the opposite of Mom's: he was sociable, intellectual, witty, charming. He read Shakespeare, Ibsen, *The New Yorker*, and Will Durant's eleven-volume *The Story of Civilization*. Unlike Mom, whose only wish for her children was happiness, his objective for his four kids was that we be "achievers."

Without realizing it, I had taken on the goal of living out some of Dad's dreams. As a youth, he had aspired to follow his father and brother to Princeton, but the Depression made that impossible. Princeton went coed just in time to accept my application, and he was thrilled. Although Dad became a retailer, he aspired to write books. When I was a child, he encouraged me in my love of writing stories. And he was the one who suggested I pursue a career in journalism, back when I was seventeen. He helped me get my first newspaper job. Now nearly seventy, still working at his bookstore, he had begun to write books on the side.

Dad was hard on himself and judgmental of his siblings, but he had high aspirations for his kids. As the youngest, I had perhaps been the most moldable. I loved the attention and internalized his goals as my own. He read every article I wrote, but he longed for the day when I would return home to "this country." A Chinese husband was not part of that vision.

The next day, I waited until after we had returned from dinner, laughing and talkative from too much to eat and drink. We were sitting in the family room, and Dad was in his favorite leather chair. Finally, I interrupted him during a monologue about the word "heuristic."

Dad was ready. "I'm not surprised," he said. "What can I say? You're about to turn thirty-one. You can think things through for yourself."

I breathed deeply, thankful he had not overreacted. Still, he launched into a well-prepared litany of advice. Indeed, he would have preferred an American and a Christian—someone with similar background and values. But his main objections were not that Paul was Chinese.

"First, he's been married before. Some other woman rejected him, and she must have had her reasons. Beware of a man who has failed at marriage and possibly as a father as well."

My body stiffened. I had thought of Paul's first wife as unreasonable and bad-tempered, the cause of their marital problems. But had Paul failed as a husband and father? That was one way to put it. What I had seen was that he proved himself responsible by refusing, month after month, to end the marriage when the time seemed wrong. But I couldn't say that. As calmly as I could, I told Dad I knew Paul well, after two years, and didn't see any reason he wouldn't be a good husband.

"Second, he has children. Can you imagine how you would feel if I divorced your mother and married another woman? You would be a stepmother."

This gave me pause. I hadn't thought much about being a stepmother. I had not been allowed to meet his kids yet. I knew nothing about parenting and was naive about what this might mean—for them and for me. I mumbled something vague about how I had heard they were nice kids and hoped to get along with them.

"Third, any children you might have will have mixed blood. You may be very idealistic about how the world has changed, but a lot of people won't accept you in society."

This one, I dismissed as old-fashioned. I was confident that American society had changed so that our mixed-race children would never face discrimination. I was hoping for the best, actually—assuming, as many young people do, that progress would continue forever.

All his comments were, in fact, reasonable questions a caring father would ask. This is what good parenting looks like: when your adult child makes a life decision that seems unreasonable, you calmly ask the questions he or she might not have considered. You can't stop an adult from an unwise marriage, but you can make her think about it more deeply.

My clenched jaw did not relax until I was finished hearing him out. Even though my heart was racing, I sensed things might be all right. He didn't like the idea, but I wouldn't lose him. Maybe I had played my cards right. When your parents doubt the wisdom of your marriage choice, give them time to get used to it. Break them in gently.

My two worlds—my family in Ohio and my beloved in China—might yet come together. Somehow.

CHAPTER NINETEEN:

Persistence

⚙⚙⚙⚙⚙

船到湾頭自然直, *chuán dào wāntóu zìrán zhí: On its journey, a boat may be tossed in storms or rapids, but once it reaches the calmer waters of the bay, it will naturally straighten out. Things will work out in the end. A reassuring phrase, as taught to me by Paul.*

A new snag emerged after I returned to Hong Kong. Paul's bosses at Exxon preempted his job search and offered him a new position within Esso China. In Beijing.

Beijing! That was 1,200 miles away from Hong Kong—farther than Seattle to San Diego, or New York to Miami. So much for any hopes of living together.

But the offer was too good to refuse. Paul would be Exxon's deputy Beijing representative, and it was a major vote of confidence in his ability. Despite a lack of experience in the oil business, he excelled at his liaison work, and they rewarded him. He would also become an official employee of Exxon, with all the benefits and perks—far better terms than anything he might have found in Hong Kong.

He had to leave by the end of the month. After his earlier career setbacks, it seemed churlish to express my dismay. But I wanted to pound my head against a wall.

Living that far apart was even harder than I imagined. Long-distance phone calls between Beijing and Hong Kong were exasperating. I had to "book" a call about twelve hours in advance, then wait by the phone for an operator to call me and connect me with Paul in his Beijing Hotel room, usually just after dinner. I had to send him a telex telling him what time to expect my call. We assumed the Chinese government monitored these calls, but that didn't bother us. We missed each other and said so.

We felt like the universe was conspiring against us. Or maybe testing our resolve.

As soon as he transferred, I planned a reporting trip that included Beijing, so that I could see him in his new setting. I decided to visit six cities in three weeks, investigating how the overheating economy and subsequent clampdown had affected American investments in China.

But I had a second agenda for my reporting. I was eager to meet some of China's most successful entrepreneurs. I had read about several impressive ones recently. Instead of lauding selfless workers, as in the old days of Communism, the state-owned Chinese press had elevated businesspeople as new heroes to worship. Could the *People's Daily* really be championing fledgling capitalists?

To meet them, I decided to travel to some of the places where capitalism had thrived before the Communist victory: Tianjin, Wuhan, Nanjing, Hangzhou, and Shanghai, ending in Beijing. My friendly minder, Tian Bin, arranged the trip for me, located the individuals I wanted to interview, and traveled with me. Like China, she was becoming more open and modern. Her haircut was more stylish now, and she was wearing brighter colors.

Everywhere I went, I saw signs of modernization amid traditional ways: Jordache jeans, bright red lips, embroidered blouses.

Tractor-pulled carts loaded down with mini-fridges. Brick high-rises under construction, encased in bamboo scaffolding. Increasing numbers of Shanghai sedans and Liberation trucks among the still-flowing sea of bicycles and overcrowded buses. Billboards advertising face cream and hair-regrowth ointment. Street stalls overflowing with music cassettes, portable stereos, bras, and suitcases sold by vendors calling out their low prices. What started in Guangzhou had taken root in major cities across the country.

Travel was getting easier, too. Across China, ten modern hotels had opened, and in Beijing construction began on Western-style apartment buildings—the first ever for foreigners who were neither diplomats nor journalists. A school for English-speaking children was being built, and it was possible to dine on chateaubriand, as well as enchiladas and lasagna. Getting a visa, making a hotel reservation, and booking appointments became easier for foreigners.

Still, troubles galore had cropped up at the factories I visited. At one, an inspector had twice fallen through the false ceiling because of too-fast construction. At a shampoo factory, the American manager repeatedly begged workers to shut windows to keep the dust out of the bottles. And Otis Elevator, which had finally begun production after a long four years of negotiation, suddenly faced a shortage of steel.

The foreign managers I talked to complained repeatedly of materials shortages, sloppy workmanship, and low productivity. Businesses faced delays at customs. The rules of the game kept changing. Laws were unclear. Foreign exchange was hard to get. Transportation was frequently disrupted. Good English interpreters were rare. Living costs were high. Businesspeople kept speaking of the need for "patience" and "trust." Someday, doing business in China would be easier. They hoped.

But none of these setbacks slowed the influx of foreign companies. They were attracted to China like recruiters to high school football games. Most major American companies were prospecting in China because their competitors were there. Even if they lost money for years, they hoped to build up goodwill to help in future sales. It was a gold rush with no assurance of finding gold.

The strains were real, and the government had indeed started tapping the brakes. But I didn't see signs of a policy reversal—or any exodus from the China market. Like me, companies were sticking it out, in the hope that one day it would all work out.

The unbridled optimists in China were not foreign investors but Chinese entrepreneurs. The ones I met were leaping into capitalism as if it had never been banned. One illiterate seller of watermelon seeds challenged a state monopoly and figured out how to make his snack available year-round. One wheeler-dealer had set up his own factory when it was still illegal—by calling it a "cooperative"—and was now exporting machine parts to Ohio. But that wasn't enough for him; he planted evergreen trees on unused land and sold them to budding landscape designers.

The state still controlled private businesses through licenses, approvals, and taxes. Some were shut down for "profiteering." But the clampdown was limited.

Even men who had flourished as true capitalists before 1949 were daring to jump into the action. Some of them had been taunted and beaten during previous political campaigns, but now they were willing to trust the government and go into business again. One of the biggest was in Shanghai, where twelve thousand former capitalists, all over the age of sixty, formed the Patriotic Construction Corporation and started forty-four factories, fifty-four retail stores, and ten joint ventures. It was even building a high-rise with condos for sale to overseas investors. This was revolutionary in China, where the state owned all housing.

"In China," I concluded my article, "revolutions may come and go, but the entrepreneurial spirit manages to prevail."

The Chinese, some say, seem to have a gene for business. This I doubt. No sweeping generalization fits one billion people. Chinese people do have a cultural belief that hard work pays off and creates better opportunities for the next generation, but I saw more than that. For decades, these Chinese had been prevented from putting their energies into making a better life for themselves. After thirty years of constraints, they were hungry and had nothing to lose.

Many had been denied higher education, so the best way to get ahead lay in business. They had a powerful, pent-up desire—to make money and get rich, for sure, but also to use their brains. To stretch out to their fullest abilities. To achieve. Not only to dare to jump into uncertain waters, but to keep at it until they succeeded. Once they saw how the rest of the world lived, they knew what they had missed. They wanted to catch up.

Although the 1980s were seen as a "decade of greed" and Hong Kong had long been caught up in the money craze, the push for wealth meant something different to people inside China. The ability to get rich was a sign of winning the game of life. So was a nice three-story house. People in China finally had a chance to play.

Much like women of my era taking professional jobs. And like Paul, breaking out of safe government work into the riskier private sector. We, too, were determined to try something that had not seemed possible.

ৎৡৢৡৢৡ

In the midst of that big trip, Paul arranged to meet me for a weekend in Nanjing, where he had lived as a boy in the late 1940s. I booked a room in the modern Jinling Hotel, which was the tallest in China, at thirty-seven floors, when it opened in 1983. Guards at the front door prevented locals from coming in to gawk at its elevator, the first they had seen, or to ride it to the top floor, which had the first revolving restaurant in all China.

When Paul arrived that Friday evening, he had big news. Just that morning, he had received a telex from his lawyer in Portland saying, "Paul, you are a free man. The divorce is final." It was June 21, 1985, two years after we met, and we had long ago committed to each other. We celebrated with a dinner at the top of the Jinling Hotel, where we lingered by the floor-to-ceiling windows, watched the city turn, and danced to a jazz band.

I considered this our engagement, albeit a strange one. Of course, Paul had not had time to buy a diamond ring, so I took a pearl one he had bought for me earlier and put it on the third finger of my left hand. After being stymied for two years, I was eager to plan a wedding.

But the timing didn't make sense. My job was in Hong Kong, and his was in Beijing. Infected by the optimism around us in China, I figured we could solve this. Somehow.

Then the universe threw us another curveball. As soon as Paul returned to Beijing, he got another surprise telex. Under the terms of the divorce, which had not been updated when he had taken the job in Beijing, he had won custody of his son. Frustrated and angry, his ex-wife had immediately placed Steve on a plane. Within days, he arrived in Beijing, with his guitar. He was sixteen.

I was still traveling, completing my reporting trip. Tian Bin regarded me with shock when she heard. "So, you will be a step-mother?" she said. "Oh, Dori, be kind."

It had not occurred to me to be unkind. I would not be that type of stepmother! But I had not thought at all about what type I might be. My instincts leaned toward empathy. How awful for Steve to have been ejected from his home. And yet I had heard reports of terrible behavior from a frustrated boy. What would he be like?

A week later, after finishing my reporting, I arrived in Beijing late at night. Steve's lanky body was asleep on the couch of Paul's suite at the Jianguo Hotel. I met him the next morning.

"I have to go to work," Paul said. "You two can get to know each other over breakfast."

Tossed into the deep end with no swimming lessons. *Be kind*, I repeated to myself.

At the Jianguo coffee shop, after Paul left, Steve and I perused the menu in awkward silence. I had not talked to a sixteen-year-old boy since high school, and it had not been easy then. I fortified myself with coffee.

"Can I have fried eggs? With bacon?" he began. He seemed shy and uncertain.

"Did Dad tell you what happened to me?" he continued, once we had ordered. I braced myself. "Yesterday I went out of the hotel by myself, just to look around, and when I came back, the hotel guy tried to stop me from coming in. I told him, 'I live here, you asshole!'"

I laughed. "They're pretty strict here. They don't let local Chinese into hotels unless they have the right paperwork."

"I can't believe he thought I was local! What a dumb prick."

I admit Steve didn't look or act local, with his shaggy hair and baggy shorts. But the doorman had probably never seen anyone who looked like Steve.

Once the stiffness wore off, that first conversation with Steve went better than I could have imagined. He was a laid-back, easygoing teenager, talkative and friendly, and asked questions about me and my life. He seemed to have no filter, and I could not detect any resentment toward his dad or me. I heard no anger or bitterness against his mom, either. He wasn't happy to be exiled to the other side of the planet, but he never complained in front of me.

Just fifteen years younger than me, Steve had grown up in America, so I began to think I might become a bridge between him and Paul. He spoke a little Mandarin but knew almost nothing about China. He was fluent in the Grateful Dead and Bob Marley.

Steve spent that whole summer with his dad in Beijing. They had a chance to get to know each other again. We hiked up the Great Wall together, and he befriended a basket seller on a nearby street. Uncertain of my role, I took it a day at a time. They visited me in Hong Kong, where Steve went with his dad to shop for a diamond ring. It felt surreal but not bad.

When the summer ended, Steve wanted badly to return home, but his mom refused to take him back. Beijing had no English-language high school, so Steve could not stay there. Hong Kong had good English schools, but I didn't feel competent to raise a teenager by myself. Exxon benefits included tuition at a boarding school, and Paul found one that would accept Steve—in Switzerland. It was our only option. So, in yet another odd turn of events, Paul and I took Steve to Europe in September to a boarding school near Zurich. Steve didn't want to go, but he had no other options. Things were happening fast and moving in crazy directions.

The challenges we faced were formidable. Could Paul and I marry even though we lived 1,200 miles apart? That didn't make any sense. How would I integrate my work, my family, and his family into our life together? How would Steve fit into the picture?

My dad's questions lingered in my mind. Any observer would have said this was the wrong man, bad timing, a questionable way to start a marriage. All the setbacks over the years, the moments when I thought I might lose him, and the insufferable separations had made me wonder deeply: Is this man worth it?

One evening in Paris, standing on the banks of the Seine, a light breeze mussing my hair and the taste of crème brûlée lingering in my mouth, I felt Paul's arm around my shoulders and watched as Steve tossed a stone into the water. We were together, but we weren't family. My college study of French history kicked in as I looked across the water at Notre Dame cathedral. It had lasted eight hundred years, through fires and riots and revolution and occupation. Yet Paris was calm now. I closed my eyes and hoped our lives would calm down someday, too. If we ever succeeded in marrying, I decided, I would stay with this man for the rest of my life.

Resolve, like silver, is refined through fire. Tough realities can force you to think of creative solutions. I wanted to have it all, this career and this man. I had already put up with more delays than I could bear. Fate had already tossed me around enough.

So I cooked up a plan to solve the living-in-two-cities problem. What if we got married in November, and after that I could live in Beijing part-time—say, three weeks a month—and cover China from there? I would spend a week each month in Hong Kong. *BusinessWeek* would get a reporter in Beijing without moving its bureau. Dinda was ready to take on added responsibilities; she could switch to coverage of Southeast Asia while I focused on China.

It was a cockamamie idea. Not the best way to start a marriage. Beijing was known as a tough place for Americans to live, and it was far from the other Asian countries I had been covering. But Paul and I would be together—not full-time, but more than before.

Apprehensive about how my editors would react but confident about their strong interest in China, I called the chief of correspondents, Keith Felcyn. I told him I planned to get married in November, to Paul Yang, who was working for Exxon in China. That was news enough, as I had not told any of my editors about him. Then I said I would like to spend two or three weeks a month in Beijing, intensifying my coverage of China. I made the case that it would be a good move for *BusinessWeek*—an inexpensive way to get more stories out of China, since I would be living with Paul. We would still keep our bureau in Hong Kong, with its accessibility to Taiwan and Southeast Asia. But China was growing quickly, I pointed out, and its trade might one day eclipse these smaller places.

Keith was taken aback and asked several questions to clarify. He seemed more surprised that I had chosen a businessman than that my fiancé was Chinese. I gathered that journalists are supposed to marry intellectuals—or other journalists. The scheme I outlined was clearly not in *BusinessWeek*'s long-term plans for China coverage. But he said he would talk it over with Steve Shepard. After a few days, they agreed.

I could marry my Ideal Man—and keep my Ideal Job. It sure wasn't a perfect solution, but it would do. Besides, I would get to cover China from within China—not from Hong Kong, on its doorstep. I would live inside China at last.

❦ ❦ ❦

It seemed safe to plan our wedding. But that fall, Paul wasn't around to help. He was off on an adventure—a six-week trip to some of the remotest regions of China. China had invited Exxon and other oil giants to tour its onshore oilfields in Xinjiang and other distant provinces. Paul was out of touch from late September through early November, staying in rough lodgings and traveling on bumpy roads through the desert.

So I planned our wedding myself. My assistant, Janita, consulted a geomancy book to find a good-luck day, but there wasn't one that fell on a Saturday in November. Oh well. I picked Saturday, November 16, anyway. I tried to find a church in Hong Kong that would marry us, but the pastor turned me down because I wasn't a member. My only option was a secular ceremony at the Hong Kong Marriage Registry, where they scheduled a wedding every fifteen minutes. I cried bitter tears that night, feeling my lack of belonging, far from home, no longer grounded in my own culture but not part of Paul's, either. Just a minor entry on someone's busy schedule.

The dinner celebration, though, would be memorable. I chose a stunning hotel in Macau, Pousada de São Tiago. Built in 1629 on a Portuguese stone fort, it had a lovely setting for an outdoor party on the patio, overlooking the narrow waterway separating Macau from China.

My heart in my throat, I called Mom and Dad. Would they come to my wedding? Dad said they would think about it. A week later, I received a long letter from him with the answer: no. "You know how I hate to travel," Dad said. "I just can't handle the trip." The rest was a carefully worded, thoughtful reiteration of his reservations about my decision to marry Paul. I spent that night in tears. Although he had not said so, his message felt like a rejection. My imagination filled in the judgment between the written words. Mom wrote nothing. But my sisters both said they would come, even though Trudy had two small children.

There was a lot I couldn't explain to my parents. By this time in my life, this deep in my career as a foreign correspondent, I knew I had fallen in love with not just Paul Yang but China. The Chinese language, Chinese customs, Chinese idioms, Chinese strengths, Chinese eccentricities. China's disturbing and disruptive modern history. Chinese resilience. I could not have married a Chinese man without that underlying sense of awe at his origins.

Cross-cultural marriage doesn't work for everyone. But if you're determined to marry a person from a different culture, it sure helps if you're also in love with his country of origin and its complexities. That way, you value his differences and overlook the bits that don't match with your preferences. It's like the Taoist symbol of yin and yang, the unity of opposites, with a dot of the black in the white and a dot of white in the black. I was American with Chinese characteristics, and Paul was Chinese with American characteristics. I doubted my dad could appreciate any of that, so I didn't try to explain.

The wedding took two months of planning: dinner, drinks, hotel rooms, jet-foil tickets, flowers, band, photography, honeymoon plans. I invited forty people and arranged for all of them to spend the night in Macau so they could stay late and dance after dinner. I printed up invitations with wording in both English and Chinese. Finally. It was happening!

To look for a wedding dress, Cindy took me shopping in Stanley Market. We found a simple but beautiful knee-length ivory silk dress. The label was cut out, which meant it was an extra from some clothing factory. Chinese brides wore a red *qipao* with a slit up the side. I bought a blue *qipao* and decided to change into it halfway through my wedding dinner.

A month before the big date, I called my mother to ask for addresses for the announcements. She told me she had decided to come, without Dad. This time, I wept with relief. Mom would be there, with Trish and Trudy. Hallelujah!

❦❦❦

Less than a week before the guests arrived, I got a sharp lesson in why my postwedding work plan might not be so ideal. A huge story broke in Manila. Anti-Marcos demonstrators flooded the streets. The protestors claimed that President Ferdinand Marcos and his wife, Imelda, had been enriching themselves on bribes and impoverishing the country. The Philippines' raucous form of democracy produced lively elections and colorful dictators—Imelda had amassed more than one thousand pairs of shoes and eight hundred purses—but had not lifted the vast majority of Filipinos out of poverty.

So, the week before my wedding, I jumped on a plane to Manila. There, I mingled with the protestors, who blocked the major streets with their marches. More excited than angry, they chanted slogans in front of the US embassy, rallying against continued American support for the dictator. They were fed up with Marcos and wanted him to go. This story was ramping up just as I was getting ready to turn coverage of Southeast Asia over to Dinda. Living part-time in Beijing might mean I would miss big, important stories like this.

I rushed back home just in time to welcome my first wedding guests. In November, Paul's children were in school; Steve was in Switzerland, and their mom had not yet allowed me to meet his daughter. Paul's parents decided it would be too difficult to fly to Hong Kong, because of his father's health. Instead, they asked us to visit Taiwan after our honeymoon, so they could invite their friends and relatives to a Chinese banquet.

Mom and my sisters flew from the United States for my wedding; that delighted me. And my friends rallied round me. Cindy and Katy wore dresses of the same turquoise color as my sisters'. Katy prepared a small lunch for family after the ceremony. Another friend, Dinah

Lee, treated my sisters and me to a ladies' lunch at her flat on the Peak. And Dinda and her husband hosted a dinner at their home the evening before the wedding.

Mom seemed disoriented without Dad. At Dinda's party, she went out to the balcony alone, crying softly. It wasn't the wedding she had imagined for me. As mother of the bride, she had no role. She was far outside her comfort zone; the world was changing too quickly for her. I noticed her out there, and I should have gone out to comfort her. I would later regret it. But I could not deal with her sadness when I was determined to focus on my joy.

To me, my oddball wedding was perfect: an unconventional mixture of East and West, like Paul and me. The *pousada* had white walls, orange tile roofs, and Portuguese blue ceramics. The wedding suite was not what I expected: it was decorated in red velvet, like a brothel! Chinese consider white the color of mourning and red the color of celebration.

About half our guests were Chinese, half American. Several were bilingual, but many spoke only English or only Chinese. The food was a mix of Chinese and Portuguese, including fresh sardines. Mom sat at the head table, next to me. After her discreet jag of emotion, she relaxed into her usual equanimity. Trish and Trudy read a long, lighthearted poem they had composed on the plane. Under a spreading banyan tree, the soft evening breeze wafted away any hint of family tension.

After dinner, a band of moonlighting Portuguese civil servants played dance music. Late in the evening, after we were all woozy with wine, the band belted out "The Hokey Pokey" and we didn't hesitate to shake it all about. The silliness and the spirited dancing brought us all together. Sometimes, even when you can't have it all, you can create lovely memories from what you do have.

At last, I had married Paul Yang. He was hard to get and worth waiting for.

At our wedding in Macau, 1985

CHAPTER TWENTY:

Inside China at last

⌘⌘⌘⌘⌘

国内, *guónèi: inside the country, usually meaning inside China. Used by Chinese all over the world to refer to their ancestral homeland. Everyplace else is guówài, outside the country.*

After our Hawaii honeymoon, in mid-December 1985, I moved to Beijing—inside China at last! I had not only a new husband but a new identity, a new passport, and a new byline.

Yes, I had decided to take Paul's last name. This was my own decision, but it grated against my pride. I had worked hard to build up an image and reputation as Dorothy E. Jones, journalist, and was proud of my byline. Besides, I didn't look like a Yang.

But Paul, conscious of the failure of his first marriage, wanted me to take the name Yang. To him, it was a very public sign that I was committed to him for life. "Besides," he said, only half joking, on a beach on Kauai, "I'd like to see my name in *BusinessWeek*." Since it meant that much to him, I agreed. Changing my name was a way to let the whole world know that I was happy to be Paul's wife. I thought the byline Dori Jones Yang was distinctive and memorable. With three short words, it fit on one line in a magazine column.

Paul and I began our married life under strange conditions. For the three weeks per month that we would be living together, our home was a hotel. Beijing then had almost no modern apartments for foreign businesspeople. The best Exxon could arrange for us was a suite of rooms in the newly built Holiday Inn Lido Hotel.

The day I arrived, Beijing's bitter winter air was thick with particles from the charcoal fires still commonly used in home kitchens.

"You're shivering. We'll have to get you a thicker jacket," Paul said, as he paid the taxi driver.

My new home, the Lido Hotel, had a bright, glossy domed lobby. I took a deep breath and followed my husband over the threshold. Inside the revolving door, the young women at the counter wore sharp uniforms with perky hats and permed hair—a sharp contrast to the frumpy, egalitarian look at the state-run Beijing Hotel, with its shoddy carpets and cavernous hallways.

"You'll love this place." Paul was trying to impress me. "There's a whole entertainment center attached. Fancy shops, restaurants, even a bowling alley. Can you imagine?"

"Bowling in Beijing!" I said. "Can we try it?"

"Of course." He didn't kiss me in front of the bellhop, but his eyebrows flirted.

Up the narrow elevator to the top floor, the fifth, Paul led the way down the long hallway to the door of our suite. "Not fancy, but comfortable," he said, glancing at me.

I smiled and grabbed his hand, and he squeezed mine. We had defied the odds that had conspired to keep us apart. Now here we were, starting our married life in Beijing. Paul was thrilled to be living there, where they spoke pure Mandarin and served dumplings and *mantou* like his mother made. Mama grew up just ninety miles from Beijing, so this part of China felt more like home to him than Guangzhou. I wanted to love it, too.

Still, the Holiday Inn Lido Hotel was not exactly a dream home for newlyweds. To accommodate long-term stays, it had converted a few of its rooms into apartments, connecting three guest rooms and converting one bathroom into a kitchen.

The room smelled like fresh paint, with crisp cream carpeting. A blast from the heating vent warmed me. Instead of beds, the first room had a bland couch, chairs, and coffee table. The second room had a desk and a small breakfast table and chairs.

"I got them to change out the furniture," Paul said. "Check out the desk!"

On the hotel desk was an electric typewriter—an IBM Selectric, the kind with all the letters on a little metal ball. The coolest and most modern. "Perfect! Where did you get it?"

"I borrowed it from our office. They approved."

One problem solved! I gave him a long, deep hug. "Thanks! Where's our bedroom?"

He gave me a wicked grin. "First, check out the kitchen." He led me to one of the bathrooms. The tub and toilet were gone. In their place was a waist-high refrigerator and a microwave oven. Only the bathroom sink remained.

My manufactured enthusiasm dimmed. It reminded me of the primitive kitchen in my first-ever apartment in Singapore, which had only a kitchen sink and a counter. There, I had bought a two-burner propane stovetop and learned to cook Chinese food in a wok. "How will I cook? Can we buy a burner?"

"They don't allow fires in the rooms."

I wasn't the best Chinese chef, but I knew that most dishes were stir-fried with oil in a wok. A few months after we met, Paul had asked me to prepare a Chinese dinner for him, which I did, using a cookbook. But in Hong Kong, I had a gas stove.

Cooking for your husband, I thought, was an essential duty of a wife. That was the image Mom had imprinted on me by cooking dinner every night for Dad, who couldn't even make his own ham sandwich. How might that work for a feminist in a hotel room?

"Is it possible to cook Chinese food in a microwave oven?" I asked, dubiously.

Paul smiled lamely. "You can try."

Yes, the whole setup was peculiar. But so was our East-West

marriage with its fifteen-year age gap. If you are sure of what you want, sometimes you have to improvise.

The third room had a king-size bed. "Okay!" I laughed when I saw it. "I can live here."

The next day, Paul took me to the Friendship Store to buy food. This was a store for foreigners, near the heart of the city, close to the major hotels. On three floors, it sold mainly ivory carvings, jade bowls, cloisonné vases, and other souvenirs. But in the back of the main floor was a small grocery, with a few sad winter vegetables, as well as some gray-looking, frozen packaged meats. My nose crinkled at the sweet-foul smells in the grocery. We bought chicken legs, potatoes, and cabbage, as well as eggs and rice.

That night, I tried making my first meal in the microwave. It was a disaster. The chicken legs just wouldn't cook, and they were still a little bloody when I served them to Paul. The potatoes were so hard, we could barely cut them. The cabbage had just wilted into a sloppy mess. Kitchen calamities like this were the main reason I hated cooking.

The next morning, we had omelets at the hotel coffee shop. Then Paul left for his office at the Beijing Hotel. I kissed him goodbye, thinking of those 1950s wives in countless movies. As he drove off, I laughed at my ridiculous expectations. That was the era when Paul came of age. Well, my generation had rebelled against it. Even with a proper kitchen, I doubted I'd ever reinvent myself as a good cook. Even my mother hadn't. I have countless memories of burned peas.

So I returned to my comfort zone, work. Because the middle room of our "apartment" had a typewriter, I dubbed it *BusinessWeek*'s Beijing bureau. What else did a journalist need? I had brought reporter's notebooks and a list of contact names and numbers.

I sat at the desk and fingered everything. I stared at the list and flashed back to how paralyzed I had felt, five years earlier, when I had first tried to do reporting from a Beijing hotel. Surely I was more confident now. I made a few phone calls but did not reach anyone. I left messages, from "Dori Jones Yang of *BusinessWeek*."

Then I lay down on the couch and cried. I couldn't push back those feelings of being isolated and lost. Who was I, in this setting?

I felt like I was starting all over, alone again, with no mentors, no sources, no moxie. The hotel walls caged me.

After lunch, I decided to send a message to Dinda in Hong Kong. Something simple, to tell her I had arrived. Rather than endure the hassle of booking an international phone call, I decided to use the quickest means: a telex.

To do so, I went to the hotel's business center. It was wedged between a jewelry shop and a shop called Lady Fashion. Speaking Mandarin, I introduced myself to the man behind the counter. I carefully did not identify myself as a journalist, since I wasn't registered with the foreign ministry as a Beijing-based reporter. "I need to use your telex machine."

"*Bu-xing,*" he answered, in the curt tones Beijingers use to talk to one another. "Guests are not allowed to use the equipment."

I smiled patiently. "But I know how to use a telex machine. It's just a short message."

"You give me the message. I'll type it for you."

No smiles or dulcet Mandarin tones would persuade him. I had to write down my message in very clear printed English, and he told me he would finish it by the end of the day.

"*Xie-xie.*" I thanked him, though I felt like swatting him. "The sooner the better. And when they reply, please call me at this room number."

I returned to my couch, feeling defeated. If I could not even type my own telexes, how could I function as a journalist? Without credentials in Beijing, I was nobody. Little Me returned with her whips and lashes.

Far from being romantic, Beijing felt heartless.

❦❦❦

Our first Christmas together was lonely and barren. In Ohio, Christmas meant warmth and laughter, eggnog and plum pudding, a tree with lights and glass ornaments, brightly wrapped presents with ribbons, and Handel's Messiah reverberating through the stereo speakers. At the "Holiday" Inn Lido, Christmas was just another day. Paul had to go to work! It had not occurred to me that Christmas is not even a holiday in China. Hong Kong, under British rule, gave everyone a day off on December 25. But why should atheist China recognize a Christian holiday? I missed my family, the easy joking and banter of a shared holiday.

Other foreigners in Beijing had figured out how to compensate. In the following week, we were invited to six parties: with older Americans at the American Club, with journalists and diplomats at a businessman's apartment, with a Canadian diplomatic couple and their friends, and to a wild New Year's Eve dinner dance.

Of all the people we met in that holiday whirlwind, though, I was most intrigued by a group of young Chinese. I met them through an American friend who worked at *China Daily*. They were recent graduates of Beijing University and other top-notch universities: an archaeologist, two international-relations researchers, an economist, and a pianist. One of them invited us to his wedding celebration on January 1 at his apartment.

He offered us plates of sunflower seeds, peanuts, and candy on a low coffee table. The young men smoked and cracked sunflower seeds with their teeth. The young women refilled their teacups from a thermos of hot water and chatted happily, flirting with the guys. The discussion was surprisingly wide-ranging and open—from Baudelaire to Ronald Reagan to Andy Warhol. They talked of biking trips to a nearby lake and invited us to go with them when the weather warmed up. They were smart and easygoing and modern-minded—so unlike the image of the buttoned-up, cautious Chinese who didn't dare befriend foreigners. Most of them spoke English and were applying to study at American universities.

Just a few years after Deng Xiaoping resumed the traditional college entrance examination in 1977, this bright young generation seemed to think everything was possible and worth trying. Getting to know them made me long to see China from the inside—not from within a Beijing hotel room but from among a warm group of Chinese friends.

Over the next few weeks, I set about developing contacts at the US embassy, mostly in the commercial section, which supported American businesses in China. I also connected with the Beijing representatives of US companies and some other journalists. But even though it was a small community, it wasn't easy to break in. The mood was formal and guarded. I was starting to understand why Beijing-based journalists considered the capital city cold and forbidding. It was great to spend every evening with Paul, but I counted the days until I could return home—to fast-paced, free-wheeling Hong Kong.

Early in January, I went back for a week, and I felt like I could breathe again. Sea breezes always kept Hong Kong's air fresh, although its winters were cool and damp. And Hong Kong's factories, unlike Beijing's, did not spew out smoke. I feasted on terrific food at restaurants with my girlfriends Cindy, Katy, Dinda, and Dinah. In Beijing, I had missed them. But in Hong Kong, I missed Paul—especially at night.

Living in two cities felt like tearing myself in two. My heart was in frigid Beijing, with Paul. But my mind was at ease in semitropical Hong Kong. I wasn't sure how long it would be until I could get used to this bifurcated life.

❦❦❦

One Sunday in late January, I discovered another reason Paul loved Beijing so. For him it was not a forbidding city of gray walls but an invitation to explore his family's past—and to imagine what might have been, if his parents had not left in 1949.

Shortly after moving to Beijing the previous summer, Paul had written a letter to one of his mother's relatives, and the response had revealed her whole sprawling family to him—relatives cut off after the Communist victory in 1949. Many had suffered persecution and scorn because they had a relative, Paul's father, who worked for Chiang Kai-shek's Nationalist army, which had fought to prevent the Communists from taking over. Simply by association, some were accused of being rightists and spies and enemies of the people.

One uncle lived in Beijing. He invited us to visit Paul's mother's birthplace, a small village three hours' drive away, in the foothills of the Taihang Mountains. A tall, thin man with rapid gestures and an accent like slurry, Fourth Uncle had grown up in the village with limited access to schooling. He now worked at Capital Iron and Steel

Works—a good proletarian job for a man whose parents had been landowners. As a worker, he had not suffered as much as his better-educated cousins.

Beijing City ended abruptly as we entered the countryside, where more than 80 percent of Chinese people still lived and labored. Traffic on the main road to Baoding was mostly bicycles, tractors, and trucks. People bundled up in dark, padded coats occasionally meandered across its two lanes. My anticipation grew as we drove farther away from the center of civilization. Mama's life spanned from the repressive old society to the modern world. Visiting her home village felt like a rare opportunity to journey back in time.

As we turned into a one-lane country road, Fourth Uncle pointed out a hillside. "This land used to be covered with red-date trees. But during the Great Leap Forward, we were ordered to cut them all down. The state wanted to increase production of grain instead, so we had to plant millet. But this soil is rocky and not good for millet."

"Sounds like a bad decision," Paul said.

Uncle nodded, unwilling to make such a bold statement himself. "For about twenty years, the village got poorer. Even after the policy changed, we couldn't afford to plant new date trees. But just a few years ago, some villagers started to plant them again."

Sure enough, small trees were growing in neat rows on a hill. *What a waste*, I thought. Twenty years of poverty because of a decision made in the name of central planning.

We rounded a bend and saw the village of Weigongcun. Gray brick walls lined both sides of the road, with gates for each household and gray tile roofs poking above. Shared brick walls connected all the houses, about twenty or thirty of them.

When our car pulled onto the main street, a group of small children surrounded us, leaping and shouting in happy voices. Uncle had let them know we were coming. The children pointed out the way, and our car stopped in front of one gate.

Paul's aunts and uncles were waiting for us there and greeted us as we got out. There was no hugging or shaking of hands, just slight bows of the head and grinning country welcomes.

"You've come back!" they said. Although this was Paul's first visit to Weigongcun, his relatives considered that he had returned to his roots. "And you brought a foreign *xifu*!"

I cringed at the word. I was a daughter-in-law to Mama, not to this whole village. But Chinese have a more possessive sense of extended family than Americans.

Paul's aunt took my hands with warm curiosity. A tiny woman with short-cropped gray hair and white-rimmed glasses, she looked older than Mama, yet she was ten years younger. She had lived a hard country life, and her wrinkles bespoke decades of sunshine and wind.

"They've never seen a foreigner before," Fourth Uncle explained.

"That's not true!" said another uncle. "The Japanese came here during the war."

This awed me. Mine were the first blue eyes to see this village. After decades—millennia, really—of isolation, even remote parts of China were truly opening up.

The two older uncles invited us through a high gate into a walled courtyard. Paul's mother had lived here until the age of ten. I had never been in a typical Chinese country home. Inside the courtyard were identical buildings on three sides. Each had a central sitting room and two bedrooms. The central building was for the grandparents, the side ones for married sons and their families. Most space in each bedroom was taken up by a traditional *kang*, a heatable brick bed.

Before the Communists took over, this courtyard had belonged to Mama's family, who were landowners. They hired men from the village to help till their land. After Liberation, several poorer families moved in, forcing the remaining relatives to crowd into one small building. The home had only two signs of modernization: each room had a single electric lightbulb hanging from the ceiling, and in the courtyard a single spigot splashed out running water from a pipe. The floors, tiled when Mama was a child, were now just packed dirt. The Communists had brought electricity, running water, and irrational directives like the order to cut down fruit trees, but otherwise life had remained unchanged for centuries. Dirt poor.

The aunt had married a local Communist official, so her life was slightly better. They invited us to their house for a country meal with several tasty dishes.

As Paul talked to his relatives, I thought about my mother's family in Niles, Ohio. Mom's great-grandparents had immigrated from Wales and founded a small steel mill. They lived in a mansion with high ceilings and marble fireplaces. Yet a few generations earlier, perhaps my ancestors had lived remote rural lives, too. Wales was poor till the discovery of coal needed for the Industrial Revolution. Today's rich are yesterday's poor. And today's poor might well become tomorrow's rich. Or not. China had remained poor for more than one hundred years. Its huge, backward population made it seem likely to be poor forever.

After lunch, we walked around the village with the relatives. Children tagged after us, staring and giggling. They looked healthy and well fed, but their clothing was much mended. Women squatted in front of their gates in the winter sunshine, their arms tucked in their thick sleeves, watching us. Some remembered Mama.

The history of the modern industrialized world is of people leaving the farms and going to the cities, and then leaving one city for another to follow jobs. All four of Mama's brothers had found jobs outside the village; only her sister lived there now. But what of the people left behind—who can't or won't leave?

My hometown, Youngstown, was devastated in the 1970s by the closure of its major steel mills. A lot of us escaped, but those who stayed behind were unable to stop the changes caused by outside forces. Many were filled with bitter resentment at being left behind—and ultimately despair at the lack of opportunity and hope. Would these Chinese villagers one day feel that way, too? Or would they find a way to learn and prosper?

China's economy was evolving quickly. Would Deng's "socialism with Chinese characteristics" be able to create opportunities for the hundreds of millions who might want to leave rural villages—and to care for those who chose to stay? The odds against Deng's success were even more daunting than I had imagined.

CHAPTER TWENTY-ONE:

There and Back Again

☙ ঌ৩৩ঌ ☙

吃苦 *chīkǔ: eat bitterness. The Chinese term for enduring hardship or suffering.*

Meanwhile, my career was suffering. After I moved to Beijing as a married woman, my fresh new byline seldom appeared on the pages of *BusinessWeek*. The previous fall, as I prepared for my wedding, several of my stories had sat around New York for weeks, sidelined because news from other parts of the world seemed more urgent. Two of my pieces had been killed as no longer timely. Then I had taken off two weeks for my honeymoon in Hawaii.

Moving to Beijing had not made it easier to cover China. Since I wasn't on China's list of Beijing-based reporters, I did not get notified about press conferences. The name *BusinessWeek* did not have the clout it had in business-oriented Hong Kong. When I requested an interview with a bureaucrat, my calls were seldom returned.

This dry spell kept lengthening. As the months passed, I agonized over what my New York editors thought of me. They did not complain, but I could imagine them asking, "Is she still a serious journalist?" When I lay in bed at night, that harsh internal critic came roaring back, chastising me with far worse words than my editors would ever have used. By the third year, Lew had said, a reporter should hit his stride, writing great stuff, very productive. Yet I was flailing.

Marriage involved compromises, I had been told many times, but the minute I suspected I was slacking off on my job, I rejected the idea. No compromises for me!

I toyed, for a while, with the idea of quitting *BusinessWeek* to write a book or have a baby. Both were appealing, in theory. But wouldn't that prove them right, those men at my cocktail reception who predicted I would get married and stop working?

To rev up the engine, I turned to a familiar solution: travel. I contacted the All-China Journalists Association and outlined a trip I would like to take. In 1986, the places where Deng's innovations were progressing most were the Special Economic Zones. In those four southern coastal cities, factories were proliferating, turning China into the export powerhouse I had boldly predicted it would never be. They were showcases and laboratories for Deng's reforms.

One Special Economic Zone especially attracted me: Xiamen. Once called Amoy, it had hundreds of years of history as a trading port, with strong connections to Taiwan and Southeast Asia. Xiamen was known as a charming subtropical city, with colonial houses where British had once settled. Fujian Chinese were reputed to be natural-born business entrepreneurs. What better place to take the temperature of China?

In addition to Xiamen, I decided to visit two cities in the Pearl River Delta: Zhuhai, the Special Economic Zone near Macau, and Jiangmen, an up-and-coming manufacturing center.

It was a great plan, an important story. But my timing proved dreadful.

My planning was well under way when the Philippines held a presidential election on February 7, 1986. Ferdinand Marcos had called for a quick election, which he hoped would reaffirm popular support after street protests. Running against him was Corazon Aquino, widow of the opposition leader assassinated in 1983. Many

Filipinos were sick of Marcos's authoritarian style, corruption, and failure to develop their lagging economy. They were especially enraged in December 1985, when a court absolved Marcos's military supporters of the slaying of Aquino's husband at Manila's airport. Many Filipinos were convinced Marcos had ordered it.

Marcos was declared the winner of the February 7 election, as expected, but many thought the results were rigged. There were rumors of an open rebellion by military officers. I quickly called my New York editors to discuss how to respond. I had covered earlier protests in Manila, but, according to our agreement, Dinda now had responsibility for Southeast Asia. The protests might die down. My editors told me to go ahead with my plans for a trip to China's southern cities. If something major happened in Manila, Dinda was prepared to go.

On the day I landed in Xiamen, February 23, the warm, moist air felt good on my cheeks. This time, my minder was a man, about my age, chubby and round-cheeked.

"My name is Ruby," he told me, as he handed me his card at the airport.

"Ruby?" I looked at his obviously male physique. "How did you get that name?"

"I found it in the dictionary. It's the translation of my family name, Zhu."

I was about to try to convince him to pick a different name, when I noticed the headline on a newspaper at the airport: a massive street protest in Manila. Filipinos were now calling it People Power, a nonviolent revolution trying to overthrow Marcos. A photo showed a Manila avenue jammed with one million protestors, most wearing yellow ribbons to show their support.

I felt like throwing up. This could be the story of a lifetime. If Marcos cracked down, blood would flow. If the people pressured him to leave, that would be momentous. Either way, Dinda would cover it. Not I.

I called my editor, and he confirmed that he had asked Dinda to get on a plane for Manila. "Don't worry," he said. "Go ahead with your interviews. We've got it covered." This did not reassure me. I wanted to be where the news was happening.

The next day, Ruby took me to meet with a local trade official, tour the port, and visit two small factories. I heard a lot of statistics about how quickly imports and exports were growing. As usual, I took extensive notes. But this work seemed trivial compared with People Power.

"Could that happen in China?" I asked Ruby during one cab ride. He laughed. "No way."

In China, small protests about local issues were frequent, but they never grew big enough to challenge Communist rule. No opposition party was ready to take power, so the only alternative was chaos. Chinese had learned this the hard way, suffering from decades of infighting, warlords, foreign occupation, and civil war. Competition between political parties had always been a fight to the death, in which millions of ordinary Chinese were roadkill.

Two days later, Ruby and I took a bus from Xiamen to Quanzhou. On the bus, he gave me some wisdom I would never forget. "I've noticed this about foreigners visiting China," Ruby said. "After visiting here a week, they want to write a book. If they stay a month, they realize they know less than they thought, and they decide to write just an article. After living here for years, they can barely write a sentence."

I laughed, ruefully. He was right. China is huge and complex. Making quick judgments about it from a distance is easy. It's worth learning about—with humility.

At the next city, I checked out the headlines. A provincial Chinese newspaper had a big photo of Ferdinand Marcos. I grabbed it and read: Marcos had left the Philippines. His twenty years in power were over. Without firing a gun, the people had forced him out of office.

This was the kind of story that comes around once in ten years. I had missed it. The byline and the glory would go to Dinda.

The bus fumes filled my nose, and my stomach lurched. Alone and far from my bosses, I had learned how to make my own decisions and live with them. But I vowed to keep alert and not make this mistake again.

❦❦❦

Over the next six weeks, I had three bylines: a book review, a short piece on China's austerity, and a major spread called "China: Perils of Prosperity," with a sidebar from Xiamen.

I was back in print, reporting the biggest China story of 1986, about how China's leaders were dealing with such strains as inflation, a surging trade deficit, mounting debt, frequent blackouts, and hucksters and swindlers. "China's economy is speeding out of control, and Beijing's attempts to rein it in are not working," I reported.

Deng maintained his firm grip on power, but some observers feared that after his death, his opponents might curb his free-market incentives and return to Soviet-style central planning. "If China doesn't succeed in cooling its overheated economy," I reported, "the Communist nation's unique experiment with capitalism could be in jeopardy."

But my unique experiment with living in two cities still felt shaky. I was caught between my love life and my work life, squirming from my loss of the Manila story, swerving to retain control, trying to rein in the perils of pride.

What happens when you get to break through your bounds and create a new life beyond what you imagined possible? When you cross the river by feeling for each stone, sometimes you stumble and slip under the water. When you come up, gasping for air, there's no guarantee you'll reach the far shore—or live to tell the tale. It's tempting to swim back to the familiar shore.

Deng must have felt this way sometimes. I did. I didn't want to jeopardize my career or my marriage, but I needed to make adjustments.

❧❧❧

As it happened, a resolution was within grasp. Paul began to consider leaving Beijing. Because of falling oil prices, Exxon was cutting back its staff in China. Paul's bosses promised him his job was safe, but the layoffs and transfers worried him. With no background in geology or petroleum engineering, he had no future at Exxon outside China.

More important, Steve was in crisis. During his Swiss boarding school's spring break, he came to visit us in Beijing. He hated his school. The discipline was strict, the classes were hard, and his best friend had been kicked out for smoking marijuana. He spent the whole week lying on our Lido couch, barely speaking. His mom still wouldn't let him go home.

Our best option was Hong Kong, which had several English-language schools. If Paul could get a job there, Steve could live with us. I was no prize as a stepmom, but my heart went out to him. He needed a home.

The solution came out of the blue—from my close friend Katy. She was now working in the China trade division of a venerable Hong Kong company called Fung Ping Fan. The company was run by two Harvard-educated sons of the founder, and they were looking for an experienced manager to take charge of their China trading business. Katy encouraged Paul to apply.

With Katy's introduction, Paul flew to Hong Kong to meet her bosses, and they offered him the job. It didn't pay as well as Exxon, but the title sounded good—general manager of Fung Ping Fan China Ltd.—and Paul hoped it would provide a segue into the China trade advisory business, which was booming. Inspired by China's burst of entrepreneurism, he liked the idea of getting out of a corporate bureaucracy and learning about the scrum of business. Best of all, the position was based in Hong Kong. We could end our bifurcated life and begin normal married life. Well, with a teenage son. And I could keep my job, which I still loved despite my troubles.

Paul and I both breathed a sigh of relief. He had been lonely in Beijing all those weeks I was in Hong Kong or traveling. And I had not unlocked the secrets of reporting from inside China. The walls keeping foreigners out were even more formidable than I had expected. It was like trying to describe a house from deep inside its well. Maybe dipping in and out from an East-West base in Hong Kong was the best way to get perspective on this massive, complex country.

But how would Steve adapt to life in urban Hong Kong? Would he even want to live with us? And how would I adjust to having a teenager in my home? I wanted a family, but mothering a seventeen-year-old boy was definitely beyond my competence. When you open the doors of possibility, you never know what challenges you might face.

Oddly, Paul had confidence that I could handle it. He had enjoyed spending the summer with his son and wanted more time with him. Now that we were married, he hoped his daughter would be allowed to visit us, too, during her summer vacation. His life had been divided much more than mine, and now we had hope that the important streams could flow together.

CHAPTER TWENTY-TWO:

Why It Matters

☙☙☙☙☙

老家, *lǎojiā: old home, meaning the place where your father's ancestors lived for generations.*

Before we moved, though, Paul and I made another journey into the past that connected me more firmly to the family of China. In late May, we flew to the Yangs' ancestral hometown, near Lianyungang. Although Paul had never even seen this place, it was his *laojia*—old home—because his father's ancestors had lived there for countless generations.

But this visit had a stronger pull. It was also where Paul's older sister lived.

When we landed at the city's tiny airport, officials from the Overseas Chinese Affairs Office met us. Paul was one of the first overseas Chinese to visit Lianyungang, a third-tier city on the coast, halfway between Beijing and Shanghai. Also on the tarmac, looking like a wizened crone, was Paul's sister Yang Huiling. Her head barely reached their shoulders; she had blunt-cut short hair and typical round glasses, light orange with small wings. A new blue cadre jacket, with round buttons up the center, hung on her thin frame.

In his coat and tie, Paul looked more than a generation younger than his sister. After Paul shook hands with the officials, he shook her hand, too. When I came to her, I took her hand in both of mine and held it a little longer, looking her in the eyes. "Jie-Jie," I said, the word for "elder sister." This was a term of respect. It would not be right to call her by her name, Huiling.

She looked away and blinked behind her thick glasses. Sweat glistened on her forehead, and her body wavered. During the ride from the airport, I found out why. We had to stop because Jie-Jie got sick to her stomach.

"Sorry, sorry," she said afterward. "Today is my first time riding in a motorcar."

When we arrived at Jie-Jie's house, a pack of neighbors swirled around. Her grown son, called Little Tiger, greeted us stiffly. He was about my age and had thick, rough hands and an open, honest face. Next to him stood his sister, Pei-Pei, who had come to town from her home in the countryside to meet her uncle from America.

Jie-Jie's house was the nicest in town, made of smoothly cut stone blocks, with an orange tile roof and a red door. When Paul had reconnected with her in 1981, she had told him she was living in a single room in a back corner of their old family home. Paul sent $3,000 for a new house, and she had used every penny well. Her son had built it himself. Behind was an outhouse. In front was a walled courtyard with a vegetable garden. In the courtyard was a single spigot—the only running water available. That was progress compared with the way they had been living before, when they relied on wells.

Inside, the main room had electric lights and even wallpaper. Across from the door was a shelf like an altar, displaying black-and-white photos of Paul's Yang grandparents. A smaller frame held a recent picture of Paul's parents. Jie-Jie had not seen them in person since 1948.

Her son shooed the neighbors and children away, and Jie-Jie asked us to sit and talk. Although her local accent was hard to understand, her personality shone through. She was tough and resilient, someone who had endured a lot and developed a thick protective shell.

"I've eaten a lot of bitterness," she began, her eyes dark and intense.

Her father, Paul's father, was forced to marry her mother when he was only fifteen years old, an arranged marriage in the 1920s. When she was a child, he left to study in Nanjing. After he was assigned to the military and war broke out, he was never able to return. Her grandparents raised her. When the war ended, Jie-Jie was in her early twenties. Her grandparents took her to Xi'an, where Paul's father and his second family were living.

"She's your daughter. You take care of her from now on," Baba's father had told him. Jie-Jie quickly realized she wasn't really welcome in her stepmother's home. Paul's father found a young Nationalist officer who agreed to marry her. When the Red Army began to close in on the city of Xi'an, Baba quickly decided to take his new family to safety in Nanjing.

"They didn't even stay for my wedding," Jie-Jie told us, her voice bitter. "I had met that man only once. We had nothing in common. Later, we divorced."

My mind darted to Paul's son and daughter, also abandoned by their father, though not so utterly. Naively, I wanted to be a stepmother who welcomed them and loved them, hoping that would make a difference. Despite Jie-Jie's powerful example, I would not realize until many years later that childhood loss has deep roots and leaves lasting scars.

She had two children and raised them as a single mother, struggling to feed them during the famine. When the Cultural Revolution started in 1966, her children, then young teenagers, were forced to move to a poor country village, part of a national movement for all urban youth. They were not permitted to return home, so Jie-Jie lived alone for nearly fifteen years. The personal tragedies of her early years were compounded by political tragedies that created even more heartache.

Paul's visit in 1981 had changed her life. With Paul's influence, Jie-Jie was able to get her son transferred back home.

The next day, Jie-Jie took us to the grave of Paul's grandparents. On the side of a small hill was a round mound with a single headstone. On it was carved Paul's grandfather's name. Next to it, where I expected to see his grandmother's full name, were the carved characters "surnamed Hu." Like many women of her generation, his grandmother had never been given a name. I couldn't imagine.

Pei-Pei swept the grave with a small broom of sticks, and Jie-Jie and Little Tiger placed bowls of fruit, nuts, and flowers before the marker. Clearly, they had a routine.

Paul and I stood awkwardly to the side. He had grown up in Taiwan, far from any family graves, and he had never learned such family traditions. In Ohio I had visited my ancestors' graves often, but that did not help me here on this remote hillside, deep in China.

Once the grave site was ready, Jie-Jie stood facing it, then went down on her knees. She dropped her hands and tapped her head to the ground, a total of three kowtows. To my foreign eyes, it looked like ancestor worship. From my reading, I knew that it was actually showing respect to your forebears. Veneration, not worship.

Jie-Jie turned to Paul. He had never kowtowed in his life. But these were his grandparents, who had raised his father and his elder sister. Baba could never return home to visit this grave and show his respects.

Paul took his place, facing the headstone. He dropped to his knees, placed his hands, and tapped his head on the ground. Three times.

Jie-Jie's eyes softened. She glanced at the headstone and smiled, as if to say to her grandparents, "See? Your grandson came back."

Meanwhile, my heart was twisting. As a daughter-in-law, was I expected to kowtow, too?

When Paul finished, he stepped back to my side.

"Should I do it, too?" I whispered in English.

"No," he said. "It's enough."

Jie-Jie's story filled me with sorrow. But her tale—and those of Paul's other relatives—also brought to life events I'd only read about. The Japanese occupation, Liberation, the Great Leap Forward, the Cultural Revolution—those weren't just words. They were traumatic chapters in the lives of Paul's relatives. In the lives of my relatives. These were my people.

Suddenly, it mattered to me, all this stuff I had been writing about Deng Xiaoping's reforms. Life in China was still poor but much more stable now. The hope Deng unleashed was magnified when measured against the terrible treatment so many ordinary Chinese had suffered for decades before 1980. Unlike some other American reporters, I had access to people the government had not chosen for me to interview.

Once during our visit, I took a nap in Jie-Jie's bed, literally seeing the world from her perspective. I could view her life not by American standards but against the way she had lived before. From Jie-Jie's bed, I felt a rush of empathy for those plagued by bitterness—but also an increasing awe for those able to rise above it. I felt invested in China and its future. I wanted Deng's reform policy to succeed so it would make their lives better. It was personal now.

For years, I had worshipped at journalism's altar of objectivity. Be skeptical of government statements. Quote people on both sides of an issue. Find the dark side.

But now, although I didn't realize it yet, I could no longer be truly neutral about China. Mao had damaged many lives, and Deng was giving people a chance. If Deng could stare down his critics and manage dissent, if he could quash the destructive aspects of Communism and keep China stable and on track, my Chinese relatives could flourish.

I was cheering him on.

CHAPTER TWENTY-THREE:

Birth of a Family

☙☙☙☙☙

阴阳, *yīnyáng: literally "dark-bright." A Chinese Taoist concept for the unity of opposites, it expresses how seemingly contradictory forces may be complementary and interconnected. To me, it described my effort to combine two families, two cultures, two countries, in a unified whole.*

By June 1986, my problems seemed to be resolving themselves. My scattered life was coming together, and I was ready to create a nest. After Paul received his job offer, he gave notice to Exxon, although they insisted he stay until July. Both his kids were coming to Hong Kong in late June. Paul and I at last could welcome them to a home of our own.

I should have known it wouldn't be that easy.

Janita Tam offered to help me find a new apartment. One morning in early June, she arrived at our office with a big grin. "I found a flat you will like," she said, her eyes shining. Janita, young and bright, had made a smooth transition from small-time trader to newspaper clipper to office assistant. And friend—she and her husband had attended my wedding.

"Is it close to the office?" I asked, delighted to see her enthusiasm.

"You won't believe. It's right up this hill. Look!" She went to my window and pointed up behind our office building. Perched precariously on concrete columns and trusses at the top of a steep slope was a tall, skinny building—bright pink on a purple base. I had never noticed it.

"Pink?" I asked, incredulously.

"Light red, good-luck color. Flat available near the top. Good price. Shall I arrange a viewing?"

A few hours later, Janita and I left the office to walk to the bubble-gum building. We climbed straight up a set of concrete steps cut into a steep hill behind my office.

"You're kidding," I said, looking up at it. "This would be my commute?"

"Less than ten minutes. Better than a taxi. And look, light poles! No problem at night."

It was, in fact, a safe neighborhood. Most of Hong Kong was.

The pink building, Suncrest Tower, was new. On the twentieth floor, an agent unlocked a thick wooden door. As I walked in, I sucked in my breath with awe. Windows lined the north wall, with a dazzling 180-degree view of the Hong Kong harbor. The vista swept from the skyscrapers of Central across Wanchai, showcasing all of Kowloon on the far side. I could even see Kai Tak Airport, its runway jutting out into the harbor on reclaimed land. Sky, sea, and horizon.

The agent chattered away. "All wood floors. Four bedrooms down this hallway, with two bathrooms. This way."

It seemed too good to be true. One of the bedrooms would make a perfect home office—especially if I could get another one of those newfangled modems and connect to my New York office from home. One would be good for Steve. The other, with a big window seat, might make a good nursery. I was hoping for a baby.

Just off the kitchen was a tiny room, a large closet. "This is for the amah," she said.

"This is too small for a bedroom," I said.

The agent laughed. "Oh, you could fit a bed in here, no problem. Amahs don't need much space."

"It would have to be a very narrow bed," I said, skeptically.

"Back here is a balcony," she went on. "See? A washer-dryer. The amah will like that." She assumed I would have an amah. Until now, I had paid a woman to clean my flat once a week. But most of the married expats I knew did have live-in amahs, all from the Philippines. I liked the idea of someone cooking dinners for us. And cleaning the bathrooms. And maybe helping with baby care someday. But what would it feel like to have a relative stranger living with us, sleeping in that tiny closet, a full-time servant? It pricked my egalitarian American conscience.

The rent was high, but my housing allowance from *BusinessWeek* would cover most of it. I signed the lease and lined up movers for July 13.

Less than a week later, before we could move in, I had two kids.

Now that we were married, Paul's daughter, Wenni, about to turn fifteen, was finally allowed to meet me—and spend part of her summer vacation with us. Steve flew in from Switzerland, glad to be out of there.

I had longed for such a reunion and yearned for happy times together. But I knew I was being tossed in over my head. I was a novice at parenting. And I had never even met a stepmother. I bought two books on stepparenting and was relieved to read that it was possible to be a good one. Leave the discipline to the natural parent, the books said. At thirty-two, I felt awkward about having teenage kids. By age, I was about halfway between Paul and his children. An unlikely stepmom.

Before meeting me, Wenni had asked her dad if I was fashionable. I have to admit, I wasn't. She permed her hair in a mass of curls and loved stylish clothes, bright nail polish, and the *Clan of the Cave Bear* books. Steve, now taller than Paul at seventeen, loved his guitar, Led Zeppelin, and Sylvester Stallone's *Rocky* movies. Wenni got straight

A's. Steve had just flunked Algebra and Chemistry. They both had Chinese faces but were thoroughly American. They could use chopsticks but far preferred hamburgers.

As with Steve, I liked Wenni right away. She struck me as a sweetheart: lively, vivacious, self-confident, fun to be around, and easy to love. She was still kid-like enough to toss french fries at her brother and paint pictures with the mustard and hot sauce at dim sum but surprisingly mature when discussing large life issues. Steve refused to tell us much about his loneliness and alienation in Switzerland but relaxed around his sister.

Before Steve arrived, I had already contacted several high schools in Hong Kong that used English as the language of instruction. The only one that operated on the American system was called Hong Kong International School. It had openings but accepted only students with good grades. This was an issue.

The school agreed to arrange a personal interview with the headmaster. He said he wanted to talk to Steve and also to us. But the day he chose was one when Paul was traveling in China with a delegation of Houston bigwigs—a long-planned trip, his last obligation to Exxon—so I had to take Steve to the interview myself. My first act as a parent.

After speaking to Steve, the headmaster asked to talk to me alone.

As smoothly and confidently as I could, I explained what I knew of Steve's childhood, home life, and school experiences—the disruptions that explained those Fs. A man in his forties with round glasses, the headmaster sternly explained the school's high academic standards.

"My husband and I think a home environment is best for Steve," I said. "We will be there, day in and day out, to help him with his schoolwork."

The headmaster regarded me thoughtfully. "How do you see your role as stepmother?"

"Pardon?" I was not expecting this question.

"Well," he explained, "some stepmothers take on the role of mother. Others see themselves like an aunt. Or a trusted friend."

I had to think quickly. "Well," I stammered, "I'm not his mother, so I'll leave any discipline to his father." What else had those books said? "But I wouldn't be like a friend, either. I guess more like an aunt. A favorite aunt." Later, I would decide this was a good answer. A good aunt would have his best interests at heart and be willing to accept him as was.

He listened more and seemed impressed by my sincerity. "But, frankly, his grades are not good enough to qualify. I'll give you my final answer in a few days."

I felt deflated. And depressed. A Princeton graduate with a master's degree from Johns Hopkins, I had never received a rejection from a school before. If Steve didn't get into this place, the other schools were even less likely to accept him. We were silent in the cab on the way home.

The next morning, I got the key to our new flat. The floors were polished and shiny, and it was ready for us to move in. In the mailbox was a small package, forwarded from Switzerland. It was not addressed to any name but was clearly labeled for my flat. So I opened it. Inside was a note to Steve from a Portland friend, plus a baggie of marijuana. I sniffed it to make sure.

My first crisis as a stepparent. On my way home, I tossed the weed into a public trash bin. That evening, I took Steve aside for a talk. "Hong Kong is not like America. It's dangerous to have drugs here. You could end up in jail."

His eyes grew wide, and he nodded his head.

I probably overreacted, but I had read horror stories about foreigners caught with illegal drugs in Asia. I didn't want to start out with discipline, but I had to draw a line.

The following day, the headmaster called. He had decided to allow Steve to attend Hong Kong International School. There were stringent conditions, including tutoring three times a week. Steve didn't see the need for that, but I thought it reasonable. I was relieved but not sure how I would fare, living with this teenager for the next two years.

I had said I wanted kids. Now I had one.

෧෧෧෧

Happy to be back in Hong Kong, I set about resuscitating my ailing career. In June, I wrote three articles, including a book review, and made two reporting trips to Taiwan. After the kids left to spend the rest of the summer in Portland, I closed a story called "Korea and Taiwan Are Really Roaring," working with a new editor in New York, Bill Holstein. Bill had worked for UPI in Hong Kong and Beijing, so he brought knowledge to the stories we worked on together.

Dinda decided to leave, after less than two years, to join *Newsweek*. I was sad to see her go, but it was good opportunity. *Newsweek* had a bigger circulation and covered a broader range of news. I hired a promising young reporter who had worked for the *Wall Street Journal* for seven years, including three as Taiwan bureau chief. Maria Shao, born in Taiwan and raised in Boston, was fluent in Mandarin. A Penn graduate, she was serious and intellectual, and I thought we would get along well.

Maria had never covered mainland China, so I arranged for her to travel with me on my next reporting trip to Guangzhou, toward the end of July. I was planning a story on China's exports, and most of its export-oriented factories were in Guangdong Province. I arranged to visit factories that made sewing machines, electric fans, Nike athletic shoes, and Mattel toys.

"I love factory visits," I told her, as we found our seats on the airplane. "It's my favorite part of being a business reporter. I like knowing how things are made."

"Me, too," she said, buckling her seat belt.

As the plane began roaring down the runway, though, my stomach twisted and my breakfast threatened to make a second appearance. I focused on my hands in my lap.

"Are you okay?" Maria's forehead wrinkled with concern.

"Yes, fine," I said, willing my stomach to settle down. The flight was smooth, so my nausea made no sense. It shouldn't be happening. But it was.

"It's crazy how fast China's exports are growing," Maria commented after takeoff.

"Yeah, but the US still imports, um, four times as much from Taiwan as from China," I said, trying hard to shift my mind away from the turmoil in my gut. "I'm not convinced they'll ever catch up."

"I've heard China has really bad packaging and poor quality."

Now my stomach was lurching like a plane in a patch of turbulence. I extracted the air sickness bag from the seat pocket and gently opened the top.

Maria regarded me with alarm. Here I was, an experienced world traveler, with my new subordinate. I didn't want to give her a bad impression by . . . too late. I held the bag close and barfed into it, as elegantly and professionally as I could. Maria turned and looked out the window, giving me my space. I was appalled. Random barfing just wasn't in keeping with my sense of dignity. This couldn't be some ordinary stomach flu.

The next week, I went to see my doctor, Dr. Tsai, and he confirmed my suspicions. "Well, it appears you are pregnant. Is that what you want?"

You bet it was. At thirty-two, after two years of delaying marriage, I was ready. Paul and I had just moved into our spacious apartment and hired a live-in Filipina amah, Tessie. Round-faced and cheerful, Tessie didn't mind living in the tiny closet. Her previous employers had required her to share a room with their newborn. With her help—which included cooking dinner every night!—I was confident I could balance career and baby.

"What?" That evening, Paul's shock took me aback. "So soon?"

"We've been married eight months," I said, hurt by his reaction. "I can't wait forever."

"Well, I guess it's good news then. But the timing isn't great." He sounded defensive. "I haven't even started this new job. How do I know it will work out?"

I found it hard to relate to Paul's viewpoint. He was forty-six years old, with two kids approaching college, alimony, child support payments, and no savings. He knew what a lifetime responsibility it was to raise a child. I remembered something my dad had written to me in a letter: "If he agreed to let you have a baby, he must really love you."

My month with Steve and Wenni had felt more like a joy than a responsibility. Well, mostly. I really didn't know what I was getting into, but what first-time parent does? I was ready to begin this adventure.

I bought a book called *Pregnancy 9 to 5*, about how women

combined pregnancy with a demanding career. That book recommended not telling one's boss until as late as possible. It also
recommended "executive maternity" clothing, in dull colors designed
to hide the baby bump. Pregnant women in the workforce had only
recently become a topic that decent people discussed publicly. The
sight caused many men to look away in embarrassment.

The very next day, in early August, Paul and I boarded a plane for the
States. The doctor had recommended no travel in the first trimester;
the main danger was of a miscarriage, which would be terrible during
a fourteen-hour flight. But we had planned this three-week trip for
months, so we took the risk. I had already mastered the art of deploy-
ing airplane barf bags. My kid would need to learn to love travel.

The high point of our journey was a full week with my parents
in Ohio.

Mom had weathered the wedding well, but Dad had not yet met
Paul. His recent letters had seemed accepting. Because Paul and I had
married in a civil ceremony, Dad asked if I wanted a small "blessing of
the wedding" ceremony at my parents' Presbyterian church. Touched
by this symbol of inclusion, I agreed. Further underlining their welcome, Mom and Dad also invited fifty friends and relatives to their
home for a party to celebrate our marriage.

Still, I was nervous about my dad, remembering his many letters expressing reservations. When Paul and I got off the plane at
Youngstown's tiny airport, Dad shook Paul's hand stiffly. Paul put him
at ease by asking questions about Youngstown and its history. By the
time Mom pulled into their driveway, the ice was broken.

Over the next few days, Paul and Dad had lively discussions about
economics, history, China, and politics. The Republican convention
was about to begin in Dallas, and President Reagan was an obvious
shoo-in. Both Dad and Paul supported the underdog, Democrat
Walter Mondale. Fortunately, they agreed on politics, and Dad rel-
ished learning about things he didn't know. Dad even invited Paul and
me to lunch with his business friends, other retailers he saw every day,
so he could show off his new Chinese son-in-law. Ever the extrovert,

Paul had no trouble chatting up roomfuls of Americans. Dad seemed to forget his objections.

"I told you we'd get along," Paul told me. I envied his blithe self-confidence.

By now, I had only one outstanding worry: introducing Paul to my prim-and-proper grandmother, age ninety-one. Scion of a prominent local family, she insisted on impeccable manners. Pedigree mattered to her. None of her children or grandchildren had married someone of another race or religion.

As we sat at an outdoor iron table under a tree in her backyard, where I had often played as a child with my cousins, my grandmother served us lemonade before quizzing Paul.

"How do you like our country?" she began.

I blushed. Paul had been a citizen for fifteen years, so it was his country, too. But Paul didn't skip a beat. "I like it very much."

It was surreal to hear him and my grandmother having a conversation.

"What is your religion?" she continued. I squirmed. Paul had no religion.

Paul looked her in the face with his honest, open expression and gave her the answer she was hoping for: "Presbyterian."

She nodded her head and did not quiz him further. He had passed the test. On the car ride home, we guffawed.

I had learned to feel comfortable with Paul's parents, his kids, and his relatives in China. Now he was accepted as part of my family. After living in North Carolina, New Jersey, and Washington state, he had already adapted to America. But now he was inside an American family, mine. He used his charm to break through my family's reservations.

And now that Steve was moving to Hong Kong and a baby was taking shape, we would be starting a family of our own. I hoped we could meld the best of East and West.

CHAPTER TWENTY-FOUR:

Rocky Shoals

⌒⌒⌒⌒⌒

打开窗户，新鲜空气和苍蝇就会一起进来, *dǎkāi chuānghù, xīnxiān kōngqì hé cāngying jiù huì yìqǐ jìnlái: If you open a window for fresh air, be prepared for flies. A favorite saying of Deng Xiaoping in the 1980s.*

*B*ack in Hong Kong, I felt pretty complacent. The new apartment looked great. I had acquired three large plants, a Korean chest with secret drawers, and a mirrored aquarium, which Steve populated with two carnivorous Oscars, two "mohawks," and a sucker fish.

Steve started school and came home with some new friends. And I was being productive again. The Guangdong export story ran a full three pages in the magazine, which would have been great except that our predictions turned out to be flat-out wrong. "Just as China seems on the brink of great possibilities, many observers are predicting that it will never become a mighty new export machine," we pronounced. "China may be entering world markets too late to achieve the growth that Taiwan and Korea had in the 1960s and 1970s." One problem with journalism is that it leaves written evidence of your lack of foresight.

Storms blew in from unexpected directions. Just three days after our return, my editors sent me to Manila. Corazon Aquino had taken over the presidency after Marcos fled, and she was getting ready to visit Washington to meet with President Reagan. My schedule in Manila included six interviews over two days. I had no trouble arranging them quickly—Filipinos in business and politics loved talking to American journalists.

The first morning in Manila, I woke up feeling a little queasy, so I ordered only toast and tea for breakfast. I stuffed a handful of airplane barf bags in my purse. In the backseat of the taxi on the way to my first interview, my breakfast came back up, filling the first bag. After paying the cab driver, I disposed of it discreetly, collected my nerves, and went in for my first interview. I asked insightful questions, took notes, shook the guy's hand, located a restroom, and threw up again. My second interview went fine, but I needed another barf bag on the next cab ride. The next day, the same routine. On the flight home on the third day, I restocked my supply.

This was getting ridiculous. I decided to see my doctor.

"This pregnancy is interfering with my work," I complained to Dr. Tsai. "I threw up three or four times a day in Manila! What I can do to stop this?"

My doctor, a slow-moving, soft-spoken Chinese man, regarded me with a steady gaze. "I think you have it backward," he said gently. "Your work is interfering with your pregnancy."

Tears welled up in my eyes. I never wept in front of other people, but here I was, sitting on an examining table, half dressed, wiping my eyes. I tried to regain my dignity. "You don't understand. I'm the Hong Kong bureau chief for *BusinessWeek* magazine! I travel all around China and Southeast Asia. I can't slow down just because of this."

He listened till I calmed down. "You may have to slow down a bit. Think about it."

I did. Jolted into clarity, I realized it was a real person's life I was messing with. This wasn't some illness I could treat. A human body was forming inside me—that of my child—and I needed to start taking care of it. I would have to shift my priorities. I swallowed my pride and told Maria and Janita that I would work half days for a while.

Right after that, dark clouds rolled in. Paul took Steve and me to brunch at the American Club, where we ordered hamburgers. Steve told us about how his new friends had taken him to Wanchai to show him the bar scene. "They never check IDs here," he said with authority.

I looked at Paul, who shrugged. "A few beers won't get him in trouble," Paul said to me.

Just then, a friend of Paul's came over to say hello—and broke some bad news. "You haven't heard?" the friend said. "Fung Ping Fan is in deep trouble. They may have to sell the China division. Isn't that the division they hired you to run?"

And so it began. The scrum of business.

The next day was Paul's first day on the job. The company chairman, Kenneth Fung, reassured him, "We are trying everything possible to keep the China trade company in business. Whatever happens, Paul, we'll take care of you." But a lot of factors were out of his control.

Each morning that week, the headlines shouted news about the company's financial crisis. Paul was devastated. He had given up his highly paid position at Exxon, with its Cadillac benefits, for this job. We had signed a two-year lease on an expensive apartment. Steve had started school. I was pregnant. What if his new employer collapsed? Would he get paid?

As the weeks went on, the crisis deepened. One Thursday in late September, Fung Ping Fan nearly went bankrupt. Paul had to fire four people to cut costs. By then, Katy had already found a more secure job in another field.

"What a disaster!" Paul said late that night, as I curled in his arms. "I've ruined my career." He felt let down, misled, and foolish for leaving Exxon. I wanted to comfort him but had no reassurances to offer. We just had to tough it out.

The next day, the *South China Morning Post* had stunning news: Shanghai had opened a stock exchange. Not a New York–style stock market, but still a market for private securities. In just a year, this had grown from a far-fetched idea to a reality. It seemed like the ultimate in capitalism—a stock market! It took my breath away.

If there was ever a big news story out of China—for a business magazine—this was it. Could the Communist Party really give up its ironclad control over the means of production? This would be the first time in history that a centrally planned Communist state would allow individuals to invest in companies. I had never expected China's flirtation with capitalism to go this far.

Immediately, I sent a telex to the All-China Journalists Association, requesting its help in setting up a reporting trip to Shanghai and Shenyang, which had started a bond market. Fortunately, my morning sickness had stopped now that I was in my second trimester.

A few days later, I found out that Shenyang had also been dabbling in another capitalist experiment: privatization. It allowed private entrepreneurs to take over a state-owned factory and three shops. Plus, it had allowed the first bankruptcy. All this was unheard of under Communism, which had guaranteed stability and lifelong employment—and protected the state sector from the uncertainties of the market.

Whatever happened in Paul's career or in Steve's schooling, I had to fly to China and investigate. Truth be told, I didn't mind the distraction.

During my trip to China, in late October, I found out that these bold experiments, radical in concept, were really baby steps. At a tiny bank branch in Shanghai, hundreds of people had shoved to get in the door the day shares were offered in two companies. Once they bought shares, though, no one wanted to sell until the dividend came out, so no stock trading occurred. Men and women in factory uniforms grinned as they showed me their bond certificates, which they viewed as essentially lottery tickets.

But privatization had truly begun. In Shenyang, a man in a modern suit jacket told me how he'd taken over a money-losing car-parts plant and made five times as much the first year as expected.

(Such a contrast to the tiny street vendors I had met in Manchuria just four years earlier!) Because of his success, his personal income had soared to ten times that of an average factory manager. That news provoked an outpouring of jealousy and complaints of unfairness. To prove himself, he agreed to assume management of an even more challenging factory.

Another entrepreneur, who had taken charge of a state-owned store, proudly showed off his wares, including cigarettes, sausages, and shoes. He told me he had added new products, extended business hours, and fired eight shop assistants he considered poor performers. His was now the largest privately owned enterprise in Shenyang. "'Capitalist' has a bad ring to it, so we use the term 'entrepreneur,'" he told me sheepishly.

All this news was dizzying. It was like handing over the church keys to a group of atheists. True, these were experiments, not yet national policy. But they appeared to be the cutting edge of a far-fetched task that had never before been attempted: turning a mammoth, inefficient, Soviet-style state sector into a sea of dynamic, privately owned, profitable businesses.

It was music to the ears of *BusinessWeek* readers, immersed in the wisdom of markets and private-sector decision making. The capitalist faith promised that free-market entrepreneurism would lead to widespread prosperity. Deng seemed to be the newest convert.

Still, there was pushback, especially among Deng's rivals, China's remaining Communist true believers. "Ideologues argue that stock trading could lead to wild speculation and a situation in which millionaires live off others' labor," I wrote. They were right. By 2016, China had more billionaires than the United States.

The midwife to China's stock exchange, I discovered, was a mild-mannered academic. Li Yining, a Beijing University economics professor, dared to urge that all state-owned enterprises be converted to publicly listed companies. I flew to Beijing to meet him.

In his book-lined office, with his whimsical face and mischievous eyes, Professor Li showed charisma and a lack of fear. "This is the way to make enterprises lively," he told me, his wide-set eyebrows dancing above his glasses. Most state enterprises were weighed down by huge staffs with no incentive to be efficient. "Perhaps the state will decide not to let go of the existing railroads, banks, and telecommunications. But in the end, the majority of ordinary enterprises should be stock-issuing companies." This was as unthinkable as imagining that the government could take over the majority of American companies.

Li Yining was building a reputation as Mr. Stock Market. He knew the risks: during the Cultural Revolution, he was attacked as a "revisionist" and led away, his head shaved, in disgrace. As recently as 1983, during the campaign against "spiritual pollution," Party newspapers had attacked his ideas as too liberal. Yet here he was, in 1986, pointing to concrete results in Shenyang and Shanghai. From enemy of the people, he had turned into a visionary.

"You live in Hong Kong?" he asked me, examining my business card. "I will be speaking there next month." He gave me his business card and encouraged me to contact him directly, something most Chinese did not do.

My hopes kicked up. As China became more like the West, maybe one day I would be able to just call up Chinese officials and professors and talk to them. It was a novel idea in a country where the Party monitored all foreigners' contacts.

Even more far-fetched ideas were catching fire. That fall of 1986, I read about rousing speeches given by an astrophysics professor named Fang Lizhi. Rather than speaking about neutron stars, he drew crowds of students at universities across China with a message they were eager to hear. Communist dogma, he insisted, was too rigid. What China needed was more freedom and political liberalization.

A brilliant scientist, Fang Lizhi had been invited to conferences overseas, where he encountered ideas never discussed in China: human rights, academic freedom, separation of powers, and accountability of leaders. Back in China, wherever he spoke of them, students transcribed his speeches and mailed them to their friends around the country. "Frankly," Fang said at one major speech, "I feel we lag behind because the decades of socialist experimentation since Liberation have been, well, a failure!" The students erupted in cheers. His gospel of freedom fed into their heady sense that anything was possible.

Many assumed such fearless candor was at least tolerated by

someone high up in the Communist Party. Might China's two top leaders, Hu Yaobang and Zhao Ziyang, endorse political liberalization? It seemed unlikely. Yet even *People's Daily* praised Fang, admiring the "air of democracy" he had created at his university. In December, student demonstrations demanding greater openness broke out at more than a dozen universities.

Paul and I read about these events with amazement. Could China really be changing so quickly? Paul hoped the Communist Party of China would change its name, now that it was ditching Marxism. Starting in 1986, Soviet leader Mikhail Gorbachev spoke of *glasnost*, increased openness and transparency in government, as well as *perestroika*, an economic restructuring similar to what Deng had begun in China. The defining lines of the world as I had always known it, communism versus democracy, socialism versus capitalism, seemed to be blurring.

As East met West, a new idea was born: Deng's economic reforms might lead to democracy. Capitalism in China would give rise to a strong middle class, who would demand the right to vote. Western pundits predicted that was inevitable, and we were eager to believe.

After the jerky progress of the early 1980s—as China alternated between the accelerator and the brakes—this felt like the open road. Would it be full speed ahead now?

Covering an energized China was giving me new energy. I was back in the groove at work, producing stories at a good clip.

Steve was adapting reasonably well to his new school, with passing grades. He didn't like studying, so sometimes Paul came down hard on him, giving lectures. "If you don't pass this test, you'll flunk. If you don't finish high school, you'll end up digging ditches."

My approach to Steve was the opposite. I would gently suggest he study, or clean the fish tank, or submit to his Chinese lesson. What he really needed, I figured, was stable ground to stand on; then he would regain his balance. Fundamentally, though, neither Paul nor I understood Steve well. He just wanted to be left alone and live life on his own terms—but that didn't mesh with the demands of high school.

The best news of all, however, was that Paul's job traumas began to calm down. The Fung brothers found an elegant solution. They convinced the company's auditors, Ernst & Young, to become co-owners of the China trade business. That ensured a steady job and salary. The tension went out of our lives like air from a balloon.

Still, Paul had to prove himself in a new field. He had never negotiated a trade deal. At first, he took over the existing business, selling materials that China needed: fertilizers, pharmaceuticals, cloth. Then he got what might be a big break. One of his relatives, who worked in a Chinese provincial trade office, told him about a factory that needed equipment to manufacture plastic film. Paul invited the American supplier to China and negotiated a deal in just a week. In 1986, this was lightning quick.

His new bosses were impressed. The commission from one deal was enough to cover Paul's salary for a year. They promoted him to senior vice president of Ernst & Young Hong Kong, head of their China consulting business. In just a few months, his "ruined career" had risen from the dust and was back on track. He had reinvented himself as a China trade consultant.

Even I was impressed. Could I reinvent myself if I ever needed to? I was approaching my fifth year on the job, when Lew Young had predicted I would get lazy. As the baby was coming soon, I would need to take on a new role as mother, without letting up on my career drive.

❦❦❦

Just before Christmas, Professor Li Yining did come to Hong Kong. Paul and I went together to hear his speech on China's stock markets, and we went up to talk to him afterward. I had always been shy in such public settings, but Paul came right out and invited him to our home for dinner.

Two days later, Li Yining and his wife sat in our living room, with the sparkling lights of the city below. Relaxed in this home setting, he gestured boldly, chuckled amiably, and predicted a day when China's economy would look a lot like America's.

Being married to Paul had an advantage I had not foreseen.

With his native Mandarin and his outgoing ways, he could reach out easily to Chinese intellectuals and officials. Without Paul, I could never have invited this brilliant man to my apartment. I watched and listened as they carried on an in-depth conversation. I could understand about 90 percent of it, but when I occasionally jumped in with a question, I sometimes reached the limits of my language ability. Yet Professor Li regarded me with respect, listened patiently, and responded thoughtfully.

In my own dining room, I felt as if I was "inside China" at a deeper level than before. Like many other outside observers, though, I failed to fathom its depths.

The next month, in January 1987, China's full-speed rush toward an open society crashed into a wall. After two weeks of exuberant student demonstrations in multiple cities, Deng's elderly colleagues reached their limits. They blamed Hu Yaobang and dismissed him from his position as general secretary of the Communist Party. Hu became the fall guy for the most radical and promising of China's changes.

But the reaction went beyond that. *People's Daily* fired the opening salvos of a new campaign against "bourgeois liberalization"—criticizing especially "wholesale Westernization." These ideas, it said, "negated the socialist system in favor of capitalism." The next victim was Fang Lizhi, who was expelled from the Communist Party, along with two other intellectuals. From that moment, the Western press dubbed them "dissidents."

Fortunately, Li Yining held on to his job at Beijing University, although he was publicly censured for his economic theories, too. Unlike Fang, he had never openly criticized the Party.

Working with our Beijing stringer, I completed a *BusinessWeek* story predicting a "long march backward" for Deng's economic reforms. We quoted a Beijing-based banker with this gloomy prediction: "The Chinese have slipped now and lost their window of opportunity to modernize for a long time."

Once again, the pendulum had swung. Deng Xiaoping was in charge, but he had reined in the enthusiasm of the most ardent reformers, including his own man, Hu Yaobang. The men the Western press called "reactionary hard-liners"—old-style Communists of

Deng's generation—had won this round. Skeptics asked, were the bold experiments in capitalism over?

Now that I had befriended Paul's relatives and even Professor Li Yining, I hoped that Deng was just keeping things from getting out of balance. Two steps forward, one step back. But I was rooting for the energy and enthusiasm of the young reformers to win in the end.

❦❦❦

In January, Paul went with me to the doctor's office. Dr. Tsai had a newfangled machine, called an ultrasound, that could actually see inside my body. The doctor had me lie flat next to a computer monitor. He applied a thick, clear gel to my belly. Paul held my hand.

"It uses sound waves. Just watch the monitor," Dr. Tsai said. He touched a handheld tool to my abdomen and moved it slowly. "There. Do you see?"

On the monitor was an image of our little baby. Incredible! A black shadow, it was bouncing up and down, limbs fluttering, hands visible. It was alive, a person separate from me. Wonder of wonders.

What would this child look like, a mix of Chinese and Caucasian? What would be his or her personality, passions, choices? How smart would this child be, how industrious, how skilled, how good-tempered? The genetic mix was set; the personality was predetermined by heredity.

"I can't tell," I said. "Is it a boy or a girl?" I couldn't change the baby's gender, but I wanted to have a few months to prepare to welcome either a boy or girl.

"Look here," said Dr. Tsai. "If it were a boy, you could see his private parts."

Paul and I squinted at the machine. No private parts visible.

"A girl!" I was delighted. I had grown up with two sisters and gone to an all-girls high school, so I felt more confident raising a daughter than a son.

Paul was a little taken aback. "I guess I assumed it would be a boy," he told me later.

So much for Ted. That was the name we had picked for a boy. For a girl, we chose the name Emily. We wanted her to have a Chinese middle name. Paul chose Ming, in part for the meaning—"bright"—and in part because it would be easy for Americans to pronounce.

As my due date in March approached, this child was kicking and punching. In utero, she traveled to Guangzhou, Portland, New York, Youngstown, Manila, Beijing, Shenyang, Shanghai, Macau, Taipei, and Sabah, Malaysia. Quite the global traveler. She would come into the world at a time when the two countries of her heritage, China and America, were moving closer. I hoped.

By this time, the storms in my life had calmed down. As Paul promised, our "boat" had reached the smoother waters of the bay and—miraculously—straightened out.

I didn't—and don't—buy into fatalism. As an American, I believed in the strength of my own willpower to make my life better. But the bad luck just stopped, and good luck blew in. Some things, good and bad, can't be controlled. It was a lesson I learned despite myself.

That year of transition, I stayed at the helm, watched for rocky shoals, and steered into a harbor. Just as the waters calmed down in my personal life, things were roiling in China. I hoped this ugly new campaign would fade away. But, given the leadership change, that was far from certain. My little junk was nothing compared to Deng's ship of state.

CHAPTER TWENTY-FIVE:

Baby and Tibet

☙☙☙☙☙

中庸之道, *zhōngyōng zhi dào: the Middle Way or the Golden Mean. A Buddhist and Confucian ideal of moderation. A path that avoids extremes. Reconciliation of opposing views.*

No female foreign correspondent for *BusinessWeek*, as far as I knew, had ever given birth while working overseas. McGraw-Hill policy granted me a six-week paid maternity leave, and I had the option of taking additional unpaid leave up to a total of six months. But I didn't dare ask for any unpaid leave. What would happen to my expat housing allowance? Without it, Paul and I could not afford the rent on our flat.

Keith Felcyn, the chief of correspondents, had been careful when I told him I was pregnant and needed to take maternity leave. I explained to him that I had a live-in helper who would care for the baby after I returned to work. But he had let one comment slip: "I can't believe any woman would want to abandon her baby." I was annoyed but let it pass. He had probably never met a working mother; in professional circles, we were a rare species. Even Paul had expressed a similar idea, two years earlier, asking me, "Why have a baby if you aren't going to take care of it?" Fortunately, I had convinced him I could continue working and be a good mother. Not that I had ever done it before.

A memory came back to me, from my days as a college student on the *Daily Princetonian*. A woman two years ahead of me graduated and got a job at the *Wall Street Journal*, a job all of us coveted, men and women. When she got pregnant, she quit her job. As a woman, I felt devastated. She had ruined it for the rest of us. Why should the *Wall Street Journal* ever hire another promising young female graduate? Why bother investing in training "girls" when they would quit to have babies?

I had personally hired two women, younger than me, at *BusinessWeek*. Both might want to have babies someday. Damned if I'd wreck it for them. Instead, I wanted to show my bosses they had not misjudged me. They had not assigned me to this plum job—and given me a promotion and raise at the end of 1986—just to lose me to what was now being derisively called the Mommy Track. I would go back to work after my leave and get up to speed and show them that a mommy could do just as fine work as a daddy. Maybe better.

Maria had been on the job for almost a year and was ready to take up the slack during my leave. By mid-May, I would be up and running, and we'd be a two-man bureau again. A two-woman bureau, actually.

On March 18, a week before my due date, I worked a full day, sending telexes with the final fixes for a story. Then I walked home, bulky and stodgy. I found it increasingly difficult to climb those steep steps, huffing and puffing with the extra weight.

After dinner, I felt a few mild pains but wasn't sure. I packed a small suitcase, got out a clock, and tried to time the contractions. At 8:30, Paul came back from a meeting at Steve's school. He noticed the clock right away and asked how I was feeling. At 9:00 p.m., my water broke, so I grabbed the suitcase. I will still wearing my work clothes.

Steve looked panicky. "Relax! Relax!" he kept saying. I reassured him all would be okay, although I felt shaky. Paul and I got in the car, and he drove much too quickly.

"Slow down," I kept saying, hanging on tight. "I just want to get there safely."

The baby arrived just four hours after I got to the hospital. A girl, as expected. She had dark hair and looked unlike my own baby pictures. She was darling—but completely Chinese. For an instant, I wondered, *Who is this? How could she have come from my body?*

The nurses wrapped her in a blanket and handed her to me. Emily Ming Yang. In my arms. Her eyes were dark brown. She blinked at the brightness of the world, cocked her head, and regarded me with somber curiosity. We all enter the world by leaving our comfort zone.

I stared at her in wonder. Who says miracles don't happen? This little person came from nowhere. I inhaled the marvel of her. Then I conked out.

The next morning, Paul stopped by my office and told Janita and Maria, who sent a telex to our editors in New York. The news spread quickly: Dori had worked a full day, finished a story, then gone home and had a baby. Many colleagues sent congratulatory telexes. The managing editor joked at a staff meeting in New York that he expected I would probably write a story for the next week from my hospital bed. It felt a bit macho. It put a grin on my face.

My mother offered to fly to Hong Kong and help me with the baby, but I declined. It would have been nice to have her there, but I didn't have a bedroom for her. Tessie cooked special foods, including green papaya and soup with bone marrow, known to build up strength after childbirth. Both Filipinos and Chinese believe a woman should not leave the house for one month after childbirth. It's called *zuòyuèzi*, "sitting the month." I didn't entirely obey the rules.

We called her Ming-Ming, and she was sweet-tempered and good from the beginning. Calm and gentle, bright-eyed and curious. Tessie helped me figure out what she needed when she cried. Having live-in help made a huge difference. I kept meticulous records on a calendar of when she smiled, when she held up her head, grasped a rattle, rolled over, sat up, ate solid food.

Living on the other side of the planet from my mother and sister, I befriended other mothers with babies and checked in with them frequently. Is this normal? Has she missed a milestone? Paul had never even changed a diaper. I insisted he be a more involved dad this time around. He enjoyed cuddling the baby. And, yes, this time he changed diapers.

I was nervous about going back to work. I was a pioneer at trying to balance work and baby care. I couldn't find any books on the subject. How would I handle the feeding? Inevitably, I would need to travel. What then? A friend who was a nurse practitioner brought me a breast pump from New York and explained how to use it.

In May, I went back to work. Living within walking distance of my office made it easy. I could come home at lunchtime to nurse the baby. At first, I chose to write about subjects close to home—about two big hotel groups based in Hong Kong. But less than eight days after returning to work, I left on a three-day trip to Beijing. I took the pump so that my milk would not dry up. I held Ming-Ming extra close that day, sure I would miss her terribly. I still felt as if we were part of the same body. Traveling, which I normally loved, now felt like cruel hardship.

In Beijing, everyone was talking about the political struggles in China's leadership. After eight years of getting his way on daring reforms, Deng Xiaoping was increasingly facing pushback from a coalition of aging "conservatives" and Maoist ideologues, led by Chen Yun, eighty-two, and Peng Zhen, eighty-four. Deng himself was eighty-two, so it was a battle among old men for the future of the country. Clearly, Deng was not a dictator; China's post-Mao system, while not a democracy, had checks and balances. The conservatives had already forced out one of Deng's chosen successors. Would they also put the brakes on economic reform?

This battle for the soul of China required big coverage, and my editors wanted me to get to work on a cover story. A cover story! I had not written one in more than two years. If I could pull it off, it would prove beyond a doubt that I could juggle motherhood and my career.

So, after returning home, I planned another, two-week trip to several Chinese cities, including two dynamic, business-oriented coastal cities I had not yet seen. I set the dates for late July.

But just as I started arranging my travel, an unexpected opportunity popped up: a chance to go to the Roof of the World—Tibet.

Of all places inside China's borders, Tibet was by far the most alluring. This remote land in the highest Himalayas sparked intense curiosity. It had been closed to journalists and most foreigners for decades—since the Communist takeover in the 1950s. Inaccessible and isolated, Tibet had a mystique like Shangri-la, the harmonious valley James Hilton invented in his 1933 novel, *Lost Horizon*. But instead of a Buddhist paradise where no one grew old, Tibet was often described as a dystopian land where dissenters were jailed and monasteries ransacked. I was eager to see what was really happening there.

Beijing had cracked open Tibet's doors to foreign travelers in 1984, but I could not justify a reporting trip to Tibet unless I could find a US business angle. Fortunately, in June, one flew in front of my face. At a social event, I met an executive of Holiday Inns, which had taken over the management of a hotel in Lhasa, raising its familiar green sign in the land of snows. What an opportunity!

Quickly, I arranged to interview the managing director of Holiday Inns' Asia-Pacific division, Rudiger Koppen. For this iconic American brand, China was a promising market, and it was competing against the world's major hotel chains for a foothold. The Tibet property, formerly state-owned, was new, but because of poor management it was still half-empty and already falling apart. "We aren't in Lhasa with a view to making money," Koppen admitted with chagrin. "It's a long-term investment."

"I'd love to go to Lhasa," I told him at the end of the interview.

He nodded. "We can help you. When do you want to go?"

That night, bubbling like pink champagne, I ran the idea past my editor. I proposed a short news piece about Holiday Inns and a second, longer article in the format of a "Letter from Tibet" describing in more detail what I saw there.

The next day, he sent me a telex. "Go for it!"

I picked the dates, July 11–18, and began planning. That was a bit tight, since I was due to leave for Beijing on July 25. When I left for Tibet, Ming-Ming would be not quite four months old. I would have to wean her before I left, but that timing felt about right anyway, based on what other mothers did. I didn't want to leave her, but she was healthy, and it would be only a week. I didn't really think about the fact that Tibet was far away and hard to get to and from, with extremely limited phone service. Molly, a Singapore Chinese friend and a mother of two, was shocked. She did not leave her babies even one night for the first year. I felt a twinge of guilt, but this was the chance of a lifetime.

When Paul heard about my Tibet trip, he didn't object. In fact, he wanted to go with me. We spent long hours discussing whether and how we could both go away and leave the baby. Tessie seemed okay with the idea. She had proved herself caring and trustworthy. We bought two tickets to Lhasa.

Controversy swirled around Tibet, and we read everything we could. During the turmoil of the 1920s through 1940s, China had been unable to enforce its claims of sovereignty, so Tibet had been ruled the traditional way, by its Dalai Lama, who was both a spiritual and a political leader. After the Communists took control, the Dalai Lama fled in 1959 to India, where his followers set up a Tibetan government in exile. Beijing and the lama's followers sharply disagreed over who had the right to rule Tibet.

The Tibetan exiles had effectively spread their version of the truth: that the evil Chinese had sent their army to occupy an independent Tibet ruled by a benevolent Buddhist monk, who had to flee for his life. They told personal stories of imprisonment and torture, wanton destruction of holy places, and lands overrun by unwanted Chinese settlers. Any right-thinking person who believed in self-determination would surely support the Tibetans who wanted to oust the Chinese occupiers. Most Americans I knew shared that attitude. In fact, that June, the US House of Representatives adopted an amendment condemning the Chinese for violating human rights in Tibet and alleged that more than one million Tibetans had died of famine or execution since the Chinese Communists took Tibet.

What most Americans didn't realize was that there was another side to the story. China's view was that Tibet under the Dalai Lama had been full of useless monks and oppressed serfs, whom the Communists had peacefully liberated in 1951. Initially, the Dalai Lama had cooperated with them. During the 1950s, Beijing claimed, the American CIA funded an armed insurrection by Tibetan rebels—a claim that proved to be true. Only after the foreign-financed rebellion broke out did the Communist army open fire to reinforce its rule in 1959.

In Beijing's view, the Dalai Lama talked like a serene and harmless Buddhist but really had charmed Americans and Europeans into funding and arming a disgruntled Tibetan expat community in India. Beijing suspected that the Americans were supporting the Free Tibet movement in order to set up a stooge government in Lhasa that was really controlled from Washington. As far as Beijing was concerned, it had abolished the oppressive system of serfdom and theocracy and was investing in bringing this region out of the dark ages and into the modern world.

I did not have strong views on Tibet, but as an American I leaned toward the "self-determination" argument and assumed that most Tibetans must be longing to overthrow Chinese rule. I had heard that Tibetans still revered the Dalai Lama, whom they had once treated like a god-king. Beijing would not allow Tibetans to possess or even see pictures of the Dalai Lama, so my guidebook recommended smuggling pictures of him into Tibet as gifts.

Before my departure, I photocopied many copies of the Dalai Lama's picture. Smuggling his photos into Tibet felt slightly conspiratorial and self-righteous—like being on the right side of history.

Paul didn't agree with me. As a boy, he was taught in Chinese schools that Tibet was an inalienable part of China. It had been ruled from Beijing—in theory, anyway—since the thirteenth century. He knew that most of Tibet's temples and monasteries had been destroyed, but that had happened during the Cultural Revolution, when Mao-inspired revolutionaries had attacked historical treasures all over China. Paul had read in Chinese newspapers that the central government was now investing money to rebuild Tibet's temples and modernize the region with new roads, hotels, and hospitals. Now, he wanted to see for himself.

Leaving Emily was much harder than I expected. Just two weeks before our departure date, I made a startling discovery. One Saturday morning, Tessie didn't come home until almost noon. Steve told us he had often seen her at bars in Wanchai, hanging out with sailors. Tessie had been sneaking out the back door of our apartment without our knowledge. I freaked out. The thought of her having sex with strange men and then cuddling my sweet, pure baby filled me with horror. When she came home, Tessie was contrite, but I needed to be able to trust her completely. What strangers might she invite to our apartment if she knew we were out of town? I fired her.

Quickly, I interviewed several Filipina amahs and found one I liked: Anita Norico. She seemed levelheaded and reliable, and she had also cared for other infants, including two of her own back in the Philippines. She spoke English well and knew how to cook. I had high hopes for her, but my sense of trust was frayed. So I hired a second amah, older and more experienced, with good references, and paid her to stay with Anita in our home while we were gone.

It felt strange to trust people I didn't know with my precious baby. Was I making the right decision? I didn't dare tell my friend Molly. I boarded the plane with doubt and anxiety.

Our biggest concern, aside from leaving Emily, was altitude. Lhasa had a small airport, with direct service to only one city: Chengdu, in Sichuan Province. Chengdu's elevation was nowhere near high enough to help us adjust to the altitude we would experience in Lhasa, which at twelve thousand feet was more than two miles above sea level, twice as high as Denver.

Altitude sickness typically occurs above eight thousand feet. But Paul and I didn't take any medication to prevent it. In its promotional material, the Holiday Inn boasted of oxygen piped into every guest room, so we figured we'd be fine.

But my body had never experienced such a shock. The minute we stepped out of the plane into Lhasa's blue-sky sunshine, I felt dizzy. I clutched the railing as I descended the stairway. Out of habit, I had stuffed an airline barf bag into my purse.

During the forty-mile drive to the city, I softened my eyes on the green fields of barley and yellow flowers that carpeted a broad valley surrounded by barren brown mountains. Few trees grew at this elevation. Brightly colored prayer flags fluttered from the corner turrets of Tibetan-style homes, which clustered like mud-brick fortresses. The dizziness, now joined by a throbbing headache, worsened.

Paul looked at me with concern. He was fine. "They say it's not about how old or fit you are," he reminded me. "It just randomly hits some people harder than others."

That didn't make me feel better.

I barely glanced at the sprawling, blocky beige exterior of the Holiday Inn. The minute we got to our room, I reached for the oxygen. Two green tubes came out of the wall, and I grabbed one, stuffed it in my nose, and began breathing. I could feel the oxygen filling my lungs, but I still felt light-headed. I had to lie down the rest of the day.

The next morning, I could barely get up. Paul did need a jolt of oxygen in the night but had no major problem. This was particularly annoying because he was so much older than I was.

The next day, feeling better, I interviewed the hotel's general manager, a Swiss hotelier named Chris Schlittler. He told me the hotel had trouble getting meat in this Buddhist land. He had started a farm for the hotel, raising ducks, pigs, and rabbits, to ensure a varied menu. The first winter, all the ducks froze, so he had switched to chickens.

"My biggest headache is hygiene," he told me. The Tibetans he hired had never seen a modern hotel, and most of them did not have electricity or running water at home. By custom, most Tibetans seldom bathed in this dry land. This hotel, completed in 1985, was one of the first buildings in Lhasa to have flush toilets.

"When I arrived last year," Schlittler told me in his precise, Swiss-accented English, "the hotel had sixty-five vacuum cleaners, but most of them were not working. Nobody knew how to empty their dust bags." Worse, he had to unclog bathroom drains, which had left up to three inches of standing water. Power outages were frequent. Schlittler brought in four English teachers, who also helped the Tibetan women employees with hairstyling and makeup. In just three months, he had brought the hotel up to Holiday Inn standards.

During our visit, it was running smoothly. The only modern hotel in town, it had hot showers, a color television, and complete rolls of toilet paper. A string quartet, with all Tibetan musicians, was playing Vivaldi on the upper level of the spacious lobby.

Tourism in Tibet was in its infancy. When the region opened, in 1984, it attracted only 1,500 visitors. By 1986, the number had jumped to 30,000. Chinese officials were hoping for more. But occupancy was running only about 40 percent that summer of 1987. Many tour operators in the United States and Europe were scared off by reports of skirmishes on China's border with India, and landslides on the road from Nepal had cut off overland travel.

After my interviews and tour of the hotel, Paul and I took a cab across town. We passed Tibet's most famous site, the majestic Potala Palace, a magnificent, thirteen-story structure built atop a hill overlooking the city. Formerly the home to many generations of Dalai Lamas, this thousand-room edifice soared up in layer after layer of whitewashed brick and red brick, like a giant wedding cake, topped by golden roofs and towers.

We drove on to the narrow alleys of the old city. Our destination was one of Lhasa's most famous sites: the Jokhang temple. It was like traveling back in time to a medieval kingdom.

Outside the temple, with its white-brick facade and gilded roof, we stood in the bustle of Barkhor Square and absorbed the sights and sounds and smells. Tibet's most sacred temple, Jokhang attracted pilgrims from all over Tibet. Tibetan women wore long black skirts, colorful striped aprons, and black vests over bright though well-worn blouses. Old men in faded, brimmed hats mumbled Buddhist prayers as they trudged around the shrines, spinning prayer wheels and fingering prayer beads. It looked like they were free to practice their religion.

Encircling the temple complex was a route lined with shops selling yak meat, daggers, incense, Buddhist figurines, and prayer beads.

I saw only a few Caucasian faces like mine and not many Chinese. I did not see any policemen or soldiers.

There, in the crowded market, I pulled out a stack of Dalai Lama pictures I had photocopied. I handed one to an old woman standing near me. She cried out in joy and hugged it to her chest. Suddenly, dozens of Tibetans mobbed me, as if I were handing out $100 bills. I had brought only about twenty copies, having left the rest in my hotel room. Hands grabbed all the pictures, and one man bowed his gratitude. Others pushed in, thrusting their hands at me.

Paul grabbed my arm and pulled me out of the melee. "Not the best place to do that," he muttered. I just wished I had brought more. Their hunger for the Dalai Lama was passionate.

We slipped out through the crowd and back into the square, where I rested on a low stone wall. Paul went off to get me a can of soda. Nearby, I noticed a Tibetan man in jeans and T-shirt.

"Where are you from?" he asked me in perfect English.

"America. Where are you from?"

He lowered his voice. "I am Tibetan. But I live in India."

"It's okay for you to come here for a visit?"

"Yes, I came to see relatives. They are very poor."

"What do they say, your relatives?" I asked, amazed to find a Tibetan who spoke English.

He looked around at the nearby people before continuing. "Everyone wants free Tibet. Independence. We want the Chinese to get out."

Just then, Paul returned with my soda. "Sorry, I couldn't find a cold one." He noticed the Tibetan man and instinctively addressed him in Mandarin. "Are you Tibetan?" he asked, noticing the man's jeans but also his tall frame and broad, flat face.

The exile looked at me. "I don't speak Chinese," he explained in English. "Wish you a good journey!" He melted into the crowd.

For the first time in twenty-eight years, Tibetan exiles were permitted to return. I wasn't sure whether they brought their dissatisfaction with them or tapped into the distrust they found among their relatives toward the Chinese. As a foreigner, I could tap only the surface.

⚜⚜⚜

The next day, Paul and I went out into the countryside. The hotel folks helped us line up a driver with a Jeep-like vehicle, which we would need on bumpy country roads. He was another returned exile, fluent in English. To gain his trust, I explained to him that Paul was American, not someone sent from Beijing.

We visited a little-known monastery called Tsurphu, which had been destroyed but was being rebuilt by local monks. A red-robed monk took us inside the rebuilt portion, the main temple. A thangka painting hung at the center, instead of a Buddha statue. The surrounding buildings were still in ruins. The destruction looked worse than what a gang of teenage Red Guards could have inflicted.

"In old days, one thousand lamas lived here," our driver translated. "Now only one."

As the lama talked to our driver, gesturing, I saw very little emotional reaction in his face. Whatever anger and sorrow and desolation he had once felt had long since played out—or was well-hidden.

"Is anyone helping him with the rebuilding?" I asked.

"Government says it will help, but all the money is going to the big cities for now."

On the way back to Lhasa, we stopped at a mud-brick house, faded prayer flags fluttering from the roof. A woman appeared, wiping her hands on a long apron. She invited us in for a cup of *tchang*, homemade barley beer. Her husband came in from a nearby field. The walls were decorated with paper posters: Zhou Enlai, Deng Xiaoping, and the Dalai Lama.

I asked our driver to translate: "Why do you have this poster of Zhou Enlai?"

"He saved the Potala Palace," the woman answered.

"And this one, of Deng Xiaoping?"

She looked at her husband, who answered, "He is doing good things for the country."

"And this one, of the Dalai Lama?" I persisted.

They looked at each other. "It is permitted now," he answered.

Outside the city of Lhasa, deep in the countryside, I got a whiff of what Tibetan people felt. The destruction was over, and the rebuilding had begun. Under Deng, Tibetans had more freedom to practice their religion, and exiles were allowed to return to visit. Life was better than it had been ten years earlier, but they were still poor and wearing faded, unwashed clothing.

Tibet was more backward than any other place I had seen in China. The food was poor and the facilities primitive. Like rural people in most developing countries, they seemed more concerned with feeding their families than with politics. Most had never expected to have a say in governance, under the Dalai Lama or the Communist Party.

It seemed to me that both versions of Tibet's story contained elements of truth—two contrasting truths, like the yin and the yang, like the posters on that mud-brick wall. The Chinese Communists were doing more to modernize Tibet and improve lives than the Dalai Lama had done. But under Mao they had also caused great harm—to all the people of China, including Tibetans.

The Dalai Lama drew on a Buddhist concept called the Middle Way. The following year, he would propose negotiations with Beijing to bring about "stability and coexistence" between the Tibetans and Chinese, based on "equality and mutual cooperation." China's leaders were not interested. They would respond by calling him a "wolf in monk's robes," a secessionist who instigated violent rebellion.

Dissent against the Chinese government would pick up a few months after we left and reach a peak in March 1989, when, after three days of violence and looting, Beijing would declare a state of emergency and evacuate foreign journalists and tourists. After that, Beijing would close Tibet to tourism for a year. After tourism reopened, foreigners had to get a special permit for travel to Tibet, only with a government-approved guide. That policy would remain in effect for decades. Paul and I had no way of knowing how exceptional our laid-back visit was in July 1987.

When I came back home to Hong Kong, after an absence of seven days, my baby was fine. She held out her arms and greeted me with her sparkling eyes and charming, toothless smile. I reached out to take her from Anita's arms, eager to smell the baby powder and feel the soft roundness of her little body. I danced around the room, holding her hand out as if we were on the dance floor, singing "Endless Love." She grabbed my hair and wouldn't let go. I burrowed my face into her neck. As the tension drained out of me, I realized how foolish I had been to leave her with people I didn't know well. No news story could ever compare to her well-being.

She had bonded well with Anita, who proved to be smart, responsible, and loving. Anita laughed and sang with Ming-Ming and seemed to love her as much as I did. As I watched them interact, I felt reassured that I had picked the right amah. That made it easier to go to work.

I discovered I could juggle my job and motherhood, with no harm to either, but the trade-off took more out of me than I had expected. I could babble with my baby but also continue to speak in intellectual and journalistic terms about controversial issues of the day, such as Tibet and China's leadership. But the contrast was jarring. It was like playing a lullaby on the piano's high keys and then switching to a Chopin nocturne without missing a beat.

I had proved that I could have a baby, take a leave, and bounce back to a high level of travel and productivity. But I knew that the key was access to reliable, affordable childcare. Having a baby in faraway Hong Kong, with a good salary and housing allowance, insulated me from the hardships of most working mothers.

CHAPTER TWENTY-SIX:

Deng's Dilemma, Dori's Dilemma

☙☙☙☙☙

下海, *xiàhǎi: jump into the sea. The decision to leave a stable government job and go into business for yourself. In the 1980s, more and more Chinese chose to take this risk, betting their lives that increased prosperity would outweigh the increased turbulence.*

Just a week after returning from Tibet, I left my baby again—for a two-week reporting trip to four cities. This time when I packed my bags, I included something unusual: a huge package of Pampers. Not for Ming-Ming, who would be staying in Hong Kong with Paul and Anita, but for my Chinese minder. Yes, Tian Bin, married to a Xinhua reporter, had given birth just two months after I did, also to a daughter, named Tian-Tian.

This time when she met me in the lobby, I was staying at a fancy modern hotel and both of us were dressed better—she in a well-cut shirt and slacks and I in a skirt and pumps. She even had a new pair of glasses, round, in the modern 1980s style.

When she saw me, her face lit up. She introduced her colleague Little Li, who would be traveling with me this time. "I wish I could go with you again," Tian Bin explained, with her familiar, dimpled half smile. "I'm back at work but not ready to travel yet."

"I brought you a gift, for the baby," I said, offering her the bulging plastic package.

"Thank you. You shouldn't have," she said automatically as she accepted it, but her puzzled look showed she was uncertain what it was.

"Disposable diapers for your baby," I said in English, not knowing how to say it in Mandarin. "You use them once and then throw them away." In Beijing, disposable diapers were not available, so for a working mom like Tian Bin, I thought they were a perfect gift.

She nodded and smiled. "Um, very nice," she said. But I suddenly got a vision of how wasteful Pampers were. I had read that they were not biodegradable, so they lived in junkyards forever. Maybe they weren't such a thoughtful thing to bring into China.

We both laughed nervously, and I showed them snapshots of my baby, kicking in tiny Nike shoes. Tian Bin had not brought any photos to this work-related meeting.

"It will be fun to watch our two girls grow up," I said, meaning it. I did want to keep in touch, even in years to come when she wouldn't be my minder anymore. What kind of future might Tian-Tian have in a China that was no longer proletarian? Her mother had been admitted to college when "redness" was the top criterion for everything. Now, college admission was based on a tough national exam, and the competition was fierce. But more opportunities existed.

Tian Bin took my hand again, in two of hers. I think she winked. But I wasn't sure.

Decades later, in a freer era, I would ask Tian Bin what she reported about me during those years and what she was looking for. She looked me straight in the eye as she answered, "We wanted to make sure foreign journalists had a good impression of our country." It was the same sentiment I heard from corporate public relations professionals.

With Tian Bin, my minder

✦✦✦✦

My goal for this trip was twofold. First, I wanted to take the temperature of Deng's reforms in the provinces, to see the effects of the power
plays going on in the capital. I chose to visit the coastal area south of
Shanghai, a hotbed for capitalism. I arranged interviews in Ningbo,
home of many of China's pre-Communist generation of industrialists,
and in Wenzhou, an isolated region that had an astounding number
of small-scale entrepreneurs. I wanted to see how things were going
for ordinary Chinese who took a chance on the reforms and "jumped
into the sea," leaving their stable jobs for the uncertainties of starting
their own companies.

But my cover story was also timed to be a "curtain raiser" for
a historic event in Beijing in October 1987. China's Communist
Party was getting ready for a major, once-every-five-years congress at
a tense moment. Ever since the overnight demotion of Hu Yaobang
as the head of the Party, jitters about succession had increased. Deng
Xiaoping was hale and hearty but could not live forever. Before
Hu's fall, Chinese had hoped for an orderly pattern of leadership
succession—in contrast to the purges, arrests, and plane crashes that
tarnished previous transitions. But if Hu could be deposed overnight,
could succession be orderly?

As "paramount leader," Deng appeared to be in control, still pushing economic reforms, but he had to contend with a cabal of critics.
Deng had announced that he would relinquish all his official positions, and he was urging the same of the other old men in the Party.
That group of geezers, in their late seventies and early eighties, was
hanging on to power—and to life—so much that foreign observers
dubbed them the Eight Immortals.

Many of these elders were anxious. They didn't speak to the press,
but insider leaks hinted that they feared a return to full-fledged capitalism, which they associated with starvation and exploitation. Talk
of political liberalization made them nervous that the Communist
Party might be overthrown, a move that would toss the country into
chaos. Inflation reminded them of the bad old days under Chiang
Kai-shek, when money became worthless. And they worried about

growing inequality: a few people in coastal cities were getting rich, while remote districts lagged behind.

Chief among Deng's challengers was Chen Yun, age eighty-two. Although he had long championed the idea of introducing market forces to help the economy grow, even back in the days of Mao, he insisted that it should be done only within the strict limits of central planning. As early as the 1950s, he had coined the term "birdcage economy." The cage was the state plan, and the bird—market forces—should be allowed freedom to fly only within its confines. Now, Chun Yun seemed to worry that the bird was being freed from the cage. That might lead to an end to Communist central planning.

Typically, I didn't write much about politics, but in China it affected business. Fang Lizhi had been silenced, but he had made me think: Might Deng's reforms spark widespread demand for political rights? Taiwan, an autocratic one-party state, had just ended martial law and now tolerated an opposition political party. But Taiwan's people had much higher incomes and more education than China's. Most Chinese, I assumed, had no concept of Western-style democracy. But I wondered.

Wenzhou was so remote that overland roads, through the mountains, were nearly impassable. So Little Li and I had to take an overnight boat from Shanghai. This cruise was on a tough working ferryboat, with hard wooden beds, four to a room, for the privileged few like me, and sleeping spaces on the floor for everyone else. Boarding the boat was a scrum of shoving and elbowing. Mine was the only foreign face.

In my cabin, I struck up a conversation with a tired-looking woman with a wriggly little boy and an ungodly amount of luggage. She had several gold teeth, and the boy had a gold necklace with a jade pendant. She and her husband were visiting from the Netherlands, to which their parents had emigrated from China in the 1940s. For decades, they could not contact their relatives in China; now, they were bringing their parents back to Wenzhou for a visit.

"Of course, we have to bring gifts." She gestured at the overflowing luggage. I noticed four bottles of French cognac tied firmly together with pink plastic string.

The next day, driving around the city of Wenzhou, I saw signs that wealth was starting to sprout there, too. Known as the birthplace of China's private economy, Wenzhou had more individually owned businesses, known as *getihu*, than any other part of China.

Wenzhou's narrow streets were lined with open shop fronts and jammed with tiny taxis and three-wheeled pedicabs. Most famous was Wenzhou's button market, which attracted makers and sellers from throughout the region. Stacks of colorful buttons in baskets lined both sides of an alley, and the sellers shouted out their specials. I also visited a private cinema and a village-operated toilet factory.

In just nine years, since the reforms had begun to permit private enterprise, Wenzhou's annual per capita income had grown ninefold, from $15 to $138. Still low, but impressive growth. I saw gold teeth and watches, as well as Vespa motorbikes—presumably imported from Europe by wealthy overseas relatives. No one in Wenzhou seemed to have any doubts about capitalism. "The economic reforms have raised living standards, so why do some people label them as capitalist?" one button seller complained.

From Wenzhou, we drove to Ningbo over windy mountain roads. Along the way, our Chinese-made car had four flat tires. While the driver patched them, Little Li and I found a place to pass the time—in a small-town clinic. It was the coolest spot we could find on that hot August day. Not a stop that my minder had planned.

At that remote clinic, a man in his sixties, with his arm in a sling, told me he owned the car repair shop, a *getihu*. He wore a sleeveless T-shirt over pants held up with a belt wrapped twice around his skinny waist. His name was Chen, and he had been a soldier in the Chinese army during the Korean War and had won medals for killing American soldiers.

"I am American," I said. "Do I look like the soldiers you saw in Korea?"

Chen examined my face. "No. Your nose is not as big." "Big nose" was a standard Chinese definition for Caucasians, just as English-speaking people used "slant eyed" to describe Chinese. Like soldiers everywhere, he had demonized the enemy and never really looked at their faces. Only by interacting in peacetime can we recognize enemies as individual humans.

Chen was as authentic an ordinary Chinese as I could find. I decided to push the boundaries and ask about taboo subjects.

"I'm curious," I began. "What is your opinion about direct elections? Do you think they would be good for China?"

He shook his head emphatically. "Not possible. There are too many people and nationalities in China. Even America doesn't have direct elections."

"Actually, we do," I explained. "I voted for president in the last election." I decided not to get into details about the electoral college.

His eyes narrowed. "That must be because you are a special, privileged person."

My minder leaned in, as if curious to hear answers to questions he would never dare ask.

The old man seemed unafraid, so I pushed on. "What do you think of Chairman Mao?"

"Chairman Mao unified the country and made China strong," he said with conviction. "Without Chairman Mao, there would be no New China. He should be revered."

"And what do you think of human rights?"

Chen looked confused. He clenched his fist and looked at it. "*Ren . . . quan?*" The Chinese term for human rights, *renquan*, sounds the same as "people's fist." He seemed to think it was a boxing move.

A young man who had been listening jumped in. "The human rights situation is better in the cities, not so good in the countryside," he told me, eager to show he was not ignorant like the old man. "I think direct elections are possible. But not until the general education level is higher."

The young man worked with his father at another *getihu*, selling nuts and bolts. "Do you worry the policy allowing *getihu* might change?" I asked them both.

Old Chen weighed in. "We do what is approved by the policy. If the policy changes, we won't do it anymore." The young man didn't contradict him.

In the next city, Ningbo, the market economy was also alive and well. I visited a joint-venture factory that made zippers, as well as the economic development zone.

After we left Ningbo, driving along the main road to Hangzhou, I noticed a young woman standing half in the roadway, waving a red scarf.

"What's she doing?" I asked Little Li.

"She's trying to get customers. See? She was standing in front of a restaurant."

"There's another one," I said. This woman was wearing a tight T-shirt.

"Most drivers are men," my guide explained. "The restaurants and shops are all competing now. It's capitalism."

In China, anything decadent, exploitative, corrupt, or unsavory was by definition "capitalist." As the daughter of a business owner, I found this attitude mildly offensive.

Little Li laughed and shook his head. "Well, maybe it's not your kind of capitalism. But you know what Old Deng says: if you open a window for fresh air, be prepared for flies."

After I got back to Hong Kong, eager to embrace my rapidly growing baby, I wrote another cover story. I included details from my interviews in Wenzhou and Ningbo but also an analysis of the growing rift in China's leadership. They were torn between a desire for the fresh air of fast economic growth and the "flies"—sexual come-ons, gold teeth, human rights, and direct elections.

I liked the title my editors chose: "Deng's Dilemma: Ideology vs. Prosperity in China." It seemed like the main drag on his reforms was rigid, uptight Communist ideology.

❧❧❧

For me, that fall of 1987 was my most glorious year. At the age of thirty-three, I believed I had the Ideal Man, the Ideal Baby, and the Ideal Job in the Ideal City. I traveled to little-known places—"off the map"—like Wenzhou. China was growing more and more open, so it was ever easier for me to meet people who would talk about what was on their minds. I had forgotten my early fears about reaching behind the mask of the "inscrutable" Chinese who held their privacy close and distrusted foreigners. My editors, in several departments of the magazine, were eager for more frequent and longer stories. And

I loved coming home to Hong Kong, to our airy flat high above the harbor, into the arms of the man I had wanted for so many years, back to the baby I had once despaired of ever having. Steve was passing all his courses and making friends; he even had a girlfriend. I enjoyed the international sophistication and energy of Hong Kong and trusted a warm and loving amah who cared for my baby while I jetted around Asia.

Still, although Lew Young was no longer editor-in-chief, I remembered his words "By the sixth year, it's time to move on." I had come to Hong Kong on a three-year assignment, and more than five years had passed already. I did not intend to spend the rest of my life here, and Paul, an American citizen, did not either. I heard from friends in Hong Kong that expatriates who stayed overseas more than eight years had trouble returning to their home country. The reason was not culture shock. It was lack of job opportunities. The more I became an expert in China and Asia, the less qualified I was for other types of jobs in the States. Most employers transferred their people back home before that expertise hardened into a shell impossible to break out of. It was a truism we all accepted.

At this point, I wasn't ready to move back to my own country. Still, we were planning a trip to the States that October, and I knew I would be asked. I wasn't sure how to respond. Maybe I would get some perspective, as I often did, thinking through my life issues at a cruising altitude of thirty-five thousand feet.

Once again, I was sitting with Paul on a long transpacific flight, but this time we were traveling with a seven-month-old baby. Like Deng, I was pulled in opposite directions. I loved my job and could envision a path of advancement, involving other foreign postings, more prestigious publications, a reputation as an expert that might involve public speaking. But now that I had a child and a husband with a career path of his own, my options were limited. I despised limitations.

If we moved back to the States, where would we live? How would I balance baby care and a job? No one I knew in America could afford a live-in nanny. How would Paul and I both find jobs that were meaningful, in the same city? Both of us were China experts now. Would that matter to employers back home?

Our US trip included stops in many places, to see relatives of mine and Paul's. I kept my eyes open, hoping to see something that would give me some ideas how to resolve Dori's dilemma.

But among the many relatives, classmates, and friends we visited, I could not find any women who balanced young children with the kind of high-pressure, high-stakes, always-on, heavy-travel career that I had. I had read about such women in magazines; surely they existed. I wished I could find one who could give me some much-needed advice.

In the meantime, our nest egg fell out of the nest and broke. On October 19, 1987, the day after we arrived in New York, stock markets around the world crashed. On that one day, immediately dubbed Black Monday, the value of our life savings dropped by 35 percent. The crash showed how when things appear to be going well, they can change abruptly. Paul had mentioned the idea of saving up for a down payment on a house. That wasn't going to happen anytime soon. We would both need to keep our jobs for some time.

That was fine with me. I was more than ready to return to Hong Kong and resume my Ideal Life. Plus, things were heating up in China.

❦❦❦

While I was gallivanting around America, focused on my family and my future, Deng Xiaoping was hard at work pacifying his critics. From October 25 to November 1, 1987, China's Communist Party held its once-every-five-years National Congress, with nearly two thousand delegates from across China. It was the first big meeting of the Party congress since 1982, when Deng Xiaoping had gotten the official go-ahead for his policies of reform and opening to the outside world. This meeting was all about making sure those reforms would keep going long after Deng died. He was eighty-three.

In November, I went back to Beijing to see how things had changed. As expected, Deng gave up all his official positions except one: chairman of the Central Military Commission. He convinced more than eighty other elderly Communist leaders to retire from their positions, too, many of them veterans of the Long March in 1934–35. Among them were his most powerful critics, Chen Yun, Peng Zhen, and Li Xiannian. A swarm of younger technocrats was promoted, mostly college-educated men in their fifties who had risen through the ranks. Deng's remaining protégé, Zhao Ziyang, an avid reformer, was confirmed as general secretary (head) of the Communist Party. The Party reaffirmed that the economic reforms would continue. The congress was hailed as a political victory for the reformers.

The chill that began in January 1987 with the demotion of Hu Yaobang had ended. Beijing's aging hard-liners lost their official posts. The liberal reformers seemed on top again.

But the hard-line critics who had fulminated against "bourgeois" Western influences insisted that their man be promoted, too. His name was Li Peng, age fifty-nine, and he was elected to the Party's Standing Committee. Trained as an engineer in the Soviet Union, Li Peng was a technocrat who had worked on power projects and was believed to favor central planning. Most people I knew, Americans and Chinese, were suspicious of him. His promotion was a sign that the elderly Maoist ideologues still wielded influence behind the scenes.

The day I arrived in Beijing, Li Peng was named acting premier, and it was understood that he would be officially confirmed as premier at the government's National People's Congress the following spring. As premier, Li Peng was head of the government, while Zhao was head of the Party, although in fact both were high-ranking Party officials. Deng's power remained paramount, but Zhao and Li Peng were expected to succeed him.

The biggest concern of the moment was inflation. After five years of wage increases and plentiful goods, consumer expectations had risen so high that China's factories could not keep up. Excessive demand was pushing up prices, especially for food. Beijing had even started to issue ration coupons for pork and sugar. To ensure stability, Li Peng was pushing for austerity and price controls. I visited my friend the economist Li Yining at his home, a tiny apartment near Beijing University. He seemed concerned. "The biggest disaster would be to reverse direction and try to use the old, planned system to replace the reform measures."

Li Peng's promotion seemed to be a sop to the ideologues. Most of us journalists described a power struggle between the "reformers," led by Deng and Zhao, and the "conservatives," led by Chen Yun and other elders, with Li Peng as their surrogate.

But in retrospect, a better way to describe Deng's dilemma would be as one between stability and prosperity.

When Deng signed the agreement with Britain about Hong Kong's future, the two things he promised to maintain were its "stability and prosperity." Clearly, he wanted China to modernize quickly, to raise living standards. But he also wanted stability. In the twentieth century, China had lived through terrible periods of war, infighting, and chaos. Now that the country was unified under the Communist Party, its leaders were able to focus on economic growth and lifting people out of poverty.

But without stability, all that progress might stop. Signs of instability showed up as discontent bordering on social unrest: among farmers who felt left behind, among city dwellers crippled by inflation, among students eager for Western-style democracy. The reforms were working, but expectations were rising, too.

Deng himself was balancing competing interests, trying to keep this high-wire act going. Sometimes, maintaining stability required taking a few steps back from the full-on rush toward prosperity. In Chinese, the word for "dilemma" literally means "advance or retreat, two tough choices." That's how it seemed for old Mr. Deng. But sometimes a dilemma requires not a choice but a better balance of two necessary goals.

After the Party congress, his calculus seemed to be working. Economic growth accelerated to 9.4 percent in 1987, far faster than predicted. Industrial output grew even more quickly. Although inflation was a problem, especially in the cities, China's economy was robust, and after the uncertainties of previous years, China seemed to be on a fast track at last. I hoped that Deng had found the right balance: fast growth and reforms, tempered by a dose of caution.

My dilemma, too, was not a choice between career and family. It was about how to find a way forward that would balance the two. I wanted to avoid that bit about "taking a few steps back."

CHAPTER TWENTY-SEVEN:

Contrasts and Contradictions

☙☙☙☙

矛盾, máodùn: contradiction. The characters are "spear" and "shield"—meaning opposite, one against the other, two tools used for opposite purposes.

BusinessWeek's editor-in-chief, Steve Shepard, was eager to visit China. It took three years for him to get to it, while he consolidated his leadership and set a new direction for the magazine, but he finally gave me the go-ahead to plan a trip for him in April 1988. China's turnabout was big news in the States, where the Middle Kingdom had long evoked strong passions.

My dream goal was to arrange for him to have a face-to-face interview with Deng Xiaoping. This would be my chance to meet my personal hero, the old man who was changing China profoundly. If not Deng, then maybe his chosen successor, Zhao Ziyang.

It seemed possible. After all, Steve Shepard headed the most important business magazine in the United States, China's major trading partner. Knowing that "connections" (*guanxi*) are the best way to reach top officials in China, Paul began to work his contacts in Beijing. He knew a woman whose brother-in-law was one of Zhao Ziyang's personal secretaries.

Zhao was busy running the largest nation on Earth and meeting leaders of foreign countries. But this woman was able to line us up the next best thing: an interview with Vice Premier Tian Jiyun. He was Zhao Ziyang's second-in-command, in charge of the country's finance, foreign investment, trade, and economic reform.

The morning of our interview, a cool spring day with a light breeze, Steve Shepard and I took a taxi to a side entrance to the truly forbidden part of the Forbidden City: Zhongnanhai. This was the walled compound where China's top leaders lived and worked, the sanctum sanctorum, as inside China as you could get. Security was tight. Our contact met us at the gate, and we had to show our US passports and hand over our bags for inspection. This complex, I told Steve, had once been part of the emperor's palace; it contained two lakes and what was once a vast private garden for the emperor. Mao Zedong had lived and ruled there.

As we walked across a spacious courtyard, we didn't see much of a garden, but we caught a glimpse of a lake lined with willow trees. Our formal state interview was in an imposing palace-style building called the Pavilion of Purple Radiance. Walking up the marble steps to the grand hall with its red columns and curved tiled eaves made us feel like we were having an audience with the emperor—or one of his high officials. That was the point, of course.

After a short wait, we were ushered inside the pavilion, set up like a typical Chinese room for receiving guests, armchairs in a semicircle, with two larger chairs at the center. The vice premier was standing in front of one of the center chairs, and an official ushered Steve over to greet him with a handshake. Per protocol, I followed behind, as a lower official representing *BusinessWeek*. A thin and dignified man in his late fifties, Tian Jiyun wore a business suit with tie and spoke in a quiet but firm voice. Unlike many Chinese leaders, who were stiff and colorless, he had a warm smile.

Steve sat in the armchair next to the vice premier, and I sat next to Steve. On a glass-topped table between us were two lidded cups of fine tea. An official interpreter sat between Steve and Tian Jiyun. They treated Steve like a head of state. It felt surreal. I had arrived.

Steve handled the meeting with gravitas, using a list of questions I had prepared. Tian Jiyun, I had explained to Steve, was a member of the Politburo, an elite group of twenty-five men who controlled the Communist Party. He was a key mover behind the economic reforms.

Tian's answers were not news-breaking, but he did explain Party policy clearly. Steve decided to run a full-page question-and-answer with excerpts from the interview. During Steve's visit to Beijing, we also met Gu Mu, another top official in charge of economic management.

To me, these meetings were the pinnacle of Steve's trip. I had pulled every string I could to get them. But what Steve remembered most was the visit to the Beijing Jeep factory, the most well-known American joint-venture investment in China. Steve was appalled at how backward, dirty, and inefficient the factory was. It produced only 110 cars per day, and only fifteen of them were Jeep Cherokees. "The primitive assembly line moves at a snail's pace, parts lie around everywhere, and the air is foul with smoke from welders' guns. By comparison, Henry Ford's Model T plants were paragons of automation and efficiency," Steve wrote in our three-page article, "Can This Really Be China?" I had visited many Chinese factories, so it didn't look backward to me. Then again, I had never visited an American car plant, so I had no vision of clean, efficient, robotized production lines. As always, views of China are a matter of perspective.

Overall, though, Steve was amazed at how quickly China was modernizing. He was impressed with the fashionable display windows and crowded department stores in Shanghai and the many high-rise buildings under construction in Beijing, as well as the crowds jostling to buy blue jeans and sneakers in private shops. And he commented on the growing disparity in wealth between private entrepreneurs, traders, and drivers, who "easily earn more than $3,000 a year," and the forty million peasants still living in dire poverty, earning less than $44 a year. "It will take a long stretch of rapid growth to raise per capita

With Steve Shepard & Lynn Povich, 1988

income to anything approaching the levels of Asia's more advanced developing countries," he wrote.

In the article Steve and I coauthored, we declared that China's reforms seemed irreversible. "It's a slow and difficult process. But . . . there is no turning back."

After our interviews, we had time to see the sights. Steve and his wife, Lynn Povich, were amused by the red-star caps in the style of the People's Liberation Army soldiers. We took a photo together at the Ming Tombs, each of us wearing a red-star PLA cap. It was very American to view Mao memorabilia as charming kitsch.

I enjoyed their company, although I was always conscious that Steve was the Big Boss. As we sat together on the plane back to Hong Kong, he brought up the subject of my future.

"I envy you," he began. "You know, they say journalism is the first draft of history. And you are here, on the ground, covering one of the most amazing stories in the world."

I grinned. After one week inside China, he got it. "You wouldn't believe how backward it was when I got here in 1982," I added. "It's like black-and-white turned into Technicolor."

He nodded appreciatively. "Still, that car factory! China will never catch up to Japan."

"Don't be so sure. One thing I've learned in my years here: don't underestimate China."

He smiled and shook his head in doubt. "Well, anyway, you've been here six years now. Have you thought about what you'd like to do next?"

I attempted to collect my scattered thoughts. "I'm very happy in Hong Kong."

"And we're happy with you here. I didn't realize how fluent you are in Chinese."

I absorbed the praise. The harsh voice in my head often nagged me about stories I had missed, press conferences I had skipped, stacks of magazines I had not read, sources I had failed to reach. But these flaws had flown under the radar. Steve thought I was better than I was.

"You can stay here as long as you want," he continued. "But when you do leave, what would you want to do next?"

Dori's dilemma. I did not want to write about business for the rest of my life, and I had toyed with several ideas: writing a book about China, applying for jobs at the *New York Times* or *Newsweek*. But those were not options I would mention to Steve. "What do you recommend?"

He looked out at the clouds, then back at me. "Well, one of my goals is to promote women like you. That would mean moving back to New York. I can't promise anything, but does that sound appealing?"

It didn't. I had never adjusted to life in New York, and I didn't like editing. I wanted to return to the US someday but couldn't envision raising my baby in a city without grassy yards. But it was heady to be asked. "Maybe."

"You know, *BusinessWeek* has never had a female managing editor or editor-in-chief. I'd like to train some women who might one day be in line to take over the magazine."

Whoa. Editor-in-chief of *BusinessWeek*? Ambitious as I was, this possibility had never crossed my mind. "That's a little hard to imagine," I said, a bit lamely.

He laughed. "Don't hold your breath! I'm only forty-eight, and I plan to stick around for a long time. But I'd love to have you come back to New York and see if you'd like it."

"Thanks. I appreciate it."

"Just let me know. You'll know when you're ready to leave."

Afterward, I felt guilty. Now that I had a husband and a baby, did that prevent me from considering a promotion within the magazine? Why had my mind immediately gone to an image of Emily growing up in a concrete jungle? Did I owe it to the younger women coming up behind me to break barriers, especially in the male-dominated field of business journalism? It felt selfish to put family first, yet that's where my mind went. Maybe it wasn't selfish. Maybe I was ready to end the roller coaster ride. But not behind a desk in New York.

The rest of that year zipped by, with more travel, interviews, visits from friends, and another trip back home. My blue three-ring binder of clippings got fatter as I added articles I wrote. My travel schedule continued to be busy, with trips to Singapore, Taipei, and Beijing, but more of my life revolved around family. My appointment calendar filled up with personal lunch dates with girlfriends, including new friends I met because they had babies the same age as Emily. Over those meals, we compared notes.

I was always on the lookout for women who balanced career and motherhood. One friend was a Korean executive with two young sons. Another was a Malaysian Chinese banker with a baby boy the same age as Emily. We were all trying to figure it out. One would later drop out of the workforce, and the other would become CEO of Standard Chartered Bank (Hong Kong) Ltd.

Naturally, I focused much of my time and attention on Emily. She had a sweet and friendly nature but also showed signs of a strong will. Once, on Anita's day off, Paul and I both went out to the back balcony, where the washer and dryer were. Little Emily turned the key in the lock so that we couldn't get back in. She smiled at us through the glass door. Paul and I were appalled. Of course we didn't have a key with us.

"Ming-Ming, sweetheart, turn the key," I kept repeating, making a turning motion with my hand. At first, she didn't seem to understand. Finally, with a grin, she reached out and obliged so we could open the door. With kids, you sometimes lose the key to your own life.

On weekends, we took her to the playground, which, though crowded, was her only opportunity to play outdoors. These city kids had to stand in line to use the slide and swing sets. As I pushed her on the swings, I imagined a day when we would have our own sunny backyard.

That year, Maria left Hong Kong for *BusinessWeek*'s San Francisco bureau, and I hired Dinah Lee to replace her. Dinah had already become a good friend of mine. She spoke Mandarin and had years of experience in journalism in London and Singapore with the BBC and *The Economist*. Despite her Chinese-sounding name, Dinah was a tall blonde from Southern California. A Berkeley graduate with an East Asian studies degree, she was fearless and outspoken—my opposite in many ways—yet I admired her enormously.

Though a few years older, Dinah was not bothered by the fact that she would report to me. She was career-oriented, too, but sparkling

Emily meets her grandparents in Taiwan

Emily in Hong Kong 1988

and sociable, a great cook and hostess. She disproved my excuse for poor cooking, showing that it was, in fact, possible to do it all. It was a joy to work with her. She was the third journalist I had supervised, all of them women, and I had learned to be a good boss, supportive and collaborative. It bothers me when others claim that women are bad at managing other women.

My role as stepmom to teenagers was starting to feel more comfortable, too. Steve graduated from high school and returned to the States, where he had been accepted into college. Wenni visited twice a year.

Though satisfied with my personal life, I began to increasingly question the trade-offs with career. In June 1988, I had an amazing opportunity: a rare chance to report from inside Vietnam. I had applied six times in three years before getting a visa. Vietnam had been experimenting with *doi moi*, its own version of Deng Xiaoping's economic reforms. This visit would allow me to see what economic reform looked like in a different Communist country.

I reported in both the capital, Hanoi, where Communism was entrenched, and Ho Chi Minh City, formerly Saigon, which became Communist only after American troops left in 1975. What struck me most about Vietnam in 1988 was the contrast between hopelessness and hope. Its economy was a mess. Most of its people were poor, many of them starving. It was bogged down in an unwinnable war in Cambodia. Most Western nations still had a trade embargo.

Yet the view from the inside was one of possibility. People I met dared to criticize government policies. In Saigon, street markets bustled with electric fans, cassette tapes, TVs, and imported foods. As in China, Vietnam's entrepreneurial spirit was busting out, and new businesses were cropping up. I interviewed people who were making perfume, repairing motorbikes, and importing used cars to rent to foreign tourists. Vietnam's policy of *doi moi* promised to change the face of socialism less than fifteen years after the Communist victory. Deng's ideas were spreading.

Yet one night at nine o'clock in an outdated hotel room in Hanoi, I sat staring at my hands. Ming-Ming could walk now and liked to bring me books to read. She could say a few words and liked to play pat-a-cake. She lavished sloppy kisses on Anita and me equally. Tonight I was alone, and Paul would be putting her to bed. I was in Vietnam, covering a great story—and had even discovered a Hanoi restaurant with rich French flavors. But my values had shifted.

On the surface, my life was going well. I did have it all: an enviable career, a loving marriage, and a darling child. But this night, far away from all that mattered most, I felt discontent bubbling up. I wondered if my job was no longer right for me. I frequently found myself procrastinating: not planning trips, not keeping up with the news, delaying a deadline. More and more, the idea of leaving my family felt intolerable. Yet travel was essential for my work. Maybe resolving Dori's dilemma would mean a different sort of role.

Maria had told me her job in San Francisco was much more nine to five, with more phone interviews and fewer in-person interviews, greater ease of getting articles into the magazine, and a lot of office talk about weekend recreation. That sounded like heaven. I was tempted to call Steve Shepard and tell him to consider me for any reporting job on the East or West Coast.

Although Paul was pleased to hear I was willing to consider moving back to the States, he wasn't quite ready yet. He was hitting his stride in his job, now that Ernst & Young had taken over. The more China opened up, the more opportunities existed for him. But he loved living in America and had been talking for years about how we could engineer a reentry.

My contradiction: I was increasingly unsettled with the demands of my job but happy in my personal life. I loved living in Hong Kong and didn't want to leave, yet I daydreamed of moving back to the States. But I wasn't sure what kind of work I might enjoy doing there. What kind of act could follow that of foreign correspondent in China?

In December 1988, Paul and I traveled back to the States again, taking Emily to see my family in Youngstown and her siblings in Portland. Unlike on previous trips, we flew back to Hong Kong through Seattle, where Paul had friends, and we stayed for a few days. Paul loved the Pacific Northwest, and he hoped I would agree to move there someday. I was skeptical.

I had been invited to speak at a luncheon of the Washington State China Relations Council, to present my observations about how China was changing. With little experience in public speaking, I was nervous, but it went well. Many in the audience knew a lot about China and asked great questions. Seattle felt like a very Asia-oriented city, with a lot of international trade. Rainy winter days, it seemed, were conducive to reading—and perhaps to writing as well. Within a three-hour drive, you could explore ancient forests, majestic mountains, deserts, seaside, and lakes. Seattle seemed to have the advantages of a big city without the grime and crime I had disliked in New York. I could imagine it as an ideal American environment in which to raise my child.

Paul wanted to live on the West Coast because his older two kids lived there. Steve had just started college at the University of Oregon, in Eugene. Wenni had her heart set on studying television and film at the University of Southern California. For me, the West Coast meant limited horizons. Seattle was appealing, but moving there would mean stepping off the fast track in journalism and doing something else. I wasn't sure I was ready for that.

Still, on the plane ride home, I began to consider alternatives. Maybe I could freelance or work for a local newspaper. Or apply to grad school in economics.

What appealed to me most, though, was writing books. Ever since childhood, I had wanted to become an author. I had gone into journalism only when I realized that I couldn't make a living writing books. While I loved reporting and had achieved far more than I ever expected in it, Steve Shepard's vision of my climbing the ladder to become a managing editor did not tempt me. That had never been my ambition. But many journalists also wrote books.

A book idea came to me quickly: China's new entrepreneurs. Ever since my first reporting trip, they had captured my imagination. The woman who sold glasses on the street. The guy who grew trees. The button seller. The car-repair guy. Most recently, in December I had written a profile of a bright young man in Beijing,

Wan Runnan. He had founded a computer-and-software company, Beijing Stone Group, with two thousand employees and annual sales of $135 million. His story would have been impossible even to imagine back in 1982, when I had arrived. These folks inspired me because they were taking a chance. They personified the big risk Deng Xiaoping was taking to change China.

When I returned to Hong Kong, I set to work on this new dream. I went to the US consulate and researched book publishing. In early 1989, I sent a book query to twenty agents and ten publishers. I wrote the letters cold, with no one to introduce me. But I had credentials: almost seven years covering China for *BusinessWeek* during a pivotal time in its history.

Paul liked my book idea, too. After making that fateful decision in 1984 to stay in Asia—and especially after moving to Hong Kong to learn the China trade—he had found his inner businessman. He seemed to have the knack. He still relied on a salary, but he began to dream of starting his own company. Someday—when he didn't have three kids to support, with college tuition bills coming due.

We weren't ready to "jump into the sea" yet. But the seed had been planted.

🕸🕸🕸

One morning in March 1989, I was sitting at my desk, fussing over an edited version of a story that annoyed me. Dinah came into the office, glowing with happy news: she and her husband, Peter, were expecting a child.

I jumped up and gave her a hug. She was trembling with joy. We had a long talk, sharing details and dreams more like close friends than work colleagues.

Not until that evening did I realize the consequences for myself. Dinah's baby was due in October 1989. She planned to take a maternity leave until December. Since we were a tiny, two-person bureau, that meant I could not leave Hong Kong until 1990 at the earliest. I would have to put my Seattle hopes on hold. But maybe that would give me time I needed.

CHAPTER TWENTY-EIGHT:

Simmering Discontent

⚛⚛⚛⚛

让一部分人先富起来, *ràng yībùfèn rén xiān fù qǐlái:*
"Let some people get rich first," a well-known saying by
Deng Xiaoping.

The year 1989 would be pivotal in world history, and in my life, but of course I didn't know that.

For Paul and me, the year began with promise. As the country became more open, he was putting together deals and I was finding it easier to set up interviews and get people to talk to me as a reporter. His business, China trade consulting, was growing fast, attracting companies from many countries. And I was covering one of the most amazing stories in the world: the transformation of a rigid, impoverished country into a vibrant, flourishing one.

Still, we noticed signs of simmering discontent. Everywhere Paul or I traveled in China, expectations had risen. Deng Xiaoping said it was okay for some people to get rich first. But those who didn't get rich got jealous. People who lived in or near cities in the coastal regions had an advantage. They were close to ports or big markets. But people who lived in the interior or in remote rural areas could not take advantage of the boom in foreign exports or domestic demand. They thought it unfair. Paul caught whiffs of this in Luoyang and Qiqihar.

These inland regions were falling further behind. Poverty was acceptable when it was shared, but some people seethed when they saw others buying TVs and fridges, cassette players and cashmere sweaters they couldn't afford. Now that the market, not the state, was setting prices, everything was more expensive. Those who worked for the state, on fixed incomes, could not afford higher prices. And some were being laid off in the name of economic efficiency.

The growing gap between rich and poor contradicted the egalitarian socialist values the Communist Party had taught for decades. The stories I had written in the mid-1980s—how China was advancing two steps forward, one step back—were increasingly replaced by reports about how the runaway pace of reforms was sparking frustration and threatening disruption.

The most obvious—yet elusive—of these discontents swirled around China's political system. Ever since Deng had first announced the Four Modernizations, in 1978, a few dissident voices had called for a "fifth modernization": democracy. A few Chinese villages were experimenting with direct election of local leaders.

But the Party was not about to permit opposition parties or direct challenges to its authority. Those who suggested it should, notably the astrophysicist Fang Lizhi, had been shut up. As I discovered in Wenzhou, most ordinary people did not care about direct elections and human rights. But some college professors and students, inspired by America, Europe, and Japan, began to talk vaguely of "democracy," without defining what it meant.

China's Party newspapers were clear. The Party favored "economic reforms" but had stopped any discussion of "political reforms." After the Fang Lizhi expulsion in January 1987, it was clear that most top leaders strongly opposed any move toward Western-style democracy. Still, many Americans assumed that economic freedom would lead to demands for political freedom.

To many observers, it seemed inevitable. As night follows day. After all, both South Korea and Taiwan, once autocratic states, had adopted multiparty elections in the 1980s, at the urging of the United States. True, those experiences were rocky, with violent street protests and fistfights in the legislature. Japan had successfully made the transition to a functional democracy, and now Korea and Taiwan were on their way. Someday, surely, China would follow the pattern. The Asian examples seemed to prove that the prerequisites were a growing economy, an expanding middle class, and widespread education. In a country of more than one billion people, this would take time. But with three thousand years of recorded history, China could be patient.

As always, I was optimistic—about China's future and my own. But tensions were rumbling under the surface, and I underestimated them. So, I believe, did Deng.

As reporter colleagues, Dinah and I had long talks about discontent in China, especially the growing gap between rich and poor. We began to plan for a cover story on the topic, debating the right approach and sketching out where we might travel for reporting.

In the spring of 1989, Dinah and I pitched a theme we called "the two Chinas." New China was coastal and entrepreneurial, able to get rich by taking advantage of economic reforms and trade with foreign countries. Old China was inland and dependent on agriculture or state-run factories and more vulnerable to high prices and job losses. While Deng's reforms had benefited millions of ordinary Chinese people, many others were being left behind. We saw the flashpoints in China as inflation, retrenchment, and resentment.

Our editors gave us the go-ahead. Dinah planned a reporting trip to Beijing. Hoping to get more fodder for my book, I chose to travel to areas of the South that had benefited greatly from the reforms. Clearly, though, we needed to get away from the coast and deep into the heart of the country to reach people left behind in the Old China. But how? Obviously, we did not expect our government minders to help us set up interviews with discontented people.

I decided to take the train to Hunan in May to test the pulse of the people in that poor inland province. To see beyond the official line, I knew I would have to reach out for "man on the street" interviews and keep my eyes and ears open. I decided to include a trip to Mao Zedong's hometown, Shaoshan, to reach people still attached to old-style Communist values.

Just as we were booking our travel, lightning struck. On Saturday, April 15, Hu Yaobang, the former general secretary of the Communist Party, died of a heart attack. He had already fallen from power. To me, he was a has-been, sidelined and semiretired, and his death at age seventy-three didn't mean much.

But students in Beijing didn't see it that way. The day after he died, some college students gathered in the streets. Big-character posters on campuses mourned his death, declared Hu had been misjudged, and demanded his legacy be reassessed. The next day, more posters appeared, calling for freedom of the press and an end to corruption and nepotism.

I was taken aback, as were Paul, Dinah, and my other China-watcher friends. So were China's leaders, it seemed. These protests were a rare in-your-face challenge of high-level decisions by the Communist Party.

We had seen student demonstrations before. The previous time, in December 1986, Deng and his cronies had sacked Hu Yaobang because he refused to crack down on the protestors. Back then, we at *BusinessWeek* had predicted a reversal of economic reforms and a lost opportunity for modernization, but that had not happened. After a slight retrenchment, Deng Xiaoping's bold free-market reforms had regained momentum. These 1989 protests seemed like yet another growing pain, which we could mention briefly in our cover story. Nothing more.

So Dinah and I did not alter our plans. I arranged two days of reporting in rapidly modernizing Shenzhen and three days in Guangzhou in late April, and after that Dinah would go to Beijing for two weeks. When she got back, I would go to Hunan, starting May 10.

Soviet leader Mikhail Gorbachev would be arriving in Beijing on May 15, 1989. We knew this would be a watershed moment, marking the reconciliation of China and the Soviet Union after a hiatus of thirty years. But we, like many journalists, assumed his visit would be uneventful, with a lot of official ceremonies and predictable speeches. Student protests and state visits were political news, not business news, and the dailies would cover them. As a weekly, we would focus on ongoing, underlying trends, things that mattered more in the long term.

But this time, the students didn't quiet down. *People's Daily* seemed to respond to their demands when it praised Hu Yaobang as a "loyal Communist fighter" and announced a state funeral on April 22. China-watcher pundits assumed this would satisfy the protestors. Most students went back to class, but on Tuesday, the day I left for Shenzhen, two thousand students marched to Tiananmen Square, chanting slogans, and hung a banner next to wreaths honoring Hu at the Monument to the People's Heroes. One young man shouted out a list of demands, calling for a reevaluation of Hu's legacy, a crackdown on corruption, and freedom of speech. Students resisted police efforts to disperse the crowd. Early the next morning, the remaining protestors staged a sit-in before the main gate to Zhongnanhai, headquarters of the Communist Party. A provocative challenge.

I immediately thought of People Power in the Philippines, the peaceful street demonstrations that had overthrown Marcos. Could that happen in China? It seemed unlikely. The Communist Party claimed to represent the masses but had never shared power. Still, these students did not demand an overturn of the Party or Western-style democracy with multiparty, direct elections. They asked to be heard.

The student demonstrations in Beijing died down but then grew exponentially that next weekend. On the day of Hu Yaobang's funeral, April 22, more than one hundred thousand students gathered in Tiananmen Square. They listened on loudspeakers to an emotional eulogy by General Secretary Zhao Ziyang, who had been Hu's close partner in promoting reforms. Many students wept. After the funeral, three students knelt on the steps of the Great Hall of the People and symbolically presented a seven-point petition to the government. They asked to see Premier Li Peng, but he did not show. Something big was going on, and no one knew quite what. The

Beijing protests were peaceful, but rioting was reported in two other cities, Changsha and Xi'an.

Mesmerized by these amazing events, I went ahead with my plans to travel to Guangzhou the following week. That's where I was—interviewing an entrepreneur amid the pounding and whirring of a welding machine shop—when the next shoe dropped. On April 26, a front-page editorial in *People's Daily* condemned the student protestors, saying they were unpatriotic and "anti-Party"—meaning they were conspiring to overthrow the government. "It is necessary to take a clear-cut stand against disturbances." This seemed ridiculously overstated, since the students were clearly just pushing for greater freedom and accountability.

The hard line backfired. The next day, more than fifty thousand students marched to Tiananmen Square again, calling for the retraction of the *People's Daily* editorial. This time, they had the sympathy and support of many Beijing residents. Dinah arrived in Beijing in time to catch the tail end of that massive march, which attracted not just students but hospital workers and workers' unions. She had lined up a series of interviews and could report on the significance of what was going on in the streets. One of her Chinese interviewees hinted that his own son was demonstrating outside.

Discontent continued festering but went below the surface for a while; no more protests occurred in Beijing the following weekend. I lined up a full three days of interviews in Hunan for May 10–12, including a long overnight train ride from Guangzhou to Changsha, hoping I could talk to ordinary people on the train and get them to open up.

On May 3 and 4, Zhao Ziyang, who had been out of the country when that controversial *People's Daily* editorial had been published, gave two speeches. He didn't denounce the editorial, but he also didn't criticize the protestors. He seemed to be trying to take a balanced approach to please everyone. About one hundred thousand students marched to commemorate the anniversary of the May Fourth Movement, but afterward student leaders announced that they would end their class boycott. I felt reassured. Most Chinese I knew respected Zhao Ziyang. Surely he could talk reason with the hard-liners in the leadership.

On May 10, Dinah returned from Beijing and I left for Hunan. Dinah had planned a romantic getaway vacation with Peter, starting May 17, so we knew we would have only a few days to work together on our cover story. I called my editors in New York, and we decided to recraft the theme as "China in crisis." That topic was broad enough to include our original story line on inequalities, as well as the student protests, which were getting a lot of television coverage in the United States.

My trip to Hunan proved to be poorly timed—but it was an eye-opener. From May 10 to 13, I documented the "other China"—the people who felt left behind. I visited a state-owned computer factory that perfectly illustrated our two-Chinas point: although it had imported expensive equipment in a high-priority industry, most of it sat idle as the factory awaited a promised $2.7 million cash infusion from Beijing. What a huge contrast to the go-go entrepreneurs of Guangdong, who found private-sector funding to fuel their rapid growth. The resentment was obvious. "It's not fair that Guangdong gets special privileges; they already have better conditions for trade," complained one Hunan official. "Guangdong is like the pampered son, and Shenzhen is like the pampered grandson."

On the long train ride to Changsha, I got an earful from other passengers. A young Hunanese woman, dressed in a silky flowered pantsuit, told me she had moved to Shenzhen three years earlier, full of enthusiasm. Now, cynicism had set in. All her city friends were feverishly saving money and studying English, hoping to emigrate.

Across from her, a young military man in a running suit told me China had been full of hope in 1984, when silos overflowed with grain. Now, he said, "power buys money and money buys power. The reforms have hit a dead end and can't go ahead unless there are political reforms." Not what I expected from a soldier.

A young train attendant weighed in with his view: "The whole political system needs to change. We need to overthrow the Communist Party."

Wide-eyed, I listened, astonished by their frankness, dispirited by their pessimism. As a business reporter, I had not heard such comments before. Had these concerns just popped up? Or had I been covering the wrong story, asking the wrong questions, talking to the wrong people?

"The students are still full of hope," explained the young woman. "Those of us who are working already know that society can't be changed."

Another woman piped up: "But I think Deng's policies have been very good."

"Yes," replied the soldier. "But they haven't been implemented right. Deng is an old man, and his thinking is no longer clear. Only when he dies will there be real change in China."

For the first time in the seven years I had been covering China, ordinary people felt empowered to speak their minds to me on highly sensitive subjects and tell me bluntly what they thought of their leaders. No one held back. I scribbled down every word.

Here I was, deep inside China, far from my handlers, and ordinary people opened their hearts to me.. Something remarkable was happening in China, and it wasn't confined to Tiananmen Square.

CHAPTER TWENTY-NINE:

China Erupts

ဢၜၜၜ

民主万岁, mínzhǔ wànsuì: long live democracy. The Chinese term "minzhu" means, literally, "the people as masters." In China, it has historically meant increased participation in government by the people—not necessarily multiparty elections or individual rights.

Two days later, when I returned to Hong Kong with my bulging notebooks, most of my reporting was irrelevant. By then, more significant events had overtaken my "two Chinas" story idea.

On May 13, 1989, just two days before Gorbachev was to arrive, the students began a hunger strike in Tiananmen Square. That evening, when I arrived home in Hong Kong after my Hunan trip, I watched the news and saw masses of young Chinese protestors covering the square. Reporters estimated the crowd to be more than three hundred thousand people.

I called Bob Dowling, the senior editor in New York who coordinated international coverage. Should I go to Beijing? When? He advised me to stay in Hong Kong, working with Dinah to get my cover done as soon as possible. I promised to deliver it within a week.

In the meantime, our Moscow correspondents were also preparing a cover story. Gorbachev was trying to ramp up his own private-sector reforms to jolt his economy out of stagnation while pushing as well for *glasnost*, political openness including multicandidate elections. Although China's economy was doing better, Gorbachev inspired China's protestors, who considered him bolder than Beijing's leaders by advocating political transformation.

As Dinah and I jockeyed with the Moscow reporters for the right to the next cover, hundreds of journalists from all over the world flooded into Beijing to cover Gorbachev's visit.

The ceremony welcoming Gorbachev to Beijing had to be held at the airport, since the students occupied the square. The protestors would not leave. They brought in buses and slept there. Some strikers refused water, as well as food, and they were the first to be rushed to the hospital. I learned that the human body can go for a more than a week without food but cannot last more than a few days without water.

We feverishly finished writing a draft of our two-Chinas story and filed it to New York on Wednesday, May 17. On that day, close to one million Beijing residents joined the students in the streets and the square. Protests sprang up on campuses and in more than four hundred Chinese cities. Multitudes of reporters who had come to cover Gorbachev's visit now had a much bigger story. Viewers around the world were watching live on television, mesmerized by the scene playing out before their eyes. Yet the leadership of China stayed silent. Clearly, they must be meeting behind closed doors. Pundits tried to imagine the debates within the Chinese leadership, but no one knew what they planned to do—or what they could do.

What the heck was I doing in Hong Kong? I flew to Beijing on May 18.

That afternoon, I dropped my suitcase at the hotel and walked to Tiananmen Square. Despite pouring rain, it was filled with protestors; not a single soldier or police officer was in sight. The atmosphere was festive but determined. Trucks packed with workers drew cheers from the crowd as they displayed rain-soaked banners made from sheets, supporting the protestors with messages in red and black. The hunger strikers sat limply in buses.

The next morning, the rain had stopped, but the sky was still cloudy. Standing under the famous portrait of Chairman Mao Zedong on Tiananmen Gate, I tried to estimate the size of the crowd. Thousands, tens of thousands, hundreds of thousands. How could I count?

Many ordinary citizens had come to support the protestors. Everyone was eager to talk—to me, to each other, to anyone who would listen, after years of silence. The hunger strike was continuing, and the students were jubilant, sure their voices were being heard around the world. Parents were anxious; bystanders were apprehensive.

One Chinese mother, tears in her eyes, spoke to my heart: "These are our children! They are starving to death, and no one is doing anything about it. Every mother in Beijing feels the way I do." The woman grabbed my arm—and appealed to my responsibility as a journalist. "Thank you for reporting this news. You must tell the world. These are peaceful protests."

The words of an old man also struck me: "Old Deng doesn't care."

At Tiananmen Square May 1989

Old Deng was no democrat; that was obvious. But no one cared more about China's future. He had defied the old guard and made changes that amazed the world. To me, ten years after seeing him on that Kennedy Center balcony, he seemed familiar and benign, though distant. I admired what he had done, opening China to outside influences and enabling Chinese to take control of their lives. However this protest ended, I felt sure, Old Deng would never allow the army to shoot its own people. That would risk undoing all the good he had done.

The next morning, May 19, I woke up to remarkable news. Just before dawn, Zhao Ziyang had come to the square and spoken to student hunger strikers inside a bus. Using a bullhorn, he had acknowledged their good intentions and begged them to end their hunger strike. Some said he had tears in his eyes. He apologized for coming too late.

I returned to Tiananmen Square and plunged into the sea of tents. The hunger strike did end that day, but more students poured in from all over Beijing, setting up a cluster of tents for each university. The ones I talked to were outraged, certain that Zhao had been sacked, that their leaders did not care about their concerns, that the army was coming.

One student injected a note of caution. "My father is certain it's all over. He wants me to go home."

"But you're not?" I asked.

"Not yet," he said, glancing at a nearby friend, as if hoping to convince him.

"Our voices must be heard!" his friend said, flashing the V-for-victory hand sign.

When people heard that I could speak Chinese, they jostled around me. But this time, they did not quietly wait to hear what other people said, as they had in the early 1980s; instead, their comments gushed forth like water from a burst pipe.

"They just want to scare us. The People's Liberation Army would never hurt us."

"We represent all the people. We can't leave."

"Who has the guns? When people die, tell the world who killed them."

An older man sidled up to me and whispered, "It's not safe for journalists. You'd better go quickly."

The next morning, May 20, the phone rang beside my bed at the familiar Jianguo Hotel. It was my editor, Bob Dowling, calling from New York, worried about my safety, eager to talk over the news. He had heard that martial law was imminent.

Suddenly, a helicopter buzzed directly overhead. I cringed at the loud sound.

"What was that?" Bob shouted.

"A helicopter. It's starting."

"No! Don't go out. Keep your head down!"

"Don't worry," I said, but my voice trembled. I had never feared the sound of a helicopter. The whirring faded as the chopper flew on.

I emerged onto the street, Beijing's main avenue, and joined a river of people flowing away from the square, out of the city center.

"What's happening?" I asked the nearest person.

"The soldiers have come into the city," a man answered. "We are blocking them so they won't get to the square."

Overnight, the army had entered Beijing from many directions, but unarmed citizens had forced them to stop. I followed the crowd to a major overpass at the Third Ring Road. There, a convoy of armored personnel carriers loaded with soldiers stood still, their guns pointing toward the city center. Civilians surrounded each carrier, pressing up against it and telling the soldiers not to go farther.

"It's a peaceful demonstration!" people said. "It's not an armed revolution. Don't believe that!" Women put flowers into the barrels of the soldiers' guns.

"Can you see the faces of those soldiers?" one resident said to me. "They are so young. Eighteen, nineteen years old. They are all country boys. Soldiers from Beijing would never follow orders to occupy the city."

That day, Beijing was in anarchy. Yet it was joyful. Inside the city, there was no functioning government, yet there was also no looting. In the absence of police, citizens stood on platforms and directed traffic.

Every citizen of Beijing, it seemed, supported the student protestors. I didn't hear anyone criticize them. The closest anyone got was one man who said, "It's too late. They should go home now, or they will all be killed."

Despite the army's presence, more people poured into the streets, including many who were not students. Each group marched down Chang'an Avenue in an orderly way, behind a banner declaring their school or work unit. I even saw people marching behind a banner for *People's Daily*—reporters from the Communist Party's propaganda machine, demanding freedom of the press.

Over the next few days, the square got more crowded. Day after day, I went out to the streets. That was the best way to find out what was going on. No one had a cell phone, but the news spread through the crowd mouth to mouth. Rumors continued to fly about what might be going on behind closed doors. Everyone I approached was eager to talk to me, a foreign reporter. Like them, I lost all sense of shyness.

For me, it was a heady experience, a lovely time. It didn't seem possible that these young soldiers would use live ammunition on their fellow citizens. Yet it was hard to imagine what might convince the crowds to disperse. Not for one minute did I feel unsafe. We were in this together.

Using the hotel telex, I managed to close my cover story, which had morphed into a joint Sino-Soviet cover called "Communism in Turmoil." The two-Chinas message was still there, but it got buried in the bigger news of the day. The world as I knew it, split between Western democracies and Communist dictatorships, was cracking under my feet. The Cold War, backdrop to my life so far, was melting away like snow in the springtime. Good outcomes seemed possible.

Paul called me every day, worried sick about my safety. In Hong Kong, he was watching nonstop coverage on CNN and the local English-language channels. When would the army open fire? Were reinforcements coming? The student leaders were openly squabbling with one another. Some called on their fellows to withdraw from the square, but others insisted they stay. Many original protestors went home, replaced by people who came from other parts of China.

On May 24, I heard fresh news: the troops had been ordered to withdraw. On the streets, some people were ecstatic. Others were glum, predicting that the soldiers were just regrouping, preparing their assault. The situation came to a tense standstill.

The protests were losing momentum. Tiananmen Square was a mess, covered with litter and garbage. The government seemed to be waiting for the rest of the students to get tired and go home. It looked like the whole thing might fizzle out.

The struggle for democracy seemed like a lost cause—for now.

The story was not over, but I had a two-year-old baby waiting for me. On May 25, after a week in Beijing, I flew home.

Paul met me at the Hong Kong airport with little Ming-Ming on his shoulders. She opened her arms and shouted, "Mama!" I ran toward them and grabbed them like a starving student after a hunger strike. I didn't want to ever let go.

That weekend, Hong Kong erupted in protest as well. On Sunday, local political leaders led a march from Central down Queen's Road East, right below our windows and in front of my office. Paul and I took Emily down, and we stood on an overpass and watched the crowds march past. They were flashing V-shaped peace signs with their fingers, supporting the students, opposing a military crackdown. We proudly taught Emily to say what the protestors were all shouting: *"Minzhu wansui!"*—"Long live democracy!" Local newspapers reported that more than 1.5 million people marched in Hong Kong that day. That was about one-quarter of the population.

The next day, May 30, students from the Central Academy of Fine Arts erected a Goddess of Democracy statue—reminiscent of the Statue of Liberty—built of foam and papier-mâché over a metal frame in Tiananmen Square. It reinvigorated the Beijing protestors, who vowed to continue their occupation.

Like me, Paul was caught up in the excitement. But it was mixed with a deep sense of unease. After years of being embarrassed at how backward his homeland was, he had cheered as he witnessed China growing into a thriving nation he could be proud of. Now, it was in danger of falling apart. If China sank into disarray, it would be dev-astating for him. But if China's leaders could somehow respond to student demands and open even faster . . . That sounded promising. Yet it seemed unlikely, now that Zhao had been deposed. It was hard to be hopeful.

On Saturday, June 3, Paul and I went to a wedding. It was surreal: a joyful event, planned long in advance, celebrated during a time of turmoil.

That night, in the middle of the night, my phone rang. It was Bob Dowling. "They're shooting in Beijing. You need to get on a plane and go."

I had been expecting the news, but I was still shocked. "But we're a business magazine. This is not a business story." That's what I had been telling Paul. After all, I was a wife and mother.

"Do you want me to call Dinah instead?"

That got my competitive juices flowing. "No! No! I'll go."

Paul was appalled. Flying into Beijing when everyone in their right mind was leaving? Yet I had to go.

We turned on the television and watched the coverage. Most of it was voices over blackness. There were no TV cameras in Tian-anmen Square that night. TV reporters were calling in from their mobile phones. We could hear gunshots in the background. My heart pounded. I hadn't signed up to cover military assaults.

When the sky grew light, we put our sleepy toddler in the car seat and Paul drove me to the airport. He waited to see if I would be able to get on a flight. Surprisingly, flights to Beijing had not been canceled. Not surprisingly, there were plenty of empty seats. I stood in line behind a camera crew from ABC News. Reluctant to leave, I hugged my husband and kissed my little girl and headed off. Toward what, I wasn't sure.

The plane, almost empty, sizzled with tension. It was a CAAC flight, the airline owned by the Chinese government. All the flight attendants were Chinese citizens, but all had been watching the news in Hong Kong, which had press freedom under British rule.

When we got close to Beijing, the pilot announced that he was diverting to Tianjin, a nearby city, because he was not certain about the situation in the capital. I had heard reports of differences between army divisions. Had a civil war begun? I had no way of knowing.

As soon as we landed in Tianjin, the plane's movie screen crackled to life, showing national TV coverage. The passengers got to hear the same news as the crew. It was the evening news, as reported in China, in Mandarin, of course. I listened carefully to every word, but I figured I must have missed something.

"Excuse me," I asked a flight attendant after it ended. "He said that fifteen soldiers were killed. How many citizens were killed?"

She flashed me a look of grim understanding. "Of course he didn't say. The soldiers had all the guns. Which side had more killed?"

❧❧❧

It was near dark when my plane landed in Beijing. I had no trouble getting a taxi to the Great Wall Sheraton Hotel. The roads were blocked to other hotels closer to the square. Most international reporters were working out of the Sheraton, a little farther from the turmoil.

Finding the other journalists at the hotel was easy. Many were gathered in a big room, watching CNN and talking to one another. Occasionally, someone would get news from another journalist over the phone and share it with us. We had so little solid news that any sense of competition was gone. We all just wanted to know the truth. I took notes on everything I heard and talked to everyone I saw. But most were other journalists. Oddly, I ran into one of my old friends, from that group of young Chinese graduates I had met in 1986. The rest had moved to the United States to study, as they had hoped. He was back in Beijing, assisting a foreign reporter.

The only useful reporting was being done in the city's hospitals, where reporters tried to get an accurate count of the dead and injured. We heard rumors that some bodies had been burned in a bonfire in the square. Some of the injured were afraid to go to a hospital. It was hard to know which figures to trust, as different numbers were released at different times. The hospitals were more concerned with treating the injured than with responding to our queries.

My heart twisted as the horror permeated my bones and tissues. These were my children, too, or my nieces and nephews. Many of those killed were not even protestors but ordinary people of Beijing who dared to come out of their safe homes to stop the army and protect the students. They were no different from the ordinary people I had spoken to over these years of optimism, now turned to despair.

The next morning, I was ready to go out and see for myself. Naturally, most taxi drivers were afraid to drive around the city, especially with a foreign journalist.

Somehow, I found a bold driver who was willing to take me around, for a hefty fee. He had what the Chinese call a "bread car"—a minivan shaped like a loaf of bread. His minivan was not marked as a taxi. Driver Wang told me to sit in the backseat, where the windows were tinted.

"If I see a soldier, I will tell you," he said. "You put your head down." I gripped my reporter's notebook and sat stiffly out of sight.

First, he drove west as far as he could on the main avenue, toward Tiananmen Square. This thoroughfare, Jianguomenwai, which I had traveled dozens of times, now looked like a war zone. The metal barriers that had once separated the bicycle lane from the car lanes were twisted and displaced. Citizens had used them to try to stop the army. Burned-out buses and military vehicles loomed like dead hulks.

It felt eerie to see such a place, once as familiar to me as my hometown, covered with the wreckage of war. Imagine Times Square devoid of people, with bullet holes in the buildings around it. Imagine Pennsylvania Avenue littered with burned-out tanks. I had loved this city like an old uncle. Now it was on its knees, clutching its chest.

When he reached the roadblocks, Driver Wang headed south, taking small streets. In the southern part of the city were signs of a pitched battle: bullet marks on the buildings. None of the news outlets had talked about this part of town.

I wanted to see Tiananmen Square, but a row of tanks blocked it off. The closest the driver could get was from the west. Near the western entrance to the square, three soldiers stopped the minivan and I ducked as low as I could. My insides clenched like an iron fist, but I willed myself to melt into a small, soft ball, like a pile of clothing on the floor. My driver was telling some sort of lie; I had put him in danger. He managed to convince them to let us drive by the roadblock.

Finally we got to where we could see the square. But the square itself was inaccessible, protected by a row of armored personnel carriers in defensive positions, with their guns pointing out toward me. I poked my head up to see the tanks. It was on this western part of the avenue, I knew from the news coverage, that most of the killings had taken place. Here, ordinary citizens, local residents, resisted, throwing bricks and rocks at the troops, who gunned them down. It chilled me to be on the site of this massacre.

Driver Wang then turned north, away from the square, toward the university district. The army had not yet occupied the campuses of Beijing University and adjacent Qinghua University. Huge banners still hung across their main gates, denouncing the bloodshed. No soldiers were visible here, but few civilians or students were, either. With a pang, I thought of Professor Li Yining, of the students I had talked to on the square, of the many well-intentioned people I had interviewed over the years. Their dreams for an open, modern China had been shot dead.

After this, the driver took me back to the hotel, completing a circle around the city center. I paid him well for his daring. I had seen all that I could. Most of the troops had withdrawn and the killing was over. Mostly.

My phone rang the minute I returned to my hotel room. Paul was frantic. He had heard on TV that a sniper had sprayed bullets on the main diplomatic compound on Jianguomenwai, where foreigners lived. I had driven by there but had not heard any gunfire. If I had passed it a little earlier or a little later, I might have been shot. But I didn't know that at the time. Paul, watching the news and hearing about the worst that was happening, feared his wife was in danger. He urged me not to go out again, especially after dark.

I immediately typed up my observations and sent them by telex to New York. They were raw and heartfelt, not a well-crafted story. But Bob said that was all they needed. They would write the rest from there. For once, I was fine with that.

My main concern at the time was to make sure my editors did not say that the student protestors had tried to overthrow the government. They were peaceful protestors, not rioters or armed rebels. Yes, they had erected a Goddess of Democracy statue, but most Americans did not understand that in Chinese, "democracy" does not mean one-person-one-vote, multiparty elections. When the students called for *minzhu*, they really meant they wanted more voices, especially those of intellectuals and students, to be heard in the country's top decision making.

What confounded me most was that the army had not used rubber bullets or tear gas. In the United States and Europe and Japan, police officers dispersed protestors using these nonlethal weapons. Why hadn't China? I could only guess. Its army was trained to fight foreign invasions, violent terrorists, or armed insurrection—not to stop peaceful protests. The use of live ammunition shocked people in Beijing and throughout the world.

෯෯෯෯

I could do little more in Beijing. My reporting was in. I could not bring the protestors back to life. I could not get a definitive count of how many were killed. The next story for my magazine would be about the secondary effects on American business, which I could report from Hong Kong.

My return ticket was for Thursday, but Paul begged me to go home on Wednesday. His voice was shrill with worry. All flights out of Beijing were overbooked as Chinese and foreigners fled in fear. The US government had sent in special flights to evacuate nonessential diplomatic personnel and families, as had many other countries. But individuals like me were on our own. Hong Kong Chinese were especially fearful, since their travel documents offered them no protection from Beijing's authority, so I knew the flights to Hong Kong would be full. No one knew whether or when flights might be halted.

As Paul urged, I decided to try to leave on Wednesday. The Beijing airport was in disarray, packed with panicky foreigners and Chinese desperate to flee. Passengers crowded around the check-in counters, everyone elbowing to get to the front of the pack. Clutching my heavy portable computer, I pushed and shoved with the best of them. Everyone was holding a ticket and shaking it over other people's heads, trying to get the attention of the counter agent.

At one point, when I was close to the counter, I looked into the face of another passenger in the mob—a tall American man. He smiled and nodded his head upward. "Notice the music?" It was carnival music. I shook my head and laughed. Then I pushed another half inch forward.

By some miracle, I got a seat on that day's flight to Hong Kong. Many people had to wait for another flight. I got a taste of how it felt when refugees flee for their lives. What Paul and his family had felt in 1949. A metallic tang of terror and foreboding.

When I boarded the plane, I still feared the flight might not take off. Everyone around me seemed edgy, too. As the plane pulled back from the gate, I clasped the armrests. My heart pounded in my ears. The plane took forever to taxi to its spot on the runway and wait for takeoff. Finally, the engines revved up and picked up speed. At last, the wheels lifted off.

The passengers cheered. We were safe, on our way out of China. I could feel how much tension I had been holding in my body for four days. But I couldn't relax. Although I was in the middle section, I looked out the window, sad to see the landscape of Beijing slipping away. I wondered if I would ever return. I loved this city so much.

Shortly after takeoff, the flight attendants came by with a tray for food service. On it: a small plastic packet of butter, paper packets for salt and pepper, a tiny tub of ketchup, some silverware and disposable chopsticks wrapped in a napkin. All so modern! Nothing like the service in those first planes I had flown in China in 1979, where they passed out apples from a metal bucket. I recalled my interviews at Beijing Air Catering Service Company.

I picked up the packet of butter—such a Western food, in such Western packaging. Some Chinese worker in a factory somewhere had manufactured it for the airline, one of thousands, millions, of Chinese who went to work every day to help make China modern. I thought of people I had met: the outspoken young people on the train in Hunan, the worried mother at Tiananmen Square, the hopeful journalists marching for press freedom, Paul's struggling relatives, the plucky entrepreneurs whose stories I had been so eager to tell.

All those who had staked their future on Deng's daring plan to reform and open China. They had put their trust in this hope: that Chinese people might one day have wealth and opportunities like those in the West. That they might have the freedom to create better lives for themselves and their children.

And now, those hopes were crushed, along with the bodies of the protestors. By the very army that had claimed to liberate them from oppressors forty years earlier.

At that moment, holding that mundane butter packet, I felt overwhelmed by the immensity of the tragedy I had just witnessed. My own fears melted away. Grief engulfed me. I wept.

CHAPTER THIRTY:

The Aftermath

⚬⚬⚬⚬⚬

過則勿憚改, *guò zé wù dàn gǎi: When you've made a mistake, do not be afraid to change. From The Analects of Confucius. The sage taught that a leader maintained the right to rule only as long as he showed virtue and benevolence.*

Nearly four hours later, when our flight landed on the familiar finger of a runway in Hong Kong, the passengers again burst into applause. Muscles relaxed. Here at last, in this British colony, we were safe. Even though I had a reliable US passport, I clapped, too. After the slaughter of the innocents, being outside China's borders was much preferable to being inside.

When I walked out into the familiar airport waiting area, Paul was not there with Emily on his shoulders. He didn't know what flight I had managed to take, and I had no way to inform him.

Instead, I encountered waiting hordes of local journalists, many with television cameras, who eagerly sought passengers arriving from

Beijing who might have eyewitness accounts. Outside China's borders, Hong Kong people cared more than anyone about the military assault on Chinese citizens. After all, their post-1997 future was at stake. As a journalist, I related to them, so I stopped to answer their questions. Speaking into their microphones, I described what I had seen in my drive around Beijing: bullet holes, twisted metal, burned-out military vehicles, banners of continuing defiance.

Hong Kong's newspapers, with their connections inside China, had more news than Western journalists could unearth. They warned of civil strife, reporting that certain military leaders had defied orders to crack down on fellow citizens. When troops based near Beijing refused to open fire, China's commanders had called on less sophisticated soldiers from distant regions, more likely to obey orders. Military leaders, it seemed, disagreed on how to respond to the protests. One report mentioned the possibility of civil war, but I hadn't seen any signs of it.

As eager as I was to embrace Paul and Emily, I had a story to close. So I took a taxi straight to my office, where I called to reassure Paul I had arrived safely. Before going home, though, I needed to review the latest version of our piece and send in my last-minute fixes.

"China: The Great Leap Backward" was the cover language my editors chose, accompanied by a photo they had found of a young Chinese man weeping in bitter grief. Much of the main story was written by my editors, who had been glued to the television, watching minute-by-minute coverage by CNN and other networks. The whole world had been watching, and everyone was suddenly an expert on China. The main story, a group effort with six bylines, predicted civil war. When I objected, they softened it with words like "might" and "could." But who knew what would happen next, really? Writing for a weekly, we were often pressed to make predictions. We could only guess what was going on behind the scenes.

The notes I had submitted about my drive around Beijing in the aftermath of the assault appeared with my solo byline, as a sidebar called "Banners, Bravery, and Bloodshed." *BusinessWeek* could prove that it had on-the-ground reporting. Although I had not been in the square when the soldiers opened fire, I had run into the fray and provided my eyewitness account.

My dad, back in Ohio, was furious with my editors for dispatching me into danger.

My husband, in Hong Kong, was exhilarated to welcome me home with a hug.

My editors were thrilled with my reporting and our cover story. No, it wasn't business news, but it was news that would affect business for a long time to come.

The day after I returned, I got a call from Steve Shepard, who told me how pleased he was with my work and our coverage—two covers in a month. "Remember what I said: Journalism is the first draft of history. You were there. You'll remember this for a lifetime."

"Thanks, Steve." His praise warmed me after the chill I had felt at the signs of open warfare in Beijing.

"So, how are you doing?" he continued. "It must have been a lot to take in."

My mouth responded before my brain: "I'm ready to go home." Despite the many times Paul and I had discussed this option, it surprised me to realize I had made up my mind.

"Really? When?"

"How about tomorrow?"

He laughed, surprised at my vehemence. "Let's talk about it later. Get some rest."

But for me, the choice was suddenly clear. On the plane, I had thought about what it might mean to continue to cover China. For seven years, I had cultivated contacts there, getting to know people who gradually came to trust me and talk more openly with me. Some I had met initially through my handlers, and others through Paul or on my own.

Now, I knew with dread certainty that all those good people would be in danger if a foreign journalist contacted them. As a reporter, I would be the one to have to call them up. As a human being, I didn't want to get them into trouble. In fact, I found the idea repulsive. They might be thrown into jail or "struggled against" because of their contacts with me, and I wasn't willing to risk it. Keeping them safe mattered more to me than getting the story.

For a journalist, that was considered a bad attitude. But I felt privileged that I had seen China from inside the family. I wanted the best for China, whatever that might turn out to be. If that meant I could no longer be objective, well, maybe it was time to go home.

Besides, those tanks had crushed my optimism. For a decade, I had admired Deng Xiaoping—a leader twice purged for speaking his mind, an old revolutionary determined to lift his country into the modern world. But Deng, as paramount leader, had ordered the assault—to preserve the power of the Communist Party. And at what a cost! The People's Liberation Army, once admired by millions of Chinese for overthrowing the oppressors, had turned its guns on its own people. How could such a government maintain legitimacy?

All these years, my reporting had shown China getting stronger, richer, more developed. Chinese people now had many more freedoms: to decide what work they wanted to do, to set up private companies, to make money for their families. They could speak their opinions, contact foreigners and former "class enemies," travel and study abroad. Like a peony bud, China had, under my watch, opened and bloomed. Even the setbacks had been stumbles along a forward path.

Now, it seemed, all that was over. Deng himself had crushed the flower he planted. I was sure that China would be going backward, toward a repressive state where thought police would seek out and punish anyone who protested. Also, amid strong US sanctions because of human rights violations, a wedge between the United States and China was deepening. America's passionate embrace of China had turned to revulsion.

The 1980s had been a wonderful interlude of hope, and I had covered those years. From now on, the story of China would be dismal. Let someone else cover it. I was ready to go home.

After I hung up the phone, I went into my daughter's bedroom and stroked her soft cheek as she slept. After all the news of life and death, nothing mattered more to me than my child.

❧❧❧

A few days after my return, a Hong Kong English-language TV station asked me to appear on a talk show—my first television appearance. As a makeup artist dabbed powder on my face, I tried to calm my tapping fingers. Once the little red light was on, would I stumble over my words? But despite my skittish nerves, I spoke smoothly. Many friends saw me on the small screen and complimented me. That whetted my appetite for higher visibility. I was now a TV pundit, but not under circumstances I would have wished.

Hong Kong was in turmoil, with huge street protests. Paul and I took Emily to the biggest of them, in Victoria Park. She towered over Paul's shoulders as we mingled with tens of thousands of local people bearing signs condemning the butchery in Beijing. If China's leaders could fire on the people of Beijing, how likely were they to live up to their promises to Hong Kong? Might there someday be blood in the streets of Wanchai?

Paul and I marched in solidarity with the protestors. Paul's dreams had been crushed, too. His birth country and his adopted country were at odds. His family—my family now, too—would be divided yet again. Our daughter's heritage, both Chinese and American, had a stake driven into its heart.

A spontaneous group in Hong Kong, we learned, had quietly provided safe houses so Beijing student leaders could slip out without the government's detection. Some of the most famous of the student leaders, including Chai Ling and Wu'erkaixi, moved to the United States. The most famous dissident, Professor Fang Lizhi, took refuge at the US embassy in Beijing, where my old professor James Lilley had taken over as ambassador just as the protests began. Lilley protected Fang and his wife, but their presence in the embassy exacerbated tensions between China and the United States.

"Tiananmen massacre" became the term widely used in English to describe the tragedy—then and for years to come—but many journalists challenged that wording. Most of the killing happened not in the square but in nearby streets. To most Americans, this distinction sounded like splitting hairs, but to many Chinese, it mattered. To them, Tiananmen was not a concept but a place. The huge plaza in front of the Gate of Heavenly Peace was the center of the protests, but not of the killings. In Chinese, the massacre came to be called the June Fourth Incident.

Just before the soldiers opened fire, in the dark early hours of June 4, few students had remained in the square itself; many had left after hearing loudspeakers warn protestors to vacate the square. Eyewitnesses said that soldiers did kill some in the square, but they also provided safe passage for some students to leave. On the main avenue west of the square, ordinary citizens had tried to stop the armored personnel carriers from reaching the square. Some frightened soldiers, we later learned, had abandoned their vehicles, which the citizens then burned. Other soldiers, though, had fired indiscriminately at people on the street in the dark hours of night, including bystanders from nearby homes. It appeared to be a chaotic military operation in which disoriented soldiers made on-the-spot decisions to either run away or open fire. But it achieved Deng's goal: clearing out the protestors and pacifying Beijing.

Clearly, many citizens were killed, and enraged citizens attacked a few soldiers, but it was hard to get a good estimate of the dead and injured. The Chinese government said that about three hundred civilians and soldiers had died. Foreign reporters in Beijing visited hospitals and pooled reports, but their estimates were confusing and contradictory. Had hundreds been killed? Thousands? Hong Kong newspapers quoted angry, anguished observers guessing a death toll in the tens of thousands. The Chinese army had removed dead bodies, so the outside world seemed unlikely ever to get an accurate count.

Regardless, the early guesstimates began to seem exaggerated. The *New York Times* estimated that four hundred to eight hundred civilians had been killed, as well as about a dozen soldiers and police. Other reporters and diplomats made similar assessments, ranging between three hundred and one thousand. I began using the term "hundreds, perhaps thousands." Others said "untold hundreds." Whatever the true number, to me, even one killing was far too many. All the civilians killed were unarmed.

In the weeks that followed, my editors assigned me to report on the question of what this meant for US business. That answer was not hard to find. Business thrives in stability, so street protests, military crackdowns, and political uncertainty bring it to a standstill. American citizens and their dependents had been evacuated from Beijing. Planes into China were mostly empty. Those companies that had already committed to production in China kept going quietly, if they could. Those who hadn't yet committed turned tail and went home.

So covering US business in China, which had also once seemed promising, now looked dismal as well. All the enthusiasm and optimism, all the opportunity and risk taking, had died the night the People's Liberation Army opened fire. The story I had covered for ten years, from outside and inside China, was over. That's what I thought.

From now on, it seemed, China would be moving backward.

CHAPTER THIRTY-ONE:

Leaving for Home

☙☙☙☙☙

低头思故乡, *dī tóu sī gù xiāng: "When I lower my head, I think of my old home"—last line of a famous classical poem, "Quiet Night Thoughts," by eighth-century poet Li Bai.*

Though eager to move back to the States, I knew I'd have to wait. Dinah's maternity leave was coming up in October through December, so I would need to hold down the fort during her absence. Besides, it wasn't obvious where I would go next.

Paul's career in the China trade seemed to be over, too. If China was going to shut itself off from the world again, there wasn't much future in putting together trade deals. Paul still wanted to move back to the West Coast, to be near his older kids. He had already been away from them for too long. But *BusinessWeek* didn't have any openings for me in that region.

Depressed about China, I turned my attention in two other directions. First, I wrote articles on other parts of Asia, which were still thriving.

Second, I doubled down on my book proposal. Now that world-wide attention was focused on China, it seemed the perfect time to pitch a book. I wanted to catch the wave. My earlier proposal, about daring entrepreneurs, now felt dead in the water—out of date and off-base. One of those I had interviewed, Wan Runnan, head of Stone Group, China's largest private company, had fled Beijing for Paris, where he joined a pro-democracy group. For now, everyone in New York, and around the world, was focused on the bigger story in China—the protests, widespread dissatisfaction, instability in the nation's leadership, and the very legitimacy of its government.

China in Crisis became my working book title. I rewrote my query letter and sent it out to four agents by the end of June. Two responded with enthusiasm, and I arranged to meet with them in New York in August. Their interest encouraged me.

A clump of instant books on the Tiananmen crisis popped out quickly: by the staff of *TIME* magazine, *Newsweek*'s Melinda Liu, and veteran foreign correspondent Harrison Salisbury. Each time one appeared, I worried about my own prospects. But those books were just about the events of May and June 1989. I wanted mine to explain the pivotal era of the 1980s, the remarkable reforms that had raised expectations and upset the whole Communist system. These, I argued, were as important as demands for democracy.

🎋🎋🎋

In August, Paul, Emily, and I flew back to the United States, primarily to visit family. At age two, Emily was now talking in full sentences. She was lively and sweet and could relate to people, and we wanted her to form connections with her siblings, cousins, aunts, uncles, and grandparents.

But Paul and I had a second motive. We planned visits to Seattle and San Francisco to see how we felt about moving to those two cities, which I did not know well. I wanted to informally check in with *BusinessWeek* colleagues in the San Francisco bureau, whose exciting beats included hot Silicon Valley tech companies with names like Apple and Sun and Intel. It seemed unlikely that we could move to Seattle, since *BusinessWeek* did not have a bureau there, but my friend

Jeanne had invited me to give a talk at a conference there about the future of China after Tiananmen Square. So we flew to Seattle first.

Seattle in late summer was lovely: sunny and warm but neither hot nor humid. Snowcapped mountains gleamed sharply on the horizon in all four directions, and boats and kayaks dotted the smooth waters of the lake and the sound. Seattle's economy was thriving, thanks mainly to Boeing and lumber, but increasingly boasted a successful tech startup called Microsoft. *BusinessWeek* had featured its geeky, boyish founder, Bill Gates, on the cover several times before he even turned thirty. Several other big companies were based in the Northwest, too, such as Nordstrom and Nike. There were even some tiny companies with potential for national growth: Starbucks and Costco. It looked like an up-and-coming city with fodder for lots of good business stories.

After my speech, Paul took me to a restaurant featuring fresh local seafood.

"We should look at houses here," he said, as I helped myself to Quilcene oysters.

"But we don't have jobs lined up," I argued sensibly. "We can't just buy a house and hope we'll figure out how to pay for it."

"I can go back to real estate. You'll find something. We should at least look."

We spent a relaxing week with my parents in Ohio, and then I flew to New York to meet with the two book agents. Both were interested, and I signed up with one of them, who planned to contact publishers right away. I was thrilled.

Meanwhile, Paul took Emily back to Seattle to look at houses. By the time I met up with them in San Francisco, he had already made an offer on a house in a Seattle suburb. I was shocked; that move seemed hasty and premature. Paul was undaunted.

"It's subject to your approval, but we have to let them know within a week. Check out the pictures!" The house looked bright and airy, in a new neighborhood of Bellevue. It had a flat, grassy backyard with a sunny patio, protected by a row of bushes, perfect for our little girl. We could afford it only with a "jumbo" mortgage that would require two good incomes.

"What if I can't find a job in Seattle?" I asked, feeling dubious.
"We'll figure something out."

The next weekend, we looked at houses in the Bay Area but couldn't find anything nearly as nice for the same price. So we took a chance, defied the odds yet again, and firmed up the offer on the house in Bellevue.

It seemed zany, but we took the plunge. A few weeks later, I flew back to sign the papers to take out a mortgage and buy the house.

I didn't dare tell my editors. Not yet. I had to figure out the best way to approach them about it. Paul wanted me to ask them to create a full-time or even part-time position with *BusinessWeek* in Seattle. But that idea intimidated me. It seemed disloyal. Steve's unfailing support was a major reason I had succeeded in journalism. How could I give him an ultimatum?

🍧🍧🍧

As I equivocated over my future, I threw myself into work and travel with a burst of gusto, conscious that I would probably be leaving soon. In October, I arranged my highest-level personal interview to date, with Corazon Aquino, president of the Philippines, in Manila. We ran a full-page transcript, as well as a story on the progress and setbacks since she had become president, in February 1986. She had paid off much of the debt incurred by Marcos, tackled inflation and crony capitalism, and the economy was growing again. Not bad for a former housewife!

As China was still tied in knots, I traveled to Taiwan several times and wrote a cover story on its much rosier economic prospects, with the title "The Other China." As always, I took the cover to a local shop, which blew up the image and created a wall hanging for me. My office wall was now crowded with covers. I loved this visible manifestation of my achievements.

In October, Dinah gave birth to a healthy baby boy and began her maternity leave. The clock was ticking.

Finally, on October 30, I screwed up my courage and called Keith Felcyn, *BusinessWeek*'s chief of correspondents. Taking a deep breath, I confessed that Paul and I had bought a house in Seattle, and I asked if he would consider creating a new position for me there. To make it less expensive for the magazine, I offered to work part-time from home. His voice hinting at disappointment, he offered to think about it and get back to me within a week.

The days crawled by. I wondered if I'd made a terrible mistake. If they said no, I was about to be unemployed. The following week, as promised, Keith called. They agreed! I would have the title of Seattle bureau chief, and I would cover companies based in the Pacific Northwest, three days a week.

My long shot had paid off. After two months of uncertainty, I had a plan, a future with *BusinessWeek*, a transition back to the United States and to Seattle. My salary would be cut by 40 percent, but I would still have a job, an income, an identity. A name card.

Plus, the part-time schedule would leave me time to write my book. But news on that front was not promising. The first few publishers said no. There were too many new books about Tiananmen Square and no interest in deep analysis behind the headlines. American attitudes toward China had shifted to blanket condemnation. My agent told me not to lose heart, but it seemed unlikely. My book dream, too, fell victim to the Tiananmen tragedy.

❦❦❦

Then, just days after I learned about my future in Seattle, the Berlin Wall fell.

By odd coincidence, I heard the news at the studios of Hong Kong TV-B. Yet again, I was being interviewed, this time about whether Deng Xiaoping was dismantling liberal economic policies and reverting to rigid Communism.

Our talk show was interrupted as the feed switched to televised images of Germans from East and West dancing atop the wall. Border guards were letting East Germans stream through checkpoints where refugees had once been shot. The journalists around me cheered.

This news was so huge, I couldn't believe it at first. Since I was seven years old, the Berlin Wall had stood firm and heavily guarded, the solid line between the Communist East and the free Western world. Now that the wall was breached, it seemed possible that

Communism would fall, even in the Soviet Union, where it had started more than seventy years earlier.

"What will this mean for China?" the interviewer asked me.

I was totally unprepared to answer. We were on air, live.

"Will Communism fall in China, too?" he persisted.

"It's hard to say," I stumbled. "Anything could happen."

In fact, everyone wondered, but no one knew. It didn't seem likely, at least for now. Deng Xiaoping and the military had made it glaringly clear that no more protests would be allowed. Plus, there was no alternative—no opposition leaders like Lech Walesa or Vaclav Havel. But there was no alternative in Russia, either.

Thirty years later, analysts would try to explain why Communist rule ended in Russia but not in China. One difference: China reformed its economy first, not its political system, while the Soviet Union under Gorbachev rushed into political and economic reforms at the same time. As a result, the Soviet government lost power before it had a chance to restructure the economy, leading to a decade of hyperinflation and widespread privation. China's Communist Party wagered that providing economic freedoms to the people would stave off further demands for political freedoms. Eventually, China's leaders would claim that Deng's suppression of the protests actually created the stability China needed to continue the economic restructuring that enabled widespread growth and prosperity.

Most protestors in Beijing were not trying to seize power, but the subsequent overthrow of Communism in Europe would make that outcome seem possible—though hardly desirable. If China's government had fallen, China, like Russia, might well have descended into chaos and paralysis. Deng and his old-man colleagues remembered how China, after the 1911 revolution, suffered more than thirty years of civil war, foreign occupation, and failed government. They also vividly recalled that the previous time students rebelled en masse, at the start of the Cultural Revolution, China had devolved into ten years of political violence and economic stagnation. Those painful memories may have driven their decision to call in the army in 1989.

But what if the Chinese military had dispersed the protestors using water hoses and tear gas, instead of bullets? For years, I wished they had done so. But when the Hong Kong police used these non-lethal means against protestors in 2019, the protests grew more violent. Better yet, what if Zhao Ziyang had not been deposed and had responded more humanely to the protestors and found a way to make the government more responsive to the people? Might China still have enjoyed years of strong growth—but evolved into a democracy? Unfortunately, no one will ever know. South Korea and Taiwan did not become democracies until after thirty years of fast economic growth under an authoritarian government, and not until education levels and living standards were much higher than China's in 1989.

None of these thoughts crossed my mind on November 10, 1989, certainly not when the television camera was pointing at me. But it did occur to me that five months had passed since my last visit to China. I could not move back to the States without going back inside China, to find out what was happening there now.

❧❧❧❧

Returning to China was distressing. As a reporter, I took two final trips to Beijing and one to Guangdong Province in late 1989 and early 1990. The mood was glum.

In eight years, I had never felt paranoid, had never looked over my shoulder as I interviewed Chinese people. And I had never heard of anyone getting into trouble for talking to me. That may seem odd, but it's true. As a business reporter, I was not assigned to interview dissidents or investigate political corruption. Chinese entrepreneurs, economic officials, and those who did business with Americans were happy to speak to me, eager to get out their views. My job was to balance what Chinese people told me with what I observed on the ground, get input from outside observers, and then analyze it in a larger context.

But in December 1989, I found myself in a coffee shop in Shenzhen, the only foreigner there. I was talking softly with a Chinese friend who worked at a company headed by a relative of Deng Xiaoping. My eyes widened when I heard that it had lost $3 million trading in foreign stocks and that investigators from Beijing were crawling all over. Suddenly, my friend's eyes darted to a man sitting behind me who had been trying too hard to listen to us. We quickly changed the subject.

I felt guilty for asking probing questions in a public place. Any political slip could torpedo my friend's application to study in the United States. Unauthorized interviews were hazardous.

Guangdong had always been the least fettered, most go-go province. Its citizens cared little about politics. Many were unabashed capitalists, focusing their lives on getting rich like their cousins in Hong Kong. Even local Party officials had followed the unspoken motto "If it isn't expressly forbidden, try it." But now, orders were dropping because of the political disruption and some new austerity measures from Beijing.

The biggest change, though, was a loss of heart. The Cantonese I spoke to no longer had that no-holds-barred enthusiasm, that firm confidence that each year would be better than the last. Several griped that the student protesters had wrecked everything.

"Guangdong wasn't unstoppable. And neither were China's reforms," I concluded, in an article titled "Where China's Sweetest Dreams Went Sour." After my byline, my editor added the words: "Hong Kong Bureau Chief Jones Yang has some dashed hopes of her own about China."

Beijing was equally gloomy, but I saw one sliver of hope. In the past, periods of fear, paralysis, and political infighting had often followed Chinese government crackdowns. Scapegoats were accused of political crimes and sent away, for months or years.

But this time, one Beijing friend told me, was different. In every office, every factory, every "work unit," people were asked to identify which of their colleagues had marched in the streets. This time, no one snitched. Frequently at meetings, the leader would ask, "We've been asked to identify the counterrevolutionaries in our midst. Who from our office marched in the streets?" Everyone knew who had marched, but no one pointed fingers. "Well," the leader would say, "I don't have any names to report, so let's move on to the next item on the agenda."

I was moved when I heard this. Chinese people had learned from history. This time, they were protecting one another and preventing the damage from spreading.

After its brutal suppression, Beijing had imprisoned some pro-democracy activists on charges of fomenting "chaos." Their parents and international human rights organizations worked hard to get them out. The government showed no compassion for the families of those killed or wounded. But civil war did not break out. Deng's economic and foreign policies were not reversed. China's private businesses were not shut down. Foreign joint-venture investments in China continued, with no drastic rule changes. Diplomats and their families dribbled back into the country. And I, as a journalist, dared to phone a few of my contacts, though not all.

The most draconian predictions, it seemed, were wrong. Maybe things would get better.

Saying goodbye to Hong Kong was hard. It was my home now, my community. In early March 1990, Paul flew to Seattle to get the house ready. I stayed behind to supervise the movers.

As I planned my farewell dinner, I thought of how I had come to love this city in its waning days as a British colony. The streets of Wanchai, with their jumble of Chinese signs, now housed familiar memories: my first office, opposite that stinky public toilet; my second office, in Dominion Centre on Queen's Road East, where the demonstrators had flooded down to the blocky Xinhua building that housed China's authorities; the vast dim sum restaurants of glassy blue Admiralty Centre, where I had once fed duck tongue to my baby.

Paul and I went back to the Regent Hotel for one last mango milk shake overlooking the harbor lights. In this shop he had bought me sneakers, in that one a gold braided necklace. I recalled where we had purchased our wedding rings, Steve's fish tank, Emily's crib. The outlying islands held memories of fresh-air dinners, scenic walks, and stolen kisses. In Repulse Bay, we had celebrated Wenni's fifteenth birthday. On the Peak, Dinah had hosted ladies' luncheons.

After my farewell dinner, Emily and I boarded a plane for Seattle on March 28, 1990. At the age of three, she was leaving the land of her birth, and I was heading back toward mine.

As our plane taxied along that familiar runway jutting into Hong Kong's harbor, I didn't cry. On this fourteen-hour flight, I would be talking not to Paul but to our little daughter—and her Filipina nanny, Anita, who had eagerly agreed to move to America with us. As I handed Emily her sippy cup, I marveled yet again at her fine brown hair, now curling at the ends. Like me, she was a little chatterbox at home but shy around other people—as reserved as I had been as a young woman starting out in my career.

How different I was from that young woman! In my earliest days in journalism, I had been paralyzed and afraid to pick up a phone and bother people. I couldn't recall when that fear had dissipated. Certainly it was gone the day I had interviewed the president of the Philippines and the day I had entered the Forbidden City to interview China's vice premier.

And yes, as I had promised Lew Young, I had managed to gain people's trust by putting them at ease, by asking the right questions in language they could understand. Rather than confronting authorities, I had pursued a quiet approach to everyday folks on the streets, who opened up the story behind the story. Somehow, I had learned to be a reporter without being aggressive or confrontational or self-aggrandizing. Introverts have more power than they realize, even in careers that seem hard-charging; sometimes they can succeed by stealth—and curiosity.

I remembered that afternoon in June 1982, almost eight years earlier, when I landed at this same airport, full of anticipation and apprehension. In those early days, I wondered if I could ever break through the secretiveness and suspicion of the Chinese—the walls they put up against foreigners—and really get to know Chinese people. Toward me, they were polite but distant.

Somewhere in the 1980s, the mysterious Chinese became no longer mysterious. When had that happened? Perhaps over that mango milk shake with Paul Yang. Or when his parents invited me to their house to eat *guiyu* fish in Taipei. Or delivering disposable diapers to my Chinese minder.

I thought of a comment by my first Chinese teacher, Yu Hou, in Singapore. "Tones is very important," he told us. "You say tones wrong, they will know you are not Chinese." My Caucasian classmates and I had guffawed at the absurdity of that.

Yet by now, sometimes, deep in a discussion in Mandarin about the future of China, I forgot that I wasn't Chinese. I was the wife of a man whose native language was Mandarin, the daughter-in-law of a man who had fought to defend China, the aunt of people who had suffered through the Cultural Revolution. I would never be a true insider. But because of Paul, I could see what China looked like from the inside out, without the filter of American assumptions.

During my eight years in Hong Kong, I realized that the farther you wander from home, the more perspective you gain on yourself. I love flying to distant shores. I love going off the map into "the middle of nowhere." I relish the distinctive views of people from diverse cultures. But I realized that I also loved home and family. I had deep roots in my *laojia*.

I wanted both deep roots and far-flung tendrils. Perhaps deep roots give you the stability it takes to travel far afield. But they do draw you back, eventually. After eight years based in Hong Kong, after falling in love with China, only for it to break my heart, I was ready to return to my homeland.

Single-minded pursuit of a career from a young age has its advantages and can help you develop expertise. But remaining an expert on China only was not all I wanted to do.

Perhaps the yin and yang, the traditional Chinese Taoist symbol, represented me best: a swirling union of opposites. The term Mommy Track still made me squirm, but I aimed to find a balance between my work in journalism and my joy in family. As a working mother, I wanted to focus more on Emily in the coming years. For fortunate women like me, it is possible to have it all, but in seasons.

The June Fourth Incident had rocked me to the core. I could never see China with the same shining optimism. But I had met many good people over the years and watched them reach eagerly for new opportunities. I wanted the best for them. By immersing myself in their language and culture, I had developed an empathy for and deep understanding of them not available to those who simply read the news.

Many Americans weren't ready to hear anything positive about China, but I retained a desire that someday I could help my people to better understand Paul's. To realize that Chinese are individuals, too, with worries and hopes, and that Deng's economic reform policies might just succeed in allowing them to break out of their past and achieve something beyond their dreams. Ideally, I could someday write books that would build a bridge between my two worlds, the United States and China—just as my articles had connected American readers with the remarkable folks I had met in Asia.

I had set out to go "out there," to expand my horizons. What I learned is that the world looks different from outside your own country, especially when you get deep inside another culture. Actual experience on the ground often proves expectations and stereotypes wrong. If you try to understand another country only by reading—or reporting—what the experts say, without talking to ordinary people living it, you'll get a warped view. While generic descriptions of people from certain cultures do have some truth, every culture is made up of individuals, many of whom don't fit the stereotype.

Traveling and living outside your comfort zone can help overcome binary thinking. No country is all good or all bad. The same is true for systems of government. I love my country, but, having seen the effects of its foreign policies on people of other countries, I will never perceive it in the same simplistic way as I did before living abroad. Freedom fighters and Communist rebels look a lot alike.

I'd like to say I had moved past individual ambition to a greater purpose in life, less self-centered and more other-centered, but I didn't have it all figured out. At thirty-five, I had no desire to give up on my quest for recognition. What is true is that I had achieved the dream I set out to achieve: to be a foreign correspondent in China. It would take time before I formulated another.

As our plane took off over the harbor, I bade farewell to the skyscrapers lining Hong Kong's dramatic waterfront. I had no idea how long it would be before I came back, but I knew I would. I vowed to return in 1997, to witness the hand-over of Hong Kong to China. I hoped for the best.

Epilogue

⚭⭗⭗⭗⭘

The tragic events of 1989 altered the trajectory of my life. Disheartened and discouraged about the country I had come to love, I left China in 1990 and gave up on my cherished work as a foreign correspondent. In Seattle, I reported on Pacific Northwest companies for *BusinessWeek* and on West Coast technology for *US News & World Report*, and I wrote my first book—not on China but on a fast-growing local company, Starbucks. Later, I wrote five more books that introduced American readers to aspects of Chinese history and Chinese in America.

In May 2019, an invitation to speak at an Overseas Press Club panel on the anniversary of Tiananmen Square pushed me to analyze my thoughts about China, then and since. Once again, cruising at high altitude on my flight to New York, I battled with conflicting emotions as I planned what to say. Sadness lapped over me as I recalled both the excitement of May and the crushed optimism of June 1989.

Like most Americans, I had been certain that that bloody crackdown marked the end of Deng's great experiment in economic reform. But I was wrong. Most of us were wrong. In early 1992, Deng reemerged, making his famous "southern tour" and reasserting his commitment to rapid economic reform. "We've been poor for thousands of years, but we won't be poor again," he said. After that, China started growing again, faster and faster, an economic miracle that brought higher standards of living and raised China from "the sick man of Asia" to a world power. Deng and his successors once again forced us to rethink our assumptions.

Today, it's clear that the 1980s were a turning point in the history of China, Communism, and the world. The China I witnessed in 1982, when I arrived as a journalist, was backward and poor, a third-world nation of dirt floors and oxen, outhouses and dim lights, streams of bicycles and heavy loads carried on shoulder poles. Thirty-three years of Communism had created a classless society with a per capita annual income of less than $300 in today's dollars. China had the atomic bomb but no modern highways, few computers, and a lot of steam locomotives. More than 80 percent of all Chinese worked in farming, which required backbreaking labor in small patches of earth. From the train windows, for miles on end, you could always see peasants in every field.

In recent years, on our frequent visits back to China, Paul and I have seen modern malls packed with shoppers—the sons and daughters of those peasants. Even third-tier cities pulse with new subways, dance clubs, neon lights, and skyscrapers. Thousands of miles of highways connect sprawling urban areas, whose ring roads are jammed with foreign-brand cars. Ordinary folks zip around on the world's largest high-speed-rail network. From the train, it's hard to see even one farmer in the rows of highly mechanized fields.

To me, Deng's legacy is astounding. His decision to order troops to fire on civilians knocked him off the pedestal where I had once envisioned him. It will forever tarnish his reputation. But never in the history of the world have so many poor people prospered in such a short time. According to the World Bank, more than 850 million people in China have risen out of poverty since 1978, and half of them have reached middle class. According to the World Bank, China's poverty rate fell from 88 percent in 1981 to less than 1 percent by 2015. Worldwide, China's progress accounted for more than 70 percent of the decline in global poverty.

I saw this transformation happen with my own eyes, over the course of forty years of journalism and travel around China. It was far from inevitable. It was the result of hardworking, risk-taking citizens and policies that enabled and supported them. I agree with the words of former World Bank president Jim Kim: "This is one of the great stories in human history."

Paul rode this boom, starting with a single sale of machinery in 1992 and building a thriving business representing an American company selling its oil refinery equipment all over China. For years, he shuttled across the Pacific and rode gritty trains across many provinces in pursuit of contracts. Despite his frequent absences, our marriage lengthened and deepened, strengthened by those early years when we weren't sure it would ever happen. Paul's mother moved to Seattle, and I kept up my Mandarin by talking with her and taking her back to see her home village near Beijing. Emily grew up thoroughly American but with a strong pride in her Chinese heritage, choosing to study Mandarin in high school and college. And yes, I took her back to Hong Kong in 1997 to witness the peaceful transition to Chinese sovereignty.

Listening to others speak at the Overseas Press Club event, I could see that I had a different perspective than most Americans looking back at the events of June 4. First, I had a different lens. I had been sent to China as a business reporter, so I had focused on Deng's economic reforms, the growing private sector, and US-China trade and investment—not on human rights or politics. I was never kicked by Chinese soldiers, berated by my handlers, or tailed by security goons. As a result, I tended to see China's progress in terms of economic development, and the human rights I counted were basic ones of food, shelter, and opportunity to create a better life. Although the government continues to detain dissidents and restrict news available on the internet, it's also true that, in terms of typical days in typical lives, most Chinese today are far better off than they were before Deng's reforms started in 1978.

More important, I had a personal and historical perspective. Paul could remember the wartime disruption of his early childhood. His relatives told us of the years of privation and persecution under Mao. We had witnessed the early days when the world's largest Communist Party promoted private enterprise and stock markets. The "great leap backward" in political rights did not lead to a "great leap backward" in China's drive for shared prosperity.

During countless trips to China over the decades, Paul and I grew closer to his relatives in different parts of the country. Most of them had suffered under Mao and had no government connections yet thrived as China grew. One cousin, deprived of an education for political reasons, started a taxi company, invested in real estate, and pursued his far-fetched dream of opening a winery. Another cousin built up a Chinese-medicine distribution company and saved up enough to send her daughter to study fashion design in New York. Another, who grew up barefoot in the countryside, makes soundproof booths for retail hearing-aid vendors across China. Many own both a home and a car—unthinkable luxuries in 1982. Thirteen of Paul's cousins flew from China for Emily's wedding in Seattle in 2016, many of them visiting America for the first time. They all returned home— called back by family, food, and familiarity.

During China's boom years, American businesspeople were on the front line of cheering it on, finally able to sell to the huge market they had imagined decades earlier. They objected to demands for technology transfer, but most learned how to evaluate the trade-offs and protect themselves. US importers and retailers profited from its cheap labor, back when Chinese labor was cheap. American universities benefited from an influx of Chinese students who could afford to pay full tuition. Chinese money bolstered US treasuries and Bellevue real estate.

For four decades, under eight presidents of both parties, the United States supported and engaged with China as it developed. The two economies became so closely tied that people began using historian Niall Ferguson's term "Chimerica" to describe the symbiotic relationship.

But in 2018 and 2019, American sentiment reversed, veering toward animosity. Some Americans had predicted that China would gradually evolve toward a democracy as its people prospered. Although I had not bought into this "China fantasy," I was, like many, dismayed when President Xi Jinping in 2018, after years of tightening censorship, convinced his congress to change the law so that he could serve an unlimited term—overturning the system of clear succession engineered by Deng Xiaoping and enabling one-man dictatorship for life. That same year, US President Donald Trump began a trade war with China, slapping tariffs on US imports from China and accusing China of cheating and theft.

Educated at Johns Hopkins to believe that global trade increases efficiency—and that tariffs distort it—I opposed Trump's tariff war. As predicted, it harmed many American businesses. Still, leaders in both parties stepped up their disparagement of China, and the carefully calibrated American approach of mutual respect and cooperative engagement was tossed aside.

This shift in sentiment reminded me of a comment I once heard from Howard Schultz, then CEO of Starbucks: the American public cheers you on when you are small and scrappy but turns against you when you grow large and successful. No longer viewed as a striving younger brother eager to catch up, China is now feared as a strategic competitor—or even an enemy. Although China's per capita income is only on par with that of Mexico, one-sixth that of the United States, its sheer size and fast growth cause some Americans to assume that Beijing's goal is to replace the United States as a world power. That makes some want to contain China or seek to stop its progress.

A better approach to maintain America's lead, I believe, is to invest in technology and support our entrepreneurs who do. China appears to have increased its espionage against US companies in recent years—necessitating increased vigilance on our part—but it also graduates four times as many students in science and engineering each year and obtains twice as many patents. Its government subsidizes targeted technologies, but its high-tech sector remains private and fiercely competitive.

Engagement with China was very good for the United States and could be again in the future, along with vigilance and investment in our own infrastructure and technology. The way to deal with rising powers is not to try to quash them, but to protect our own strengths and ensure that they have a big stake in keeping the system going. If we want to persuade the Chinese leaders to live by the "rules-based system" we Americans helped create, we need to live by those rules ourselves. Globalism provides opportunities for entrepreneurs and innovators around the world, and the United States has always had more of those than any other country.

I'm not alone in my dismay about the new belligerence. In 2019, more than one hundred prominent American experts on China from the scholarly, foreign policy, military, and business communities signed an open letter called "China Is Not an Enemy." I agree with their premise: "We are deeply concerned about the growing deterioration in US relations with China, which we believe does not serve American or global interests."

In the long run, as *Financial Times* commentator Martin Wolf said in 2019, "We are more likely to get a China that we will feel comfortable with if we are open, fair, and reasonable in dealing with it—and not paranoid and crazy."

When I hear ordinary Americans expressing fear or disdain about China, I tell them something I learned from my years as a foreign correspondent. By definition, the news is what's new, so often it is startling and negative. When we hear news about our own country, we see it in perspective, so bad news, like school shootings, does not necessarily affect our view about whether our country is basically good. But when we read disturbing news about decisions that foreign leaders make, some are quick to label that whole country as "evil." This is as true about Chinese looking at America as it is about Americans regarding China. Only when you live inside the walls of someone else's home for a while can you understand the world from their viewpoint.

"China" is not just the Chinese government. Cutting off a whole nation because of its government policies is also cutting off all its people. China-bashing arouses fear and hatred, which can lead to violence and war. As Harvard professor Graham Allison pointed out in 2015, when a rising power rivals a ruling power, the most likely result is war. To prevent that outcome, he recommends careful management of the US-China relationship and deeper mutual understanding. What's needed is more listening and communicating, less waving of fists. War would be terrible for the people of both countries.

The entire history of US-China relations, as journalist John Pomfret wrote in his 2017 book, *The Beautiful Country and the Middle Kingdom*, has been a turbulent love story of two nations whose passions swing violently between extremes. "Both sides experience rapturous enchantment begetting hope, followed by disappointment, repulsion, and disgust, only to return to fascination once again." I've seen two cycles of that in my lifetime. Yet, he added, "No problem of worldwide concern . . . can be solved unless Washington and Beijing find a way to work together." As we learned in 2020, this includes finding better ways to contain and prevent pandemics.

As I neared completion of this book in 2020, a fog of sadness settled over me. Street protests in Hong Kong had continued for months and morphed from peaceful to violent, and China's congress passed a national security law that would curb Hong Kong's freedoms of speech and assembly. Xi Jinping and his "wolf-warrior" diplomats were stirring up resentment in neighboring countries. And in Washington, Trump was stoking anger against China as the origin of the deadly new coronavirus, in part to detract criticism from his mishandling of the outbreak in the United States. The tariff war continued unresolved, and Washington was imposing new sanctions and export restrictions. The US military had been practicing war games against China. US-China relations had deteriorated to their worst point since those terrible months after Tiananmen.

One afternoon, my heart heavy, I walked into Paul's home office and plunked myself on his brown couch. "I see no reason for hope," I told him. Paul swiveled around to face me as I enumerated my worries.

"It does look bad," he responded. "There's no way the situation between the US and China could change easily or quickly. A lot of Americans are paranoid that China will overtake us in the next generation of technology. That's hard for Americans to swallow— especially since China is a non-white nation that was poor and backward not long ago. Still, I see reason for hope."

"Really? Like what?" I asked.

"Well, look at China's younger generation," he continued. "Before the pandemic, about three million Chinese came to the US every year as tourists. More than 300,000 Chinese students are enrolled in US universities. In recent years, more and more of them have been going home after their studies, finding good jobs in China. The next generation of China's leaders will be different."

Paul's ease with statistics did not surprise me; in his retirement, he spends hours each day reading major US newspapers and checking the online forum WeChat, exchanging information and views with more than a hundred people in China.

"Most Chinese are pretty savvy about the outside world," he continued. "A lot of them know how to circumvent that Great Firewall and get uncensored news. Most Chinese I know want closer relations with the US. The inherent goodwill is there."

"But I can't see attitudes in America changing any time soon," I said. "It seems everyone running for office is hostile toward China."

"It's really hard to predict. But maybe, once the election is over, cooler heads will prevail. If Joe Biden wins, he might dial back on the tariffs and work with China on big issues like climate change. A new administration may see the bigger picture and realize that the most practical approach for the US is not to try to block China, or thwart it, but to find ways to cooperate, ways that are win-win. China's a huge market and it keeps getting bigger. Just think how much the US can benefit from a good relationship in the future."

I sighed. For the sake of millions of ordinary people in China and the United States, as well as our new Chinese-American grandchild, I fervently hope he's right.

It would not be the first time that China has defied the odds.

Acknowledgments

࿔࿔࿔࿔࿔

My writing mentor, author Brenda Peterson, encouraged me to write this memoir decades ago, and I resisted, insisting I needed time to digest and make sense of my experiences in Hong Kong and China. What got me going was the publication of her book, *Your Life Is a Book: How to Craft and Publish Your Memoir*, in 2014. When I got stuck in 2017, I found renewed inspiration in an online class with Brooke Warner and Linda Joy Myers, Write Your Memoir in Six Months. Brenda has been my biggest champion over three decades, and Brooke got me over the finish line by accepting this memoir for publication among an impressive list of authors at She Writes Press. My gratitude to these mentors!

I also feel deeply grateful to my mentors in journalism, especially former *BusinessWeek* editor-in-chief Lewis H. Young, who believed in my potential from a young age, and his successor, Stephen B. Shepard, who supported and encouraged me with enthusiasm. I also appreciate my editors Bruce Nussbaum, Bob Dowling, and Bill Holstein, who held me up along the way. And many thanks to my delightful Hong Kong colleagues, Dinda Elliott, Maria Shao, and Dinah Lee, for their expertise, insights, and companionship.

Many thanks also to my late parents, William B. and Margaretta H. Jones of Youngstown, Ohio. Bill Jones, the bookseller, pushed me to consider the path of journalism when I was only seventeen and cheered on every article I wrote. Both Mom and Dad welcomed Paul into our family and loved their "China doll" from the moment of her birth. My parents-in-law, Yang Ping-Nan and Chu Ping-Wen, welcomed me into their family with warmth and explained China from their perspective.

I benefited from invaluable editing by Meredith Bailey, Leslie Helm, and Brooke Warner, and helpful feedback from Brenda Peterson, Bruce Nussbaum, Steve Shepard, John Holden, Cindy Caldwell, Dinda Elliott, Maria Shao, Dinah Lee, Trish Jones, Katy Ehrlich, Jeanne DeMund, Paul Yang, Emily Yang Yuhas, and Steven Yang. Thanks to Yen Liu Fogarty for reviewing Chinese words and sayings.

I am also grateful to Brooke Warner and the team at She Writes Press for encouragement and support through the publishing process. I value the community of women writers you have fostered and am proud to count myself among them.

Deepest thanks, of course, goes to my husband, Paul Yang, who opened my eyes to the complexity and depth of China and continues to regale me daily with its latest advances. And to my darling daughter, Emily Yang Yuhas, light of my life, who reads and improves every book I write.

About the Author

*D*ori Jones Yang is a Seattle-based writer who aims to build bridges between cultures and between generations. Author of a wide variety of books for different audiences, she specializes in introducing China to Americans, explaining complex issues in understandable language, and making history come alive.

Born in Ohio and educated in history at Princeton and in international relations at Johns Hopkins, Dori worked for eight years as a foreign correspondent for *BusinessWeek*, covering China during its pivotal years, the 1980s. She also worked as senior technology correspondent for *U.S. News & World Report*. Fluent in Mandarin Chinese, she has traveled throughout China over forty years. She is married to a China-born husband, Paul, and has a Hong Kong-born daughter, Emily.

Learn more about her earlier books at www.dorijonesyang.com.

Author photo © Chris Loomis/SparkPoint Studio

Questions for Book Group Discussion

⚙⚙⚙⚙⚙

1. Dori's relatives had little experience living overseas or pursuing journalism. Why do you think she was drawn to a career as a foreign correspondent? What women do you know who chose to live overseas or pursue an unlikely career? What are the advantages and disadvantages?

2. Dori says she was introverted and reserved, so she found it difficult to become a good journalist. To what extent did she overcome this—or did she just work around it?

3. To what extent do you think Dori's career was hurt or helped by being a woman? How does this differ from your experience in the workplace?

4. Why was Dori attracted to Paul? Were you surprised at the kind of man she married?

5. Why do you think Dori's parents were hesitant about her marrying a "Chinaman"? How similar or different were your parents' attitudes about marriage?

6. In Chapter Twelve, the author writes "Why should any of us look behind the next hill, or across the border, or across the ocean, into the warm living rooms of people who don't look or think or talk as we do?" How would you answer that question?

7. In an era where few women did so, Dori returned to a high-pressure career six weeks after the birth of her baby. What are the pros and cons of doing that? What have you observed about the lives of your friends who have made various choices about motherhood and work?

8. Why did Dori leave Hong Kong/China when she did? Why do you think she never went back to work in China? How might her life and career have been different if she had?

9. Why could Deng Xiaoping, a lifelong Communist, allow capitalism in China? What makes a country "communist"?

10. Deng Xiaoping faced a dilemma when the protestors would not disperse. Why do you think he ordered the military to open fire, after six weeks of relative tolerance? How else might he have responded?

11. China's Communist government has never embraced free elections or multi-party democracy, yet its policies modernized the lives of hundreds of millions of citizens. How do you view this tradeoff? Do you think China should have prioritized political reform and evolved into a Western-style democracy, even if it meant instability?

12. During Dori's years in China, many American leaders and businesspeople were enthusiastic about China, although sometimes frustrated. How and why have American attitudes about China become more negative since then?

13. In what ways did your understanding of China change after reading this book?

14. Since this book was written, Hong Kong has erupted in protests and China has adopted a national security law for Hong Kong, sparking outrage around the world. How has this book affected the way you think about Hong Kong and its future?

SELECTED TITLES FROM SHE WRITES PRESS

She Writes Press is an independent publishing company founded to serve women writers everywhere. Visit us at www.shewritespress.com.

How Sweet the Bitter Soup: A Memoir by Lori Qian. $16.95, 978-1-63152-614-5. After accepting an exciting job offer—teaching at a prestigious school in China—Lori found herself in Guangzhou, China, where she fell in love with the culture and with a man from a tiny town in Hubei province. What followed was a transformative adventure—one that will inspire readers to use the bitter to make life even sweeter.

Accidental Soldier: A Memoir of Service and Sacrifice in the Israel Defense Forces by Dorit Sasson. $17.95, 978-1-63152-035-8. When nineteen-year-old Dorit Sasson realized she had no choice but to distance herself from her neurotic, worrywart of a mother in order to become her own person, she volunteered for the Israel Defense Forces—and found her path to freedom.

Learning to Eat Along the Way by Margaret Bendet. $16.95, 978-1-63152-997-9. After interviewing an Indian holy man, newspaper reporter Margaret Bendet follows him in pursuit of enlightenment and ends up facing demons that were inside her all along.

Filling Her Shoes: Memoir of an Inherited Family by Betsy Graziani Fasbinder. $16.95, 978-1-63152-198-0. A "sweet-bitter" story of how, with tenderness as their guide, a family formed in the wake of loss and learned that joy and grief can be entwined cohabitants in our lives.

Renewable: One Woman's Search for Simplicity, Faithfulness, and Hope by Eileen Flanagan. $16.95, 978-1-63152-968-9. At age forty-nine, Eileen Flanagan had an aching feeling that she wasn't living up to her youthful ideals or potential, so she started trying to change the world—and in doing so, she found the courage to change her life.

This is Mexico: Tales of Culture and Other Complications by Carol M. Merchasin. $16.95, 978-1-63152-962-7. Merchasin chronicles her attempts to understand Mexico, her adopted country, through improbable situations and small moments that keep the reader moving between laughter and tears.